DeKalb County, Tennessee

Chancery Court Records

—

1844-1892

Compiled by:

Thomas E. Partlow

Please direct all correspondence and orders to:

www.southernhistoricalpress.com
or
SOUTHERN HISTORICAL PRESS, Inc.
PO BOX 1267
Greenville, SC   29601
southernhistoricalpress@gmail.com

ISBN #0-89308-761-0

Printed in the United States of America

This Book

Is

Respectfully Dedicated

To

My Friends

JACK CATO

&

JAMES V. MILLER

PREFACE

Chancery Court records are of great value because they contain estate settlements of people who have died intestate. Oftentimes, such information cannot be found elsewhere. In addition to estate settlements, these records also include divorces, and after 1865, some Civil War information.

Thomas E. Partlow
December, 2000

TABLE OF CONTENTS

Be it remembered that pursuant to the requirement of an Act of Assembly, passed by the Legislature of Tennessee at the regular session of 1843-1844 establishing a Chancery Court to be held at the town of Smithville in the County of DeKalb, Honorable Broomfield Ridley, Chancellor for the Fourth Chancery Division, organized said court by appointing Thomas Whaley, Clerk & Master for the term of six years, whereupon, said Whaley took an oath to support the Constitution of the State of Tennessee and the Constitution of the United States. Mar 1844. (Pp. 1-3)

WILLIS W. and PLEASANT M. WADE versus HARDIN P. BOSTICK. The equity set up in the bill has been met. Sep 1844. (Pp. 3-4)

SOLOMON C. DAVIS versus ABRAHAM BURGEN. The demurrer is overruled. Sheriff James McGuire of DeKalb County is appointed receiver. Sep 1844. (P. 4)

SAMUEL WILLIAMS, Administrator, versus MATHEW GRIFFIN's heirs. Petition to sell land. Goodman Griffin, John Griffin, and Mary Griffin are minor heirs of Priscilla Griffin. James McGuire is appointed guardian. The heirs of Franklin Garrison and his wife, Charlot, are minors and are non residents. R. A. Thomason is appointed guardian. Elias Griffin also appears to be a non resident. Sep 1844. (Pp. 4-5)

Chancery Court met in the town of Smithville on the third Monday in March 1845, it being the 17th day of the month. Broomfield L. Ridley, presiding. (P. 5)

LEONARD LAMBERSON versus DANIEL FORD and others. This cause is dismissed. 17 Mar 1845. (Pp. 5-6)

A number of causes are continued. (Pp. 6-7)

WILLIAM W. WADE and P. M. WADE versus HARDIN BOSTIC, assignee in bankruptcy, and others. The Clerk is to give an account of the amount paid to complainants. 17 Mar 1845. (P. 7)

M. M. BRIEN and D. FITE versus BENJAMIN TAPP. Complainant's bill is dismissed. 17 Mar 1845. (Pp. 8-9)

BERNARD RICHARDSON versus DAVID (KOGER). The Clerk is to take an account and report to the court. 17 Mar 1845. (Pp. 9-10)

WILLIAM M. (MODAY) versus BERNARD RICHARDSON. The injunction is granted. 17 Mar 1845. (P. 10)

JOHN CANTRELL, Guardian of Abram Cantrell. Petition praying for a sale. 17 Mar 1845. (P. 11)

Chancery Court met in the town of Smithville on the third Monday in Sep 1845, it being the 15th day of the month. Broomfield L. Ridley presiding. (P. 11)

A number of causes are continued. (Pp. 11-12)

SAMUEL CAPLINGER versus WILLIAM PATTERSON. There have been various transactions and dealings between the complainant and the defendant. 17 Mar 1845. (Pp. 12-13)

MANSON M. BRIEN and THOMAS V. ASHWORTH versus ROBERT HILL, Administrator of Eli A. Fisher; THOMAS RICHMOND, JAMES H. FISHER, JAMES EWIN, and PASCHAL W. BRIEN. Defendants were partners in trade. Complainants were partners as charged. Complainants pay the costs. 17 Mar 1845. (Pp. 13-14)

WILLIAM ADAMS and wife versus JOSEPH CLARK. 17 Mar 1845. (Pp. 14-15)

J. H. JOHNSON versus H. and M. DAUGHERTY. Complainant is given time to take depositions. 17 Mar 1845. (P. 15)

JOHN COLLEY versus ALEXANDER ROBINSON. Leave is given to complainant to execute a new bond. 17 Mar 1845. (Pp. 15-16)

WILLIAM WRIGHT, Administrator of Baker, versus WILLIAM FLOYD. The intestate, John Baker; was not possessed of a sound, disposing mind, but he became childish and imbecile, and was incapable of making a contract or valid disposition of his property. The bill of sale from the deceased John Baker to the defendant, William Floyd, for the slaves is cancelled and annulled. The slaves have been in the possession of the defendant since the death of the intestate in May 1844. The defendant has been guilty of no fraud. 17 Mar 1845. (Pp. 16-17)

BERNARD RICHARDSON versus DAVID HAGER. Complainant has ceased to be an indebtor to defendant. 17 Mar 1845. (Pp. 17-18)

HARDIN BOSTICK versus DAVIS and TATE. L& Mary 1845. (P. 19)

Chancery Court met in the town of Smithville on the first Thursday after the third Monday in Mar 1846, it being the 19th day of the month. Broomfield L. Ridley presiding. 19 Mar 1846. (P. 21)

HENRY (BASS), Administrator of A. M. Bass. Ex Parte. The petition of Henry Bass, Administrator of Archeable M. Bass, to sell slaves. In the year 1845, said Archable Bass died in De-Kalb County, intestate, leaving a considerable amount of property. Said Archable died seized and possessed of the following slaves, six in number, to wit, Lucy, Hartwell, Israel, Sussex, Amzi, and Argan. Said Hartwell was aged about 15 years. Israel was about 13 years. Sussex was about 10 years. Hartwell, about 15. Israel was about 13, Sussex was about 10. Amzi was about 6. Argan was about 3 years. 19 Mar 1846. (Pp. 21-22)

HENRY BASS, Administrator of Archable M. Bass. The slaves are to be sold to pay the debts of the intestate. 19 Mar 1846. (Pp. 22-23)

PARALEE A. STOKES by her next friend Jordan Stokes versus THOMAS J. SNEED and others. This cause is dismissed. 20 Mar 1846. (P. 23)

WILLIAM WRIGHT, Administrator of John Baker, versus WILLIAM FLOYD. Complainant reports his sale of the slaves. 20 Mar 1846. (Pp. 23-24)

2

JEFFERSON H. JOHNSON versus MARK and HENRY DOUGHERTY. Final Decree. There is no proof to justify the bill. 21 Mar 1846. (P. 24)

SOLOMON C. DAVIS versus ABRAHAM (BENGEN) and PLEASANT A. THOMASON. Final Decree. Complainants' bill is dismissed. 21 Mar 1846. (P. 25)

JAMES TUBB versus WILLIAM and SAMUEL WILLIAMS, SAMPSON BRASWELL, and W. W. BRIEN. 20 Mar 1846. (Pp. 25-27)

JOHN MARTIN, Administrator of Richard Butcher, versus JOSEPH RAMSEY. The Clerk is to give an account as to the executions which Milly was subject under the decree of the Supreme Court. 21 Mar 1846. (Pp. 27-28)

MANSON M. BRIEN, Administrator, versus WILLIAM MARTIN and others. The demurrer is sustained. 21 Mar 1846. (Pp. 28-29)

BERNARD RICHARDSON versus DAVID KAGER. The bill is dismissed. 21 Mar 1846. (P. 29)

SAMUEL CAPLINGER versus WILLIAM PATTERSON. Final Decree. The bill is dismissed. 21 Mar 1846. (Pp. 29-30)

BENJAMIN LEWIS versus BERNARD RICHARDSON. Motion to dissolve injunction. 21 Mar 1846. (P. 30)

SAMUEL WILLIAMS, Administator of Mathew Griffin, versus D. FITE and others. Mathew Griffin has departed this life. The defendants are his heirs. The complainant was appointed administrator. There is a debt due Samuel Williams, Sr. 21 Mar 1846. (P. 31)

Chancery Court met in the town of Smithville on the third Monday in Sep 1846, it being the 24th day of the said month. Broomfield L. Ridley, presiding. (P. 32)

HENRY BASS, Administrator of Archable M. Bass. Ex Parte. Petition to sell slaves. Rachel Bass purchased the boy Sussex for $350; John Bass purchased the boy Amzi for $252.50; Fountain ( ) purchased the boy Israel for $535.25; Thomas Lawrence purchased Hartwell for $569.50. 21 Mar 1846. (P. 32)

SAMUEL WILLIAMS, Administrator, versus DANIEL FITE and the other heirs of Mathew Griffin. The cause is continued. 21 Mar 1846. (Pp. 32-33)

JOHN (HUTTS) versus DAVID FISHER and WILSON UPCHURCH. The cause is dismissed. 21 Mar 1846. (P. 33)

WILLIAM C. MARTIN versus WILLIAM H. MAGNESS, WILLIAM B. CANTRELL and wife HANNA, WATSON PATTON and wife HARRIET, DANIEL W. WEBB and wife SARAH, PERRY GILLESPIE, JR., RANSOM A. YOUNGBLOOD and wife MARY, MARTHA MAGNESS, ELIZABETH BYERS, LEROY MAGNESS, CHARLOTTE MAGNESS, RICHARD MAGNESS, heirs of Bethel C. Magness. Watson (Potter) is appointed guardian for the minors Peggy G., Martha, Elizabeth, Leroy, Charlotte, and Richard. 21 Mar 1846. (Pp. 33-34)

3

HARDEN BOSTICK versus SOLOMON C. DAVIS and JAMES TATE. Title is divested out of Davis and vested in James Tate. 24 Sep 1846. (Pp. 34-35)

BENJAMIN LEWIS versus BERNARD RICHARDSON. Final Decree. The equity set up in the complainant's bill was fully met. 24 Sep 1846. (P. 35)

JOHN MARTIN, Administrator of Richard Butcher, versus JOSEPH RAMSEY. Final Decree. Complainant recovers. 24 Sep 1846. (Pp. 35-36)

Chancery Court met in the town of Smithville on the first Thursday after the third Monday in Mar 1847, it being the 18th day of the month. Broomsfield L. Ridley, presiding. (P. 37)

JOHN MARTIN, JR., Administrator, versus JOSEPH RAMSEY. Leave is granted to the defendant to file his answer. 18 Mar 1847. (P. 37)

MARY A. D. SULLIVAN versus LENT BUTLER and the other heirs of Simon P. Hughes. Defendants, William Hughes and Simon Hughes, are minors without guardian. Thomas Whaley is appointed guardian. 18 Mar 1847. (Pp. 37-38)

SAMUEL WILLIAMS, Administrator of Mathew Griffin, versus DAVID FITE and the other heirs of Mathew Griffin. Decree. There was no indebtedness from the said Mathew Griffin in his lifetime to Samuel Williams, Sr. It appears that there is no other indebtedness. 18 Mar 1847. (P. 38)

WILLIAM C. ETHERIDGE versus HENRY FRAZER. Defendant was guardian of complainant. Complainant was 21 years old previous to bringing said suit. 18 Mar 1847. (P. 39)

JOSEPH CLARK, Guardian, versus JAMES TUBB and others. Defendant Tubb and one Samuel Turney became the purchasers of the Skelton tract. 18 Mar 1847. (Pp. 39-41)

JOEL E. CHEATHAM versus ENOCH LOCKHART and others. The bill is taken for confessed. 18 Mar 1847. (P. 41)

SARAH BAY versus RICHARD BAY. Defendant has been guilty of cruel and inhuman treatment towards complainant. The bonds of matrimony are dissolved. 18 Mar 1847. (P. 42)

WILLIAM C. MARTIN versus WILLIAM H. MAGNESS and others. The bill is dismissed. 18 Mar 1847. (P. 42)

JORDAN STOKES, Executor of Spencer Kelly, versus WILLIAM FLOYD and LEVI HERROD. The equity in the bill has been met. 18 Mar 1847. (P. 43)

JOSEPH RAMSEY versus JOHN MARTIN, Administrator of Dillard S. Payne and Asa Smith. The equity in the bill has been met. 18 Mar 1847. (P, 43)

JOHN COLLEY versus ALEX H. ROBINSON. Final Decree. Plea of infancy of defendant. The defendant was a minor under the age of 21 years. The defendant's plea of minority is sustained. 18 Mar 1847. (P. 44)

A number of causes are continued. (Pp. 44-45)

GEORGE H. WALTON and ELISHA MONROE and wife KITTY. Ex Parte. Petition for partition. Devisee departed this life as charged in said petition. Petitioners are the only persons entitled to said land. The same can be immediately partitioned. Commissioners are appointed to partition the land. The said George H. Walton and Elisha Monroe and wife, Kitty, are the ones to receive the land. 24 Sep 1847. (Pp. 45-46)

JOHN MARTIN, Administrator, versus JOSEPH RAMSEY. The cause is continued. 24 Sep 1847. (Pp. 46-47)

NANCY J. SNEED by her next friend James Wood versus THOMAS J. SNEED and others. It is the intention of the complainant not to prosecute further. 24 Sep 1847. (P. 47)

WILLIAM ADAMS and wife versus JOSEPH CLARK, Administrator of Wills Adamson Et Al. The Clerk is to report whether the negroes can be divided without a sale and also the land. 24 Sep 1847. (P. 47)

JORDAN STOKES, Executor of Spencer Kelly, versus LEVI HERROD and others. The bill is taken for confessed. 24 Sep 1847. (P. 48)

GEORGE W. GASTKANS versus J. YOUNG and others. 24 Sep 1847. (P. 48)

JOEL E. COCKERHAM versus ANDREW LOCKHART and others. The bill is taken for confessed. 24 Sep 1847. (P. 48)

JAMES A. RICHARDSON, Administrator of Bernard Richardson, versus JOHN FRAZER. The death of complainant's intestate has been suggested at a former time. 24 Sep 1847. (P. 49)

WILLIAM G. ETHERIDGE versus HENRY FRAZER. Final Decree. 24 Sep 1847. (Pp. 49-50)

MARY A. D. SULLIVAN versus LENT BOLTON and other heirs of Simon P. Hughes. Defendant Herbert H. Sullivan has disclaimed any interest in the land mentioned. The other defendants, as heirs at law, had an equitable interest in the same. 24 Sep 1847. (P. 50)

This day is assigned by law for holding the Chancery Court at Smithville, but the Chancellor has not arrived. The Clerk adjourned until tomorrow morning. 23 Mar 1848. (P. 51)

GEORGE H. WALTON and ELISHA (MANSON) and wife Kitty. Ex Parte. Petition to partition land. 24 Mar 1848. (Pp. 52-53)

JEFFERSON LINK versus THOMAS ALLISON and others. 24 Mar 1848. (P. 54)

JAMES A. RICHARDSON, Administrator of Bernard Richardson, versus JOHN FRAZER. There is no evidence sustaining the charges. 24 Mar 1848. (Pp. 54-55)

WILLIAM ADAMS and wife versus JOSEPH CLARK. This cause is continued. 24 Mar 1848. (P. 55)

DAVID A. McEACHERN and LINDLEY M. BRANSFORD, Administrators of John Bransford, versus MARY A. D. SULLIVAN. This is a proper case for the filing of a cross bill. 24 Mar 1848. (P. 55)

JOEL E. CHEATHAM versus ENOCH and ANDREW LOCKHART and J. A. RICHARDSON. Complainant was the lawful assignee of Bernard Richardson. Complainant had the right to enforce his lien by a sale of Lot No. 39 containing 5520 square feet. 24 Mar 1848. (P. 56)

ELIZABETH HALL by her next friend B. Anderson versus JACOB FITE and WILLIAM HALL. The complainant has shown no grounds of relief, the said defendant Fite having fully paid to complainant's husband before the filing of this bill, their interest in the estate of John Anderson and has paid also to Benjamin Avant, the assignee of the husband of said Elizabeth all their interest in the negro woman, Rhoda, mentioned in the bill. 24 Mar 1848. (Pp. 56-57)

JOSEPH CLARK, Trustee, versus E. WRIGHT and others. The Clerk reports that he has sold the land ordered to be sold except for one tract of 56½ acres. 24 Mar 1848. (P. 57)

JOHN MARTIN, Administrator of Richard Butcher, versus JOSEPH RAMSEY. This is a proper case for the Clerk to make a report. 24 Mar 1848. (P. 58)

LEWIS LAWRENCE versus EDMUND FOSTER. The exceptions are not well taken. 24 Mar 1848. (P. 58)

MARY A. D. SULLIVAN versus LENT BOLTON and others. The Clerk has sold all the interest that the heirs of Simon P. Hughes held in a tract of land to Eli Rowland. 24 Mar 1848. (P. 59)

GEORGE W. EASTHAM versus JOHN YOUNG and JAMES EASTHAM. 24 Mar 1848. (P. 59)

ELIZABETH HALL by her next friend versus JACOB FITE and WILLIAM HALL. 24 Mar 1848. (P. 60)

Chancery Court met in the town of Smithville on the 21st day of Sep 1848, it being the day assigned by law for holding the Chancery Court. The Clerk & Master, Thomas Whaley, issued his report. (Pp. 61-62)

JOSEPH CLARK, Trustee, versus E. WRIGHT Et Al. The land was sold to Nathan Ward and Edward Evans. 21 Sep 1848. (Pp. 62-65)

BRANSFORD and McEACHERN versus MARY A. D. SULLIVAN. Cross bill. 21 Sep 1848. (P. 65)

JOSEPH RAMSEY versus JOHN MARTIN and ASA SMITH. The defendant Martin as administrator of Dillard T. Payne was entitled in his proper person as a creditor of said Payne to have the sum of money. 21 Sep 1848. (P. 66)

LEWIS LAWRENCE versus LINA and EDWARD T. FOSTER. A tract of land is ordered sold. Defendants are enjoined from cutting down any of the timber. 21 Sep 1848. (P. 67)

JOEL E. CHEATHAM versus ENOCH LOCKHART and others. Final Decree. Complainant became the highest bidder of Lot No. 39 in the town of Smithville owned by Enoch Lockhart. 1 May 1848. (Pp. 67-68)

MANSON M. BRIEN versus STEPHEN H. COLMS and others. Application for an attachment. 21 Sep 1848. (P. 69)

JOHN ROSE versus SARAH ROSE. The bill is taken for confessed. 21 Sep 1848. (P. 69)

WILLIAM WILLIAMS, Administrator of Mary Williams. Ex Parte. Petition to sell slaves. It is in the interest of the heirs that the slave, Abraham, be sold for distribution. 21 Sep 1848. (Pp. 69-70)

JOHN MARTIN, JR., Administrator of Richard Butcher, versus JOSEPH RAMSEY. Final Decree. Complainant's bill is dismissed. 21 Sep 1848. (P. 70)

THOMAS LAWRENCE versus ELI VICK. The demurrer is overruled. 21 Sep 1848. (P. 71)

WILSON UPCHURCH versus JESSE LACK and JOSEPH CLARK, Executors of William J. Givan. Lack sold a tract of land to his co-defendant Givan in his lifetime and for several years, said Lack had been in possession of the land. 21 Sep 1848. (Pp. 71-72)

JOHN B. TUBB, Administrator, versus THOMAS LEATH and others. This is a proper cause for a report. 21 Sep 1848. (P. 73)

GEORGE W. EASTHAM versus JOHN YOUNG and JAMES EASTHAM. Final Decree. Complainant was entitled to a perpetual injunction against said John Young. 21 Sep 1848. (Pp. 73-74)

WILLIAM ADAMS and wife and other heirs of Wills Adamson versus JOSEPH CLARK, Administrator. Wills Adamson departed this life in 1838. Complainant and Ausburn Mullinax were appointed executors of his last will and testament. In 1840, they resigned. Joseph Clark was appointed in their stead. It appears that the complainants are the only heirs of the said Wills Adamson. 21 Sep 1848. (Pp. 75-76)

This day being the time assigned by law for holding the Chancery Court at Smithville and the Chancellor not having arrived, the Clerk adjourned the session until tomorrow. 22 Mar 1849. (P. 77)

Court met pursuant to adjournment. Broomfield L. Ridley, presiding. 23 Mar 1849. (P. 77)

Thomas Whaley, Clerk & Master, gave his report. 23 Mar 1849. (P. 77)

WILLIAM WILLIAMS, Administrator of Mary Williams. Ex Parte. Final Decree. In the town of Liberty on 14 Oct 1848, Leroy Williams became the highest bidder for the boy Abram. 23 Mar 1849. (P. 78)

ABRAM M. SAVAGE versus JOHN C. CANNADY. A compromise has been reached. 23 Mar 1849. (P. 78)

WILSON UPCHURCH versus JESSE LACK and J. CLARK. The Clerk reports that he has sold the tract of land mentioned to Manson M. Brien. 23 Mar 1849. (Pp. 79-81)

LEWIS LAWRENCE versus LINA and EDWARD FOSTER. Decree. The tract of land was originally sold by Bluford T. Reynolds to defendant Lina Foster. In 1845, the defendant conveyed the land to Arthur E. Reynolds, the agent of the said Bluford T. and gave possession to complainant's vendors Clinton B. and Arthur E. Reynolds. They held possession until 1 Jan 1847 at which time, the defendant Edward Foster took possession. 23 Mar 1847. (Pp. 81-82)

JOSEPH CLARK, Trustee, versus E. WRIGHT Et Al. Sale of a tract of land. 23 Mar 1849. (P. 83)

EZEKIEL BASS. Ex Parte. Petition to sell land. Ezekiel Bass is guardian of Mary A. is indebted, and so a tract of land is to be sold. 23 Mar 1847. (P. 84)

WILLIAM ADAMS and wife and other heirs of Wills Adamson versus JOSEPH CLARK, Administrator. Sale of a tract of land and the negro boy Isaac. 23 Mar 1849. (Pp. 85-86)

JOSEPH RAMSEY versus JOHN MARTIN and ASA SMITH. 23 Mar 1849. (Pp. 86-87)

MARY A. D. SULLIVAN versus LENT BOLTON and others. 23 Mar 1849. (Pp. 87-88)

N. S. BROWN, Guardian, versus JOHN H. SAVAGE and others. Final Decree. The equities set up in the complainant's bill are met. 23 Mar 1849. (P. 88)

JOHN ROSE versus SARAH ROSE. Complainant failed to sustain the charges. Complainant's bill is dismissed. 23 Mar 1849. (P. 89)

PLEASANT THOMASON, Administrator, versus LUCINDA BROWNING and others. Complainant's bill is dismissed. 23 Mar 1849. (P. 89)

HAMPTON and THOMAS JAMES versus THOMAS RUTLEDGE. The defendant has two months to answer. 23 Mar 1849. (Pp. 89-90)

JOHN B. TUBB, Administrator of Nancy W. Allen, versus THOMAS LEEK, Guardian of Elizabeth Allen, Littleberry Allen, George W. Allen, and William W. Allen, minor heirs of William H. Allen deceased; also SARAH M. ALLEN and WALTER P. McFARLANE and wife MARY. Thomas Leek was appointed guardian on 3 Dec 1842 for the six children of William H. Allen deceased. 23 Mar 1849. (Pp. 90-97)

WILLIAM ADAMS and wife versus JOSEPH CLARK and others. Appeal. 23 Mar 1849. (Pp. 97-98)

Chancery Court met in the town of Smithville on 21 Sep 1849, it being the day assigned by law for holding the Chancery Court. Broomfield L. Ridley, presiding. The Clerk made his report to the court. 21 Sep 1849. (P. 99)

8

EZEKIEL BASS, Guardian of Mary Bass. Petition to sell land. 20 Sep 1849. (P. 99)

WILLIAM ADAMS and wife and others versus JOSEPH CLARK and others. The Clerk reports that nothing has been paid for clothing, boarding, schooling or doctor's bills for the children. 20 Sep 1849. (P. 100)

THOMAS W. WEST, Executor, versus JOHN F. WEST and others. The negro boy, Daniel, named in the bill, is necessarily obliged to be sold in order to make distribution of him to the legatees. The sale is to be made on the premises of Thomas West deceased. 20 Sep 1849. (P. 101)

MILTON WARD, Chairman, versus GEORGE W. EASTHAM and others. 20 Sep 1849. (Pp. 101-102)

CATHARINE OWEN versus JOHN OWEN and EZEKIEL BASS. Complainant is poor and unable to employ counsel. John Tubb is employed as counsel. 20 Sep 1849. (P. 102)

MARY TALIFARO versus JOHN B. TALIFARO. Complainant had been married about three years and had resided all that time in DeKalb County as charged. It appears to the court that the defendant has been guilty of cruel and inhuman conduct. The complainant's condition has been rendered intolerable. It is improper for her to live with and be under his control. Complainant's name before her said marriage was Mary Dyer. She has given the defendant no just cause for his treatment of her. The bonds of matrimony are dissolved. The said Mary is restored to her maiden name of Mary Dyer. 20 Sep 1849. (P. 103)

JEFFERSON LINK, Trustee, versus THOMAS ALLISON and others. Final Decree. The negro boy, Lafayette, specified in the bill, has been purchased by Malone from his co-defendant Allison. 20 Sep 1849. (Pp. 104-105)

GEORGE W. ALLEN versus JOSEPH CLARK, Executor. Motion to dissolve the injunction. 20 Sep 1849. (P. 105)

JOSEPH CLARK, Trustee, versus EBENEZAR WRIGHT and others. 20 Sep 1849. (Pp. 105-106)

JANE KELLEY; Elizabeth J., William J., and John Kelley versus SAMUEL WILLIAMS and GILBERT WILLIAMS, Administrators, and CICERO B. DUNCAN, Executor. Said Duncan is to file an amended answer. 20 Sep 1849. (P. 106)

AMON L. DAVIS versus DANIEL SMITH. The equity in the bill is not fully met. 20 Sep 1849. (P. 106)

THOMAS LAWRENCE versus ELI VICK. Final Decree. The allegations have not been fully sustained. 20 Sep 1849. (P. 107)

JOHN B. TUBB versus THOMAS LEEK. Final Decree. The slaves are to be divided and allotted to complainant and defendants as heirs of William H. Allen. 20 Sep 1849. (P. 107)

JOHN B. TUBB, Administrator, versus THOMAS LEEK Et Al. The said John B. Tubb is the administrator of Nancy W. Tubb. The slaves are to be divided among the heirs. Sarah M. Allen, the widow, is to receive one seventh of the slaves. McFarlane and wife are to receive one sixth, the share of Cornelius deceased, it leaving one seventh to devide the remainder equally between complainant and the infant defendants. The slaves are Milly and her infant child, George; Joe; Crockett; Silvey; Henry; John; and Mary, nine slaves amounting to $3175. The widow's share if $453.57. McFarlane and wife's share of Cornelius' part, it being one sixth of one seventh or $75.59. John B. Tubb, the complainant is entitled to one seventh and one sixth of one seventh. Elizabeth, Littleberry, William H., and George W. Allen, the same each which is $539.16. Larkin, the husband of Milly, sold for $500. 15 Jun 1849. (Pp. 107-110)

THOMAS and HAMPTON JAMES, Executors, versus THOMAS RUTLEDGE. Attachment bill. Deposition to be taken of Andrew Maynard. 20 Sep 1849. (P. 110)

WILLIAM R. CANTRELL and wife CANNY: D. W. WEBB and wife SARAH: DAVID POTTER and wife ELIZABETH: WILLIAM H. MAGNESS: P. G. MAGNESS: ROBERT CANTRELL and wife MARTHA versus WATSON POTTER and wife Harietta; ELIZABETH MAGNESS, widow of B. C. Magness; LEROY, CHARLOTTE, and RICHARD, minors by their guardian W. Potter. Elizabeth Magness, widow, is entitled to one third of the land mentioned during her natural life. 20 Sep 1849. (Pp. 110-111)

Chancery Court met in the town of Smithville on 21 Mar 1850, it being the day assigned by law for holding Chancery Court. Broomfield L. Ridley, presiding. (P. 112)

On 21 Mar 1850, the said Ridley appointed Thomas Whaley as Clerk & Master for a term of six years. (Pp. 112-114)

WILLIAM R. CANTRELL and others versus ELIZABETH MAGNESS and others. Report of sale. Commissioners allot to Elizabeth Magness her dower out of the real estate of Bethel C. Magness, her deceased husband. 30 Oct 1849. (Pp. 115-116)

MARY TALLAFARO versus JOHN B. TALLAFARO. Complainant and defendant have agreed upon a division of the property. 21 Mar 1850. (Pp. 118-119)

DAVID STROUD versus NANCY G. and GEORGE GIVAN Et Al. William J. Givan became the purchaser of a tract of land. Title to the land is divested out of the defendants and vested in the complainant. 21 Mar 1850. (Pp. 117-118)

TABITHA M. POTTER versus JAMES VANNATTA. The bill is taken for confessed. The defendant has been guilty of such cruel and inhuman treatment towards the complainant, such as cursing and abusing complainant that it is the opinion of the court that it it is unsafe and improper for her to cohabit with him and be under his dominion. The defendant has abandoned the complainant and refused to provide for her. The bonds of matrimony are dissolved. The parties have an infant about five months old. The care of the child is given to the complainant. 21 Mar 1850. (Pp. 118-119)

GEORGE W. ALLEN versus JOSEPH CLARK, Executor. In 1840, complainant by grant contracted with William J. Givan for lots 11 and 21 in the town of Smithville and fifty acres of land in the County of DeKalb. The contract for the said fifty acres and Lot No. 21 was void under the statute of fraud. Complainant was the deputy of said Givan as Clerk of the Circuit Court. Givan is dead and defendant is his executor. Complainant is indebted to the estate of the said Givan. The dealings between complainant and said Givan were material and complicated. The Clerk is to take an account and report back. 21 Mar 1850. (Pp. 119-120)

THOMAS WEST, Executor, versus JOHN F. WEST Et Al. The bill is taken for confessed. The Clerk has sold the negro boy, Daniel. Mathias S. West became the purchaser. Tabitha West is the widow of the said Thomas West. After the death of the said Tabitha, all that was bequeathed to her would revert back to the legatees of the said Thomas. The slave, Alcey, was given to the said Tabitha and Elizabeth C. Garrison during her natural life and after her death to her four daughters, Mary Garrison, Tabitha Garrison, Elizabeth Jane Garrison, and Martha Delila Garrison. The court is of the opinion that all the legacies given to Nancy H. Fite, by said will, has lapsed by the death of the said Nancy H. Fite in the life time of the said testator. As to that portion of his estate that the said testator died intestate, it should be distributed among all of the distributees of the said testator accoring to the statutes of limitations. The husband or the personal representative of the said Nancy H. Fite was not entitled to any of the same. The court is of the opinion that by the 9th item of the will bequeathing all of the real and personal estate of the testator to his four daughters, Elizabeth C. Garrison, Nancy H. Fite, Martha D. West, and Tabitha J. Williams only intended to bequeath to them all of the personal and real property not previously disposed of. 21 Mar 1850. (Pp. 120-122)

F. M. OVERSTREET Et Al versus JAMES P. THOMPSON Et Al. The complainant is to prosecute the lawsuit in the name of all the complainants. 21 Mar 1850. (P. 123)

JOHN P. W. ALLEN versus EMILY HOOVER. Motion to dissolve the injunction. 21 Mar 1850. (P. 123)

SUSAN and MALVINA REYNOLDS versus DOBSON YERGER. The matter of equities has been met. The bill is dismissed. 21 Mar 1850. (P. 124)

CATHARINE WYNN versus JAMES WYNN. The cause is dismissed. Complainant to pay the costs. 21 Mar 1850. (P. 124)

JAMES REDMAN versus GEORGE W. EASTHAM and the Bank. Demurrer. 21 Mar 1850. (P. 124)

AMON L. DAVIS versus DANIEL SMITH. Injunction. 21 Mar 1850. (Pp. 125-126)

M. M. BRIEN versus SNEED, OVERALL, CLARK, and COLMS. Attachment. The suit against Colms and Clark is dismissed. 21 Mar 1850. (P. 126)

WILLIAM ADAMS and wife and other heirs of Wills Adamson versus HENRY DAUGHERTY and TILMAN BETHELL. At the sale of the estate, Defendant Daugherty purchased a negro boy and executed his note. 21 Mar 1850. (Pp. 126-127)

JEFFERSON LINK, Trustee, versus THOMAS ALLISON and others. Final Decree. 21 Mar 1850. (Pp. 128-130)

M. M. BRIEN versus SNEED and OVERALL, Administrators. 21 Mar 1850. (P. 130)

JANE KELLEY and others versus DUNCAN, Executor, and others. This cause is remanded to the rules. 21 Mar 1850. (Pp. 130-131)

ROBERT GILBERT versus F. R. OVERSTREET Et Al. The demurrer is overruled. 21 Mar 1850. (P. 132)

A number of causes are continued. (Pp. 132-133)

Chancery Court met in the town of Smithville on 19 Sep 1850, it being the day prescribed by law. (P. 133)

REBECCA HAYS by her next friend William Hays versus JOHN HAYS and others. William Williams departed this life in Jan 1850. Defendants John W. Williams and Mathew Williams were appointed executors. Complainant Rebecca Hays was a daughter of the said William Williams. She is entitled to a certain negro woman named Rose. The said Rose is to be delivered over to the complainant. John Hays, the husband of the said Rebecca, is appointed trustee for her. The slave is for the use only of the said Rebecca and her children. 19 Sep 1850. (Pp. 133-134)

A number of causes are continued. (Pp. 135-136)

A. B. BOTTS versus NANCY BOTTS. The defendant is allowed time to file her cross bill. 19 Sep 1850. (P. 136)

MILTON WARD, Chairman, versus JAMES A. TAYLOR and the other Trustees of Fulton Academy. Defendants Taylor and Allen were not appointed trustees until Feb 1848. Defendant Schurer was appointed trustee in 1847, but never acted as such trustee until 1848. Eastham and Richardson are the only trustees that acted as trustees for the year 1847. 19 Sep 1850. (Pp. 137-139)

BENJAMIN AVANT versus ISAAC BRATTEN Et Al. 19 Sep 1850. (P. 139)

JAMES REDMAN versus GEORGE W. EASTHAM. 19 Sep 1850. (Pp. 139-140)

AMON L. DAVIS versus DANIEL SMITH. The injunction is dissolved. 19 Sep 1850. (P. 141)

LEVI D. BARBEE, Administrator, versus EDWARD LAWRENCE. Defendant is charged with all the property and effects of the complainant's intestate which came into his hands after said intestate's death. 19 Sep 1850. (Pp. 141-142)

AMON L. DAVIS versus DANIEL SMITH and others. Bill and cross bill. 19 Sep 1850. (Pp. 142-144)

BENJAMIN AVANT versus ISAAC BRATTEN and others. The complainant is not entitled to the aid of this court. 19 Sep 1850. (P. 144)

CATHARINE OWEN versus JOHN OWEN. Final Decree. Defendant John Owen has taken up and was living with another woman in adultery. He left complainant in a destitute condition. The only tangible effects of the defendant was two notes on defendant Bass for $100 each. The said Bass is to pay the notes to the complainant. 19 Sep 1850. (P. 140)

BATTAIL M. JAMES versus JOEL FOSTER. Final Decree. 19 Sep 1850. (Pp. 146-147)

JAMES EASTHAM versus JOHN YOUNG. Decree. 19 Sep 1850. (Pp. 147-148)

F. R. OVERSTREET and others versus JOHN SANDERS and others. In 1834, Aaron Cantrell departed this life. He devised all his property to his widow, Martha, for the term of her natural life or widowhood with the power to sell any of the property for her own use. About 12 Feb 1841, the said Martha sold the slave, Elizabeth, to one James Webb with the knowledge and consent of William Cantrell and complainant Smith Cantrell. A bill of sale was executed to said Webb for the said Elizabeth. 19 Sep 1850. (P. 149)

HIRAM MOORE versus ALFRED L. HANCOCK and MOORE. The complainant's bill is dismissed. 19 Sep 1850. (Pp. 150-151)

Chancery Court met in the town of Smithville on Thursday, 20 Mar 1851, it being the day prescribed by law. Broomfield L. Ridley, presiding. The Clerk & Master gave his financial report. (Pp. 152-153)

JOHN REYNOLDS versus ANNE SULLIVAN and the other heirs of William Sullivan. This bill is dismissed. 19 Sep 1850. (P. 153)

A. B. BOTTS versus NANCY BOTTS. Divorce. The bill is dismissed. Complainant is to pay all the costs. 20 Mar 1851. (Pp. 153-154)

NANCY AVANT by her next friend William B. Stokes versus WILLIAM C. AVANT and others. William Williams died in DeKalb County some time in the year 1850. John W. Williams and Mathew Williams were appointed executors. The said Nancy Avant was the daugher of the testator and the wife of defendant William C. Avant. She was given a negro girl, named Milly. 20 Mar 1851. (Pp. 154-155)

MOSES MATHEWS versus MARTHA J. CANDLER. Complainant is wholly insolvent and unable to pay the defendant her rent profits. 20 Mar 1851. (P. 155)

LEWIS LAWRENCE versus SPENCER E. and WILSHIRE BOMEN. The complainant's bill is dismissed. 20 Mar 1851. (Pp. 155-156)

S. H. COLMS versus THOMAS C. (WEAR) and others. In 1843, Defendant Duncan as executor sold to defendant Brien 500 acres.

A short time after the sale from Duncan to Brien, said Brien sold all of the land to Benjamin T. Browning. Said Browning is dead. Lucinda Wear was the wife and only heir of the said Browning and she is entitled to said land. Since the death of the said Browning, she has intermarried with the defendant Wear. 20 Mar 1851. (Pp. 156-157)

ROBERT GILBERT versus F. R. OVERSTREET. The bill is taken for confessed. The charges are sustained. The contract for the land is rescinded. 21 Mar 1851. (Pp. 158-159)

LEVI D. BARBEE versus EDWARD LAWRENCE. 21 Mar 1851. (Pp. 159-160)

WILEY B. JOHNSON versus BRACKET ESTES. The demurrer of the defendant is overruled. 21 Mar 1851. (P. 160)

JANE KELLEY and others versus GILBERT WILLIAMS and others. The complainants were allowed to bring before the court the administrator of John R. Kelley deceased. 21 Mar 1851. (P. 160)

EZEKIEL BASS versus CATHARINE AMENT and others. A demurrer was filed. 21 Mar 1851. (P. 161)

WILLIAM ADAMS and wife and others versus JOSEPH CLARK, Administrator and Guardian, and others of Wills Adamson deceased. It is in the interest of the heirs that the land be sold. 21 Mar 1851. (Pp. 162-164)

WILLIAM H. JOHNSON versus W. R. D. PHIPPS and others. The cause is remanded to the rules. 21 Mar 1851. (Pp. 164-165)

Chancery Court met in the town of Carthage on Thursday, 18 Sep 1851, it being the day prescribed by law. Broomfield L. Ridley, presiding. (P. 166)

YANCY PENNEGAR Et Al versus WILLIAM ADCOCK Et Al. The affidavit of William Adcock that John L. Adcock, Martha Ann Adcock, Benjamin F. Adcock, and Casanda Adcock, defendants, are all minors and without guardian. William Adcock is appointed as guardian. 18 Sep 1851. (P. 166)

A number of causes are continued. (Pp. 166-167)

LOTT ADCOCK versus LUCINDA ADCOCK Et Al. The property attached is one wagon and one mare. 18 Sep 1851. (P. 167)

JOHN P. ALLEN versus EMILY HOOVER. About 29 Dec 1847, complainant purchased of the defendant the land in controversy and had taken from the defendant a bond. 18 Sep 1851. (Pp. 167-168)

LEWIS LAWRENCE versus SPENCER E. BOMAR. Final Decree. 18 Sep 1851. (Pp. 168-169)

W. R. JOHNSON versus J. M. BAIRD and others. Defendant James M. Washburn has leave to take a deposition. 18 Sep 1851. (P. 169)

JANE KELLEY and others versus GILBERT and SAMUEL WILLIAMS, Administrators, and others. Final Decree. The original bill is

14

dismissed. 18 Sep 1851. (Pp. 169-170)

WILLIAM L. ADAMS and wife versus JOSEPH CLARK and others.
On 30 Aug 1851, the land in question was bidded off to Moses H.
Fite. It is decreed that the Clerk pay over to Lemuel Adamson
his share of the estate in his hands or to William Adamson who
has power of attorney for him. 18 Sep 1851. (Pp. 170-171)

JOSEPH HAYS and others versus SAMUEL HAYS and others. The
demurrer is well taken. 18 Sep 1851. (P. 171)

BENJAMIN AVANT versus ISAAC BRITTEN and others. Final Decree. The complainant's bill is dismissed. 18 Sep 1851. (Pp.
171-172)

JAMES W. EVINS Et Al versus WILLIAM BLACKBURN Et Al. The
land mentioned in the pleadings belonging to Isaac Evins. The
complainants are the heirs at law of said Isaac. The land was
ordered sold. Edward Evins became the purchaser. Said Edward
Evins had no legal title that was subject to levy and sale.
Defendant Fite became the purchaser. The deposition of Reuben
Evins is sustained. 18 Sep 1851. (P. 173)

S. H. COLMS versus THOMAS C. WROE Et Al. Thomas Malone became the purchaser of the land ordered sold. 18 Sep 1851. (Pp.
173-174)

CATHARINE OWEN versus JOHN OWEN. As to that part of the
bill which seeks to impeach the title to the tract of land sold
by Owen to complainant, the Chancellor refuses to sustain the
demurrer. 18 Sep 1851. (P. 175)

JANE WARFORD versus JOHN WARFORD and others. Final Decree.
The complainant's bill is dismissed. 18 Sep 1851. (Pp. 175-
176)

A. L. DAVIS versus DANIEL SMITH. On 26 Aug 1846, complainant purchased of defendant a tract of land for $8000. 18 Sep
1851. (Pp. 177-178)

WILLIAM B. JOHNSON, Executor, versus WILLS B. DORTCH Et Al.
James M. Quarles is the regular appointed guardian of Jane Ward
by the Sheriff of Montgomery County. 18 Sep 1851. (Pp. 176)

AMON L. DAVIS versus DANIEL SMITH. The defendant has been
guilty of contempt of this court. The defendant is discharged
from the attachment for contempt. 18 Sep 1851. (P. 178)

LEMUEL BRASWELL, Administrator of Mary Williams, versus
JOHN WILLIAMS and MATHEW WILLIAMS, Executors of William Williams.
This is a proper cause for an account. 18 Sep 1851. (Pp. 179-
180)

HESTER JOHNSON versus WILLIAM JOHNSON. The defendants are
all non residents except William and John Johnson. 18 Sep 1851.
(P. 180)

Chancery Court met in the town of Smithville on Thursday,
18 Mar 1852, it being the day prescribed by law. Broomfield L.
Ridley, presiding. (P. 181)

A number of causes are continued. (Pp. 181-182)

WILLIE B. JOHNSON, Executor of Willie Blount, versus WILLIE R. DORTCH, JOHN B. DORTCH, LUCINDA JANE WARD, LUCY BAILEY, and BRACKET ESTES. Willie Blount departed this life in Montgomery County, Tennessee about the year 1835. James W. Dortch was appointed his executor. Complainant entered upon the discharge of his trust and in 1843 had legally paid out between $900 and $1000. He his asking the court to be allowed to sell some real estate. 22 Mar 1852. (Pp. 182-183)

WILEY B. JOHNSON, Executor of George Blount, versus JAMES N. DORTCH. Complainant has exhausted the personal estate. It appears to the court that it will be necessary to sell some real estate. 22 Mar 1852 (Pp. 183-186)

MOSES MATHEWS versus THOMAS SIMPSON, Executor of Martha J. Candler. It appears to the court that the deed heretofore executed by complainant was intended as a mortgage. 22 Mar 1852. (P. 187)

LOTT ADCOCK versus LUCINDA ADCOCK, SAMUEL STONE, and others. Isaac Adcock, husband of the said Lucinda, is dead and he has no administrator upon his estate. 22 Mar 1852. (P. 187)

WILLIAM KELLY versus MARY KELLY. The defendant has been guilty of adultery as charged. The bonds of matrimony are dissolved. 22 Mar 1852. (P. 187)

JANE WARFORD versus JOHN WARFORD and others. The cause is dismissed. 22 Mar 1852. (P. 188)

JANE WARFORD versus DAVID WARFORD. The cause is continued. 22 Mar 1852. (P. 188)

A number of causes are continued. (Pp. 188-191)

S. H. COLMS versus THOMAS C. WEAR and others. 22 Mar 1852. (P. 192)

ELIZABETH ALLEN versus JESSE D. ALLEN. This cause is referred to Rules. 22 Mar 1852. (P. 192)

RICHARD CROWDER versus GEORGE W. EASTHAM and others. On 31 Jan 1852 an attachment was issued restraining George W. Eastham, John L. Dearman, and Nancy Ann Eastham from selling or disposing of in any way a negro named Sarah. The said George W. Eastham did, after the filing of the attachment and in violation of an injunction sell the negro named Sarah. 22 Mar 1852. (P. 193)

YANCY PENNEGAR versus WILLIAM ADCOCK. Petition to sell land. 22 Mar 1852. (P. 194)

ELIJAH WHITELY versus AMON L. DAVIS and others. 22 Mar 1852. (Pp. 194-195)

Chancery Court met in the town of Smithville on Thursday, 23 Sep 1852, it being the day prescribed by law. Broomfield L. Ridley, presiding. 23 Sep 1852. (P. 196)

The Clerk makes his reports. 23 Sep 1852. (P. 196)

A number of causes are continued. (P. 197)

YANCY PENNEGAR Et Al versus WILLIAM ADCOCK. The Clerk sold the land on 14 Aug 1852 with Tillman Adcock becoming the purchaser. William Adcock became the purchaser of a second tract of land. 24 Sep 1852. (Pp. 197-198)

WILLIAM ADAMS and wife and other heirs of Wills Adamson versus JOSEPH CLARK, Guardian, and other heirs of Wills Adamson. When notes are paid to the Clerk, he will distribute the funds to the heirs of the said Wills Adamson. 24 Sep 1852. (P. 198)

LOTT ADCOCK versus LUCINDA ADCOCK and others. Isaac Adcock made a deed of trust to the defendant for the benefit of the complainant. Said Isaac departed this life before said not was paid. Since his death, the said same has been paid by complainant. Complainant recovers from the defendant. 24 Sep 1852. (P. 199)

MARTHA J. ENGLISH versus ARCH D. ENGLISH. Defendant English abandoned his wife, Martha J., and has neglected and refused to provide for her maintainance. He has offered her such indignities to her person that it would be unsafe and improper for her to live with him and be under his domination and control. They have one female issue named Mary Elizabeth. The name of the complainant before marriage was Elizabeth J. Martin. The bonds of matrimony are dissolved. The complainant is given custody of the child. The name of the complainant is to be changed to that of Martha J. Martin and the name of the infant from that of Mary Elizabeth English to that of Mary Elizabeth Martin. Defendant to pay the costs. 24 Sep 1852. (Pp. 200-201)

MOSES MATHIS versus THOMAS SIMPSON, Executor of Martha J. Candler. Defendant recovers from the complainant. 25 Sep 1852. (Pp. 201-202)

PLEASANT A. THOMASON, Administrator of Benjamin F. Browning, versus THOMAS C. WRAE and others. This is a proper cause for an account. 25 Sep 1852. (Pp. 202-203)

JOSEPH CLARK, Executor of William J. Givan, versus JESSE LOCK. William J. Givan purchased of the defendant a tract of land lying principally in DeKalb County, but partly in White County as well. It is commonly known as the Wilson Upchurch land. The defendant has not been able to make a good and sufficient title to the land. The defendant has broken his covennant. Complainant is entitled to recover. 25 Sep 1852. (Pp. 203-204)

MOSES and DAVID GRIFFITH and others versus AMOS and PEYTON GRIFFITH and others. The bill is dismissed. The Clerk is to take proof and report back. 25 Sep 1852. (P. 205)

RICHARD HANCOCK versus HIRAM MORRIS and BIRD SPURLOCK. Complainant is not entitled to the relief prayed for. 25 Sep 1852. (P. 206)

RICHARD CROWDER versus GEORGE W. EASTHAM. Attachment for contempt. 25 Sep 1852. (Pp. 206-207)

JOSEPH HAYES and WILLIAM HAYES versus SAMUEL HAYES and CORNELIUS HAYES. Final Decree. The bill is not sustained by the proof. 25 Sep 1852. (P. 207)

ABRAM M. SAVAGE versus GEORGE W. ALLEN. 25 Sep 1852. (Pp. 207-208)

RICHARD CROWDER versus GEORGE W. EASTHAM, NANCY ANN EAST-HAM and others. George W. Eastham was the owner of the two negroes, Sarah and Adaline, mentioned in the bill. He executed a deed of trust to defendant Brien as trustee to pay a debt to William J. Givan who was dead and Clark was his executor. It appears to the court that the said George W. Eastham and Nancy A. Eastham who is his daughter contrived and intended fraudulently to hinder and delay the complainant in the collection of the judgment. 25 Sep 1852. (Pp. 208-210)

ELIJAH BOWEN versus SHERIFF EZEKIEL W. TAYLOR and others. Complainant recovers. 25 Sep 1852. (Pp. 210-211)

BATTAIL M. JAMES versus SHERIFF EZEKIEL W. TAYLOR. Complainant recovers. 25 Sep 1852. (Pp. 211-212)

WILLIAM H. WHALEY, Administrator of Leonard Lamberson; D. C. LAMBERSON, JOHN LAMBERSON, JAMES LAMBERSON, PALLIS SMITH and wife CHRISTINA, JR., CHRISTINA LAMBERSON, SR., MARY D. LAM-BERSON, MARY LAMBERSON, AMANDA LAMBERSON, the said Christina, Jr., Mary, and Amanda by their guardian James Allen. Ex Parte. Bill for construction of the will. Mary D., widow and relict of the said Leonard Lamberson, by dissenting to the said will, has forfeited the right to receive out of said estate anything for the support of the family of the testator except that allowed to her by the statute of dower. The minor children and legatees who still continue to live with the said Mary D. are entitled to their support out of the whole estate till 21 years old. The support of Christina Lamberson, the mother of the testator, was a lien upon all of the property of the testator's except the interest of the widow. 25 Sep 1852. (Pp. 212-214)

B. L. JOHNSON and wife SARAH E., POLLY JOHNSON, ALSA GIVAN, GEORGE GIVAN, and NANCY E. GIVAN by their guardian George Givan, and JOSEPH CLARK, Executor of William J. Givan. Ex Parte. William J. Givan died about the 13th of Feb 1848, leaving a last will and testament in which Joseph Clark was appointed as executor. The above named parties are his legatees. It was the intention of the testator to give to the said Sarah E. one third of his real estate during her natural life and to give to her one fourth of the personal estate which should be unexhausted after the payments of debts. The support of Polly Johnson should be charged upon the residue of his estate and was a lien upon the same. 25 Sep 1852. (Pp. 214-215)

Chancery Court met in the town of Smithville on 24 Mar 1853, it being the date prescribed by law. Broomfield L. Ridley, presiding. (P. 216)

THE BANK OF TENNESSEE versus WILLIAM BOYD THOMPSON and others. 24 Mar 1853. (P. 216)

LEVI D. BARBEE, Administrator, versus EDWARD LAWRENCE. The cause is continued. 25 Mar 1853. (Pp. 216-217)

JANE WARFORD versus DANIEL WARFORD. This cause is continued. 25 Mar 1853. (Pp. 217-218)

JOHN W. SEATT and others versus JOHN B. CLAIBORN. Defendant has been committing waste upon the premises or tract of land willed to complainant by their father and has damaged their interest or vested remainder. The defendant is enjoined from committing further waste or using any timbers from the same. 25 Mar 1853. (P. 218)

AVERY HARRIS versus JOHN J. TRAMMEL and others. Final Decree. Complainant has failed to sustain the allegations. 25 Mar 1853. (Pp. 218-219)

MOSES MATHEWS versus THOMAS SIMPSON, Executor of M. J. Candler. Report of sale. The title to a tract of land that Martha J. Candler held during her life time and also the interest of Moses Mathews is divested out of them and vested in Robert Johnson. 25 Mar 1853. (Pp. 219-220)

JOSEPH CLARK, Administrator of William J. Givan, versus JESSE LOCKE. Final Decree. 25 Mar 1853. (Pp. 220-221)

LUCINDA GILBERT versus ROBERT V. GILBERT. Final Decree. Parties were married some seventeen years ago. Complainant has been guilty of adultery herself since her marriage with the defendant. She has also been guilty of committing acts of violence towards the defendant. The court is of the opinion that she is not entitled to a divorce and other relief prayed for. Complainant's bill is dismissed. 25 Mar 1853. (Pp. 222-223)

JOHN GRIFFITH and others versus PATON GRIFFITH and others. Defendants were not guilty of any fraud or concealments. There is a large amount of money in the hands of the administrator liable to be distributed according to the compromise agreement. An account is ordered to be taken with the daughters of the deceased of all advancements made to them. An account is to be made of the amount the widow is to have and the amount the granddaughter, Nancy Hays, is to have. 25 Mar 1853. (Pp. 223-224)

ELIZABETH J. ALLEN versus JESSE D. ALLEN. Complainant and defendant have been resident citizens of DeKalb County for two years before the filing of this bill. Defendant has been guilty of cruel and inhuman treatment towards complainant. It is unsafe for the complainant to remain longer under his control and dominion. Complainant and defendant have two children, James L. and Andrew J., one about four years and the other about two years. Defendant is a man wholly incapable and unfit to have the nurture and education of said children. Complainant is a lady of high standing and moral character. Most of the land mentioned in the bill came to complainant by bequest from her father. Complainant and defendant have mortgaged a negro boy, Leroy, to one David Dinwiddie for $450. The boy is an esteemed family servant willed complainant by her father. The bonds of matrimony are dissolved. 25 Mar 1853. (Pp. 224-225)

PLEASANT A THOMASON versus WRAE, COLMS, Et Al. The estate is not indebted to Thomason. 25 Mar 1853. (P. 226)

LEONARD HATHAWAY versus DANIEL SMITH. The defendant sold to complainant by verbal contract the lands described in the pleadings, it being 150 acres in Nov 1848 for $250. Title was to be made upon making the last payment by complainant. Complainant has made the last payment. It does not appear to the court whether the defendant can make a good title to the complainant of the land. The Clerk is to take proof. 25 Mar 1853. (P. 227)

JOHN P. W. ALLEN versus EMILY (HOBSON). 25 Mar 1853. (P. 228)

CHURCHWELL and JOHN H. ANDERSON, partners, versus WILLIAM ( ) and others. 25 Mar 1853. (Pp. 228-229)

EZEKIEL W. TAYLOR versus ELIJAH BAINES. Complainant to pay the costs. 25 Mar 1853. (P. 230)

JOHN M. LANE versus MANSON M. BRIEN. Final Report. The land in dispute was sold to defendant Brien on 1 Jun 1850. Defendant took complainant's note for $100. Complainant Lane on 29 May 1852 made search at the usual place of residence of defendant Brien, but who was not home. Complainant then paid the money for said land into the Circuit Court Clerk's office. 25 Mar 1853. (Pp. 231-232)

Chancery Court met in the town of Smithville on Thursday, 22 Sep 1853, it being the day prescribed by law. The Chancellor, not being present, the Clerk & Master adjourned court. (P. 232)

The Honorable Court met pursuant to adjournment. Broomfield L. Ridley, presiding. 23 Sep 1853. (P. 232)

The Clerk & Master, Thomas Whaley, made his reports. 23 Sep 1853. (P. 233)

JOHN MARTIN, Administrator of Martha Butcher, and his wife PATSY versus ABRAHAM ENGLISH and others. This is a proper cause for a report. 23 Sep 1853. (P. 234)

JAMES W. EVANS and others versus WILLIAM BLACKBURN and others. Final Decree. 23 Sep 1853. (Pp. 235-236)

MARTHA CHEATHAM by her next friend Elisha Conger versus ARCHABLE B. CHEATHAM Et Al. Complainant's bill is dismissed. 23 Sep 1853. (Pp. 236-237)

SAMUEL CASEY versus CLARY CASEY. Complainant intermarried with the defendant in Smith County about the year 1850. They, afterwards, removed to DeKalb County. Defendant, without any reasonable or just cause, wilfully left and absented herself from her husband. She is beyond the limits of this State. The bonds of matrimony are dissolved. 23 Sep 1853. (Pp. 237-238)

JOHN W. SEATT and others versus JOHN B. CLAIBORN. Commissioners report a waste of the timber upon the land. 23 Sep 1853. (Pp. 238-239)

LEVI D. BARBEE versus EDWARD LAWRENCE. 23 Sep 1853. (P. 239)

ABRAM ENGLISH and others and JOHN MARTIN and others versus
WILLIAM CAMPBELL and others. Bill and cross bill. 23 Sep 1853.
(Pp. 239-240)

A number of causes are continued. (P. 240)

JOHN GRIFFITH and others versus PATON GRIFFITH and others.
William Floyd, Administrator, gave an account of the estate of
Jonathan Griffith. The estate is equally divided between all
the heirs of Jonathan Griffith deceased, to wit, Moses Griffith,
David Griffith, John Griffith, Elias Griffith, Amos Griffith,
Paton Griffith, William Griffith, Allen Jones and wife, Green B.
Adams and wife, James Yeargan's children, Elizabeth Griffith,
the widow. 23 Sep 1853. (Pp. 240-243)

CATHARINE OWEN versus E. W. BASS Et Al. The bill is taken
for confessed. The defendant John Owen cannot make title to
all of the land. 23 Sep 1853. (Pp. 243-244)

JOHN P. W. ALLEN versus EMILY HOOVER. 23 Sep 1853. (Pp.
244-245)

CHURCHWELL and JOHN ANDERSON versus WILLIAM C. GHOMLEY.
23 Sep 1853. (P. 245)

WINSTON W. CROWDER versus JAMES WHITE. The Clerk is to take
proof and report back to the court. 23 Sep 1853. (P. 246)

MATHEW WILLIAMS and JOHN W. WILLIAMS, Administrators of
William Williams versus WILLIAM B. LAWRENCE, WILLIAM HAYS and
wife MARIA, JOSIAH L. BASS and wife PARALEE, JOHN SIMPSON and
wife ELIZABETH, WILLIAM C. AVANT and wife NANCY; LEROY P.,
THOMAS, VINCENT and JAMES M., WILLIAM, PARALEE, WILBURN, and
TEMPERANCE FITE and HIRAM FITE, Guardian for the three last
named, JOHN HAYS and wife REBECCA, and JOHN SIMPSON and wife
ELIZABETH. Motion to dissolve the injunction. 23 Sep 1853.
(Pp. 247-249)

ELIZABETH HAIL versus PLEASANT HAIL. Decree. The bill is
taken for confessed. Parties were married about the 6th of Sep
1852. At the time of the marriage, complainant was a widow and
had three children. Defendant was an improvident and dissipated
man. Defendant has abandoned complainant without cause. In
the division of the slaves belonging to the estate of the late
Samuel Williams, father of complainant, there has been set apart
for complainant a negro slave named Emily Harriet, a girl about
17 years old. There is a further small amount coming to the
complainant from Samuel Williams, father. Complainant is not
to be liable for the debts of the defendant. 23 Sep 1853. (Pp.
250-251)

MOSES FITE versus HENRY FITE and EBENEZAR WRIGHT. Decree.
The bill is taken for confessed. 23 Sep 1853. (Pp. 251-252)

WARFORD versus WARFORD and others. The depositions of
Cintha Warford and Jane Warford have been accepted. 23 Sep
1853. (P. 252)

GHORMLEY versus GHORMLEY. Decree. Defendant recovers of
the complainant. 23 Sep 1853. (Pp. 252-253)

RICHARD CROWDER versus GEORGE W. EASTHAM, NANCY ANN EASTHAM, and others. 23 Sep 1853. (Pp. 253-254)

LEONARD HATHAWAY versus DANIEL SMITH. 23 Sep 1853. (Pp. 254-255)

Chancery Court met in the town of Smithville on Thursday, 23 Mar 1854, it being the day prescribed by law. Broomfield L. Ridley, presiding. (P. 256)

A number of causes were continued. (Pp. 256-257)

(ANNA) WEST versus THOMAS WEST. Petition for alimony. Complainant and defendant married several years since in the State of North Carolina. Complainant was possessed of considerable property, consisting of money and slaves. They have since removed to Tennessee and settled in DeKalb County. The said Thomas has expended pretty well all of said property. The defendant is a drinking man and is likely to expend said property. 23 Mar 1854. (Pp. 257-258)

A number of causes are continued. (Pp. 258-259)

WINSTON W. CROWDER versus JAMES MARTIN. 24 Mar 1854. (P. 259)

NANCY FOUTCH versus AMOS FOUTCH. Petition for divorce. This cause is continued. 24 Mar 1854. (P. 260)

JOHN BURTIN and CHARLES BURTIN, Administrators, versus WILLIAM ROBINSON and others. The lands mentioned in the proceedings were not susceptible to partition between the heirs. It is in the interest of the heirs that the land be sold. 24 Mar 1854. (P. 260)

ELIZABETH J. ALLEN versus JESSE D. ALLEN and others. The land mentioned in the pleadings descended to complainant by the Will of her father. The land was given to the complainant for life and then to her children. 24 Mar 1854. (P. 262)

JANE WARFORD versus DANIEL WARFORD and others. 24 Mar 1854. (Pp. 263-264)

MATHEW WILLIAMS and JOHN W. WILLIAMS, Administrators, versus WILLIAM HAYES and others. The matter is referred to the Clerk. 24 Mar 1854. (P. 264)

A. M. SAVAGE, Administrator of Joseph Crowder versus JOANAH CROWDER and others. Motion by complainant for an order to sell the slave Reese and one other now in possession of the widow, Johanna Crowder. It is necessary for the slaves to be sold for a division. 24 Mar 1854. (P. 265)

CATHARINE OWEN versus JOHN OWEN and others. The report of the clerk is confirmed. 24 Mar 1854. (Pp. 265-267)

HARRIS SMITH and HARRY MOSIER versus E. A. JACKSON. 24 Mar 1854. (Pp. 267-268)

Chancery Court met in the town of Smithville on Thursday, 25 Sep 1854. Court was adjourned until Oct. (P. 269)

Chancery Court met in the town of Smithville on the first Thursday after the fourth Monday in Oct 1854, it being the 26th day of said month. This is the day that the Honorable Court was adjourned at the regular term in Sep last. The Chancellor, not appearing, the Clerk adjourned court. (P. 269)

The Honorable Court met pursuant to adjournment. Broomfield L. Ridley, presiding. 27 Oct 1854. (P. 269)

JOHN BURTIN and CHARLES BURTIN versus WILLIAM ROBINSON and others. Report of sale. John Burtin purchased the 321 acres mentioned in the pleadings with Charles Burtin as his security. 27 Oct 1854. (Pp. 269-271)

LEWIS heirs, to wit, HIRAM LEWIS and others versus BENJAMIN LEWIS, Executor. This is a fit case for an account. 27 Oct 1854. (Pp. 271-272)

ISAAC COOPER versus WASHINGTON BRYANT and LEWIS BRYANT. The defendants purchased from complainant the lot of ground with the improvements. The defendants are non residents of the State. They are indebted in a considerable sum. The land is ordered to be sold. 27 Oct 1854. (Pp. 272-273)

SARAH HICKS versus WILLIAM HICKS. Complainant and defendant have been married for more than forty years. The defendant, some three years since, maliciously and without any reasonable cause abandoned complainant and has refused to live with or provide for her. The bonds of matrimony are dissolved. 27 Oct 1854. (P. 273)

WILLIAM G. ETHERIGE versus LAVINA ETHERIGE. Complainant and defendant had been married for about thirteen years. The defendant, for more than two years previous to the filing of complainant's bill, wilfully and maliciously abandoned him without any reasonable or probable cause and still refuses to live with him. The bonds of matrimony are dissolved. 27 Oct 1854. (P. 274)

A. M. SAVAGE, Administrator, versus JEREMIAH COGGIN and others. William M. Wade became the purchaser of the negro boy William Henry for $330.15. 27 Oct 1854. (Pp. 274-275)

MARTHA JAMES versus HAMPTON JAMES. Complainant and defendant intermarried some 18 or 20 years ago. Complainant's father died in the year 1842 or 1843, leaving a last will and testament in which he bequeathed to her the tract of land on which the defendant now lives, it being on the Caney Fork River. Defendant and complainant have one other small tract of land adjoining the above tract and also a negro man named Henderson which said negro descended to complainant from her mother's estate. Said defendant was conducting himself badly and indiscreetly. Should the property remain under his control, it would be squandered. Complainant would be deprived of the only means she has to support herself and little children. The property is to be settled on the complainant for her separate use and enjoyment. 28 Oct 1854. (Pp. 275-276)

M. WILLIAMS and J. W. WILLIAMS versus WILLIAM F. HAYS and others. Each heir received $779.91 and also certain negroes.

23

The heirs were John Simpson and wife, John Hays and wife, Josiah
L. Bass and wife, William C. Avant and wife, James M. Williams,
William F. Hays, Thomas J. Williams, Leroy P. Williams, Vincent
Williams. The guardian of Paralee, Temperance, and William Fite
was paid their share. 28 Oct 1854. (Pp. 276-278)

MARTHA WOOLDRIDGE, JOHN YOUNG AND WIFE Jane, Pleasant Young,
William Young, Isaac Young, Patty Young, Polly Young, Jane Young,
William R. Billings and wife Sarah, children of Rachel Young,
formerly Rachel Cantrell, versus Polly Johnson, Eliah Durham,
Eli Sims, Dillard G. Stone, Benjamin Rowland, Jefferson Sims,
Riley Ellis and wife Sally, Abraham English and wife Cansada,
Charles Hamlin and wife Nancy, Patsy Ann Cantrell, Elizabeth
Cantrell, heirs of John Cantrell; William Cantrell, Executor;
James Cantrell, Moses Cantrell, Smith Cantrell, and Ephraim Can-
trell, being devisees under the will and having been made com-
plainants in this cause without their consent desired to Court
to have their names struck out of the bill as complainants. Jane
Young, Rachel Young, and Martha Wooldridge are daughters of Aaron
Cantrell. They were married women at the time of the making of
the will. Aaron Cantrell, then of White County, departed this
life in 1834. Before his death, he made his last will and
testament. Complainants and defendants were his only devisees.
He gave to his wife, Martha Cantrell, all his real and personal
estate during her natural life or widowhood. Martha, being too
old and infirm to manage the property of the estate, and the legatees all being of full age, Martha consented to surrender up her
life estate. The property was allotted to each legatee his or
her share. William and his mother, Martha, conveyed the slave,
Betsy, to one James Webb who sold her to Lucy Dean in 1841 who
held her adversely to the whole world to the time of her death
which was in 1849 or 1850. Sanders, her administrator, since
has died. Defendants recover of complainants. 28 Oct 1854.
(Pp. 278-282)

NANCY FOUTCH versus AMOS FOUTCH. This cause is continued.
28 Oct 1854. (P. 282)

RHODERICK DRIVER versus JAMES DURHAM AND SUSAN SULLIVAN,
Administrators of Lucian B. Sullivan; HERBERT H. SULLIVAN,
RICHARD LAMBERSON and wife DITHA ANN, PLEASANT A. THOMASON and
wife ARAMINTA, CALVIN MARCHBANKS AND WIFE JOSEPHINE, and DEWANE
SULLIVAN. On 29 Mar 1848, complainant sold to defendant's intestate the tract of land mentioned in the pleadings. It was
located in the 9th District and contained 212 acres. Complainant has a lien on the land. The land was ordered sold. 28
Oct 1854. (Pp. 283-284)

WILLIAM ROBERTS and WILLIAM R. ROBINSON, Administrators of
Elijah Robinson; MARTHA V. ROBERTS, JOHN REYNOLDS and wife MARY
versus ELIZA ROBINSON, CHARLES E. ROBINSON, BENJAMIN S. ROBINSON,
NANCY ROBINSON, JOHN J. ROBINSON, ALFRED GUINN and wife ANN,
JANE F. ROBINSON, MARGARET M. ROBINSON, and ELIZA F. ROBINSON.
Petition to sell slaves. Elijah Robinson died, intestate, in 1853.
Several of the heirs have received advancements during the life-
time of the intestate. Others have received none. The said Elijah

was seized of the negroes mentioned in the pleadings. The legal title was in him. Since the filing of this bill, the girl, Hannah has been delivered of a child which is about five months old. Two of the negroes, Saran and Beck are very old and worth, but little, if any thing. The slaves cannot be divided among the heirs. A sale is ordered. The slave, Hannah, and child are to be sold together. 28 Oct 1854. (Pp. 284-286)

ABRAHAM ENGLISH and others versus WILLIAM CAMPBELL and others; JOHN MARTIN, Administrator, and others versus WILLIAM CAMPBELL and others. In 1814, Susan Hawkins and her son, Reuben, who was of imbecile mind had joint title to a tract of land in the State of Kentucky. The said Susan sold the land to one Trible for $1000. In part payment were the slaves, Fannie, Darcus, and Allen. Susan and Reuben lived together until May 1823, retaining possession of the slaves who had increase, Lucy and Lack. About which time, the said Susan died. In Oct after the death of said Susan, her heirs and distributees, a part of whom were the ancestors of complainants met together and made a just division of the slaves to each other. Defendant Campbell has been holding the possession of the slaves under said division.adversely to the whole world till the present time. The slaves received by Butcher and wife who were the ancestors of complainants have been sent to parts unknown as well as the slaves received by John Hawkins. All the parties acquiesed in the division. Neither Butcher in his life time nor his widow, after his death attempted to disturb the same. The said Reuben Hawkins was not vested with any rights to the slaves. 28 Oct 1854. (Pp. 286-287)

Chancery Court met in the town of Smithville on the fourth Monday of Mar 1855, it being the 26th day of said month and also the day assigned by law for holding the Chancery Court. Broomfield L. Ridley, presiding. (P. 287)

A number of causes were continued. (Pp. 287-289)

ROBERTS and wife and others versus ELIZA ROBINSON and others. The tract of land mentioned in the pleadings was sold at the town of Alexandria. 26 Mar 1855. (It was slaves that were sold, rather than land. (Pp. 289-291)

JAMES M. GEORGE versus JAMES TURNER and others. Decree. (Pp. 291-292)

MARY DYER versus JOSEPH COLE and others. On 7 Jan 1850, the lands, mentioned in the pleadings, were sold as the property of John B. Tallafara. Complainant purchased the land and a deed taken for the same. James Mahan fraudulently obtained possession of an unregistered deed from Cook to said John B. Defendant Mahan is ordered to deliver up to the complainant the title papers in his hands. 26 Mar 1855. (Pp. 292-293)

RHODERICK DRIVER versus JAMES DURHAM and others. 27 Mar 1855. (Pp. 293-295)

BANK OF TENNESSEE versus WILLIAM C. J. THOMPSON and others. Injunction. 27 Mar 1855. (Pp. 295-297)

JAMES M. GEORGE versus JAMES TURNER, THOMAS REEVES, and PEGGY BELCHER. The court has no jurisdiction in this cause. 27 Mar 1855. (P. 297)

ISAAC COOPER versus WASHINGTON BRYANT and LEWIS BRYANT. Final Decree. The Clerk sold the lot to Isaac Cooper. 27 Mar 1855. (Pp. 297-298)

ABRAM M. SAVAGE, Administrator of Joseph Crowder, versus JEREMIAH COGGIN, JOSEPH CROWDER, JOHANAH CROWDER, JR., MARY A. CROWDER. Two negroes have been sold by the Clerk subject to the decree of the court. This is a proper case for a report. 27 Mar 1855. (P. 299)

RUSSELL LEWIS and other heirs of William Lewis versus BENJA-MIN LEWIS and others. It does not appear what the rents of the land would be worth during the life of the widow from the death of the husband. A report is ordered by the Clerk. 27 Mar 1855. (Pp. 299-300)

SAMPSON BRASWELL versus MATHEW WILLIAMS and JOHN W. WILLIAMS, Administrators of William Williams. 27 Mar 1855. (P. 300)

DAVID JAMES versus WILLIAM PATTERSON. The death of defendant William Patterson is suggested. 27 Mar 1855. (P. 300)

NANCY GARRISON versus JOEL M. GARRISON. Defendant by attorney moved the court to dismiss complainant's bill for the reason no security has been given. 27 Mar 1855. (P. 301)

G. M. GARRISON versus GEORGE L. GIVAN. Final Decree. Complainant's injunction is granted. 27 Mar 1855. (P. 301)

E. A. JACKSON versus WILLIAM FLOYD. On 1 Jan 1849, complainant purchased from the defendant a tract of land consisting of 400 acres. Complainant, afterwards, sold the land to Harvey J. Mosier who later claimed that there were only about 128 acres. Floyd is ordered to come to court and defend the title. 27 Mar 1855. (Pp. 301-302)

S. H. COLMS versus THOMAS C. WEAR and others. Final Decree. Title to the land mentioned in the pleadings is divested out of the heirs of Thomas W. Duncan and vested in Thomas Malone. 27 Mar 1855. (Pp. 303-304)

Chancery Court met in the town of Smithville on the fourth Monday of Sep 1855, it being the 24th day of said month and the day assigned by law for holding said Chancery Court. Broomfield L. Ridley, presiding. (P. 305)

A number of causes are continued. (Pp. 305-307)

EREN LINDER versus WILLIAM BRASWELL, JOHN LINDER, RICHARD P. BURKS, and JOSEPH BRAGG. The execution in favor of defendant Braswell has been levied upon the land of complainant, but said land was not subject to levy and sale for the debts of John Linder. 25 Sep 1855. (P. 307)

A number of causes are continued. (Pp. 307-308)

ELIZABETH WILLIAMS versus BARNETT WILLIAMS. The defendant was guilty of adultery as charged. The bonds of matrimony are dissolved. 25 Sep 1855. (Pp. 308-309)

H. C. EDWARDS versus MARY JANE EDWARDS. The defendant was guilty of adultery as charged. The bonds of matrimony are dissolved. 25 Sep 1855. (P. 309)

A number of causes are continued. (Pp. 309-310)

CATHERINE WYNN versus J. F. MORFORD and TAYLOR. There is in the hands of J. F. Morford, trustee for Mary Wynn, the sum of $210. He is required to pay over to the clerk this amount. 25 Sep 1855. (Pp. 310-311)

SAMUEL KNIGHT versus O. M. GARRISON. The complainant recovers. 25 Sep 1855. (P. 311)

CHARLES BURTON and JOHN BURTON, Administrators of Henry Burton, versus WILLIAM ROBINSON and wife ZELTHA and others. Mrs. Mary Lefever, the wife of Abraham Lefever, formerly Mary Burton, and one of the heirs of Henry Burton privately and apart from her said husband requested that all the proceeds of the sale of the real estate of her father, the said Henry Burton, be paid over to her said husband. 25 Sep 1855. (P. 312)

GILES DRIVER versus JESSE SEWEL and THOMAS L. SEWEL. Giles Driver has heretofore sold to defendant Jesse Sewel a house and lot in the town of Smithville upon which defendant Thomas L. Sewel lived at the time of filing this bill known in the plan of the said town as lot no. 17. There is a lien on the property. The land is ordered sold. 25 Sep 1855. (Pp. 312-313)

E. FISH versus C. W. KERLEY. The death of the defendant is suggested. 25 Sep 1855. (P. 313)

VINSON WILLIAMS versus M. M. BRIEN and others. 25 Sep 1855. (Pp. 313-315)

HIRAM LEWIS and RUSSELL LEWIS and others versus BENJAMIN LEWIS and others. Final Decree. 25 Sep 1855. (Pp. 315-316)

ALFRED L. HANCOCK versus HIRAM MORRIS and CONNOR. The bill was not sustained by the proof. 25 Sep 1855. (P. 316)

JOSIAH L. BASS versus MATHEW WILLIAMS. 25 Sep 1855. (Pp. 317-318)

TABITHA SMITH versus WILLIAM SMITH and others. The defendant has wilfully abandoned the complainant without cause for more than two years. The bonds of matrimony are dissolved. 25 Sep 1855. (P. 318)

THOMAS C. WEAR and wife versus A. M. SAVAGE and others. 25 Sep 1855. (P. 318)

E. A. JACKSON versus WILLIAM FLOYD. Decree. Complainant purchased from the defendant 400 acres for $150. Part of the land was covered by a better title. 25 Sep 1855. (P. 319)

FELIX N. PATTERSON versus MARY DYER and others. Decree.

25 Sep 1855. (Pp. 319-320)

J. J. WHITE versus W. OVERALL. The parties agree to a compromise. 25 Sep 1855. (Pp. 320-321)

SAMPSON BETHEL versus HENRY McROY and wife LOUISA, SAMUEL McWHIRTER and wife MARY, CELIA C. BURTON, alias CELIA C. BETHEL, and LOUISA V. BETHEL. The defendants Henry McRoy and wife and Samuel McWhirter and wife are non residents. The bill is taken for confessed against the non residents. The minors, Celia C. Burton and Louisa V. Bethel are appointed a guardian. The Clerk is to report back to the next term of court. 25 Sep 1855. (Pp. 322-323)

A. M. SAVAGE versus JEREMIAH COGGIN and others. Joseph Crowder, intestate, died in the State of Virginia in 1843, leaving certain slaves mentioned in the pleading. The widow, Joannah Crowder, removed to this State bringing said slaves. Defendant Coggins was afterwards appointed guardian for the heirs of Joseph Crowder and took the negroes into his possession, hired them out for two years and distributed the funds arising from the hire for support of the children. Complainant Savage hired the girl Rose from Coggin for the year 1851. Defendant Coggin was in possession of said slaves, one of them viz. Susan sickened and died without any fault on the part of the said Coggin. In 1852, Savage was appointed administrator and took the balance of the slaves into possession. He brought suit against Coggin for the one that had died. He finally lost the suit. While the slaves were in the possession of said Savage, three of the negroes viz Bets and her two children were burned up without any fault of the said Savage. The other two slaves viz Rose and Henry have been sold by a former decree of this court. Said Savage has paid out the money for the use of the family. 25 Sep 1855. (Pp. 323-324)

O. D. WILLIAMS versus HOLLIS and others. 25 Sep 1855. (Pp. 324-325)

GEORGE W. EASTHAM versus JAMES M. BAKER, Administrator of William Robinson and JOHN M. WHITELY. Defendants did in 1843 verbally agree and consent with the complainant that they would purchase the lands mentioned in the pleadings. The court decreed that William Robinson deceased and John M. Whitely be declared to be trustees for the sale of the said lands and the same be declared a mortgage. The court is of the opinion that complainant is not bound by the statute of limitations. 25 Sep 1855. (Pp. 325-326)

SAMUEL L. TYREE versus JOHN B. RODGERS, JAMES M. BAKER, Administrator, and the heirs of William Robinson. Decree. Complainant and defendant Rodgers are partners in the saw and grismills and timber, etc. on the lands as mentioned in the pleadings. It appears to the court that there should be an account taken between complainant and defendant Baker as administrator of William Robinson. The clerk will report to the next term of court. 25 Sep 1855. (Pp. 326-328)

Court adjourned until the next regular term. (P. 329)

Chancery Court met in the town of Smithville on the fourth Monday of Mar 1856, it being the 24th day of said month and the day assigned by law. The Chancellor failing to appear, the Clerk adjourned court. (P. 330)

The Chancellor not having arrived, the Clerk adjourned the court till the next regular term. (P. 330)

Chancery Court met on the first Thursday after the third Monday in Sep 1856, it being the 18th day of said month and the day assigned by law. The Chancellor not having appeared, the Clerk adjourned court till tomorrow morning at eight o'clock. (P. 330)

Court met. Broomfield L. Ridley, presiding. 19 Sep 1856. (P. 330)

GILES DRIVER versus POLLY DRIVER. It appears to the court that it has not been two years since defendant deserted the complainant. The cause is continued. 19 Sep 1856. (P. 331)

SAMUEL BRENT versus WILLIAM BATES. A compromise has been agreed on. 19 Sep 1856. (P. 331)

WILLIAM J. KELLEY and JOHN KELLEY versus WILLIAM BRASWELL and others. Final Decree. The charges are not sustained by the proof. 19 Sep 1856. (P. 331)

DAVID JAMES versus AMZI PATTERSON, HORACE A. PATTERSON, JOHN PATTERSON, ___ HALL, EASTER HARPER, E. M. NORTH and wife MARTHA, FELIX N. PATTERSON, WILLIAM M. BRADFORD and wife ELIZABETH. A compromise has been made. 19 Sep 1856. (P. 332)

T. C. DAVIS versus JESSE T. HOLLIS & COMPANY. Decree. 19 Sep 1856. (Pp. 332-334)

ALFRED BONE and WILLIAM BONE versus BENNETT and JOHN B. YERGAN. Complainants recover a judgment against defendants. Defendant John B. Yergan furnished materials and built a frame house in the town of Alexandria on the lot of said defendant. There is a lien on the property. A sale is ordered. 19 Sep 1856. (Pp. 334-335)

JAMES F. GOFF versus JOHN ROBINSON and others. Final Decree. The suit is dismissed. 19 Sep 1856. (Pp. 335-336)

WILLIAM GARVIN and others versus HENRY MADDLEBAUM and others. Final Decree. The clerk is to make an account and report back to court. 19 Sep 1856. (Pp. 336-340)

MONROE F. DOSS by his guardian John F. Moore. Ex Parte. Petition to sell slaves. It is in the interest of the said Monroe F. Doss that the slave, Jack, should be sold. 19 Sep 1856. (Pp. 340-341)

ETHELDRED FISH versus ROBERT CANTRELL. Final Decree. Said Robert Cantrell is the administrator of C. W. Kerley. 19 Sep 1856. (Pp. 341-342)

LUCY PARISH versus G. W. PARISH. Complainant is not entitled to any relief. The cause is dismissed. 19 Sep 1856. (P. 342)

CATHERINE CONNER versus TERRANCE CONNER. Defendant was guilty of adultery and cruel and inhuman treatment as charged in complainant's bill. Complainant is the mother of two children. Defendant is a man of bad moral character. The bonds of matrimony are dissolved. Complainant is given custody of the children. 19 Sep 1856. (Pp. 342-343)

THOMAS J. LEEK and wife and CHARLES SCHURER versus THOMAS LEEK and other heirs of Mathew Martin. The bill is taken for confessed. In 1846, complainant Thomas J. Leek purchased of Thomas Leek the lands mentioned in the pleadings for $596. The defendant, Thomas Leek, was selling the land as the agent of the respective parties, but had no regular power of attorney. Power of attorney was needed for William H. Young, Nancy Bogle, J. J. Bogle, Mathew Foster, and William M. Wilson, children of Mary Wilson, formerly Mary Martin who have one eighth interest. John Greenaigh and Joseph Melchore who have one sixteenth and Fanny Patton who has one third of one eighth. It is in the interest of these heirs that the deed be ratified. 19 Sep 1856. (Pp. 343-344)

A number of causes are continued. (Pp. 344-345)

SAMPSON BRASWELL versus JOHN W. WILLIAMS and MATHEW WILLIAMS, Administrators of William Williams. The case is referred to the Master to report. 19 Sep 1856. (P. 345)

JESSE SEWEL versus LEAH SEWEL. The complainant's bill is dismissed. 19 Sep 1856. (P. 346)

A. BONE & BROTHER and SNEED and others versus J. J. FORD and others. Several years ago, defendant Walter Bradley purchased the land mentioned in the pleading which was located near Alexandria. Defendants have several judgments against Walter Bradley. The court rules that the deed from Bradley to Ford is void and for nothing. The land is to be sold. 19 Sep 1856. (P. 347)

JAMES WHITE and others versus BRIEN and SAVAGE. Final Decree. Complainants' bill is dismissed. 19 Sep 1856. (P. 348)

MATHEW JOHNSON versus VICY JOHNSON. The bill is taken for confessed. The charges of adultery in the bill are true. The bonds of matrimony are dissolved. 19 Sep 1856. (P. 348)

JOHN CRIPS, THOMAS CRIPS, and others versus ZENITH CRIPS and others. Bill to partition land. At various times during the life time of the said Henry, John Thomas and Henry purchased several tracts of land. They were tenants in common. The transactions continued until about one year of the death of the said Henry at which time they made a partition of most of their lands. It appears that the Crips boys, John, Thomas, and Henry purchased the land from Thomas Simpson. 19 Sep 1856. (Pp. 349-350)

JOHN MASON and others versus VINSON WILLIAMS and JOHN WIL-
LIAMS. Final Decree. The parties agree to a compromise. 19
Sep 1856. (Pp. 350-351)

BENJAMIN CURTIS versus BRACKET ESTES, WILLIAM A. GARRISON,
and others. Decree. Defendant Bracket Estes was indebted to
complainant. A tract of land is to be sold for the debt. 19
Sep 1856. (Pp. 351-352)

DANIEL LASATER versus JOSEPH L. BYBEE and others. A compromise is reached. 8 Sep 1856. (P. 353)

THOMAS ALLEN and wife versus WILEY SANDERS and GEORGE W.
ALLEN. Decree. Complainants are the legal owners of the land
in dispute. Some years since, the land was sold for taxes and
bid off by defendant Allen. Complainant, afterwards, redeemed
the same. 19 Sep 1856. (Pp. 353-354)

WILLIAM GREEN versus ROBERT GORDON and WILLIAM BASSON. Decree. Defendant Gordon is possessed of the tract of land mentioned
in the pleadings. The title is held in trust for Gordon by the
said William Basson. Complainant has no legal remedy by which he
can make his said debt. The court orders the land to be sold. 19
Sep 1856. (Pp. 354-355)

SHADE TRAMEL versus THOMAS MALONE. Attachment. 19 Sep 1856.
(P. 355)

WILLIAM ROBERTS and other heirs versus ELIZA ROBINSON and
others. Petition to sell slaves. The Clerk is ordered to distribute the funds among the several heirs, making an equal division of the Central Bank money. J. W. Oran became the purchaser
of one of the slaves at the sale and executed his note. H. G.
Flippen purchased another of the slaves. The said Flippen has
since died. The Clerk is to recover from the securities of the
said Flippen. 19 Sep 1856. (Pp. 356-357)

Be it remembered that Chancellor B. L. Ridley on 31 Mar
1856 appointed Thomas Whaley as Clerk & Master pro tem until the
present term of said Chancery Court. On this the 20th day of Sep
1856, said Chancellor appointed said Thomas Whaley as Clerk &
Master of said court for the term of six years. (Pp. 357-360)

T. C. WROE and wife versus BRIEN, SAVAGE, and others. Decree. The deed of Duncan to Brien and Savage was without consideration when taken during the pendency of the suit between
Brien, Colms, and these complainants. Said deed is a cloud over
complainant's title and embarrass their defense to defendants'
action of ejectment. Said deed from Duncan to Brien and Savage
is declared null and void. 20 Sep 1856. (Pp. 360-361)

JOSEPH TURNEY versus JOHN SHEHANE and others. Final Decree.
The injunction is dissolved. 20 Sep 1856. (P. 361)

THORNTON CHRISTIE versus THOMAS DOWELL. Decree. (P. 361)

CATHARINE WYNN versus P. (   ). The allegation is sustained
as to the unfitness of the defendant to manage the trust fund.
The cause is transferred to the Circuit Court of Warren County.
20 Sep 1856. (P. 362)

JESSE MALONE versus A. NORRIS and E. W. TAYLOR. Decree. 20 Sep 1856. (Pp. 362-363)

THOMAS POTTER versus ISAAC CHRISMAN and others. The demurrer is well taken. 20 Sep 1856. (P. 364)

EDWARD LAWRENCE versus WILLIAM LAWRENCE and others. The bill was denied. The matter of controversy has been fully adjudicated. 20 Sep 1856. (P. 365)

SAMPSON BETHEL versus HENRY M. RAY and others. It is in the interest of all the parties that the land be sold. 20 Sep 1856. (P. 366)

GILES DRIVER versus JESSE and THOMAS SEWEL. Decree. On 9 Aug 1854, complainant recovered a judgment against defendant Jesse Sewel. The judgment was not paid. A town lot was ordered to be sold. 20 Sep 1856. (P. 367)

JOSIAH L. BASS versus MATHEW WILLIAMS. Defendant is justly indebted to the complainant. 20 Sep 1856. (P. 368)

Chancellor was pleased to adjourned the Court until the next regular term. (P. 369)

Chancery Court met in the town of Smithville on the first Thursday after the third Monday in Mar 1857, it being the 19th day of said month and the day assigned by law. The Chancellor not being present, the Clerk adjourned court until tomorrow morning at eight o'clock. (P. 370)

Court met pursuant to adjournment. Broomfield L. Ridley, presiding. 20 Mar 1857. (P. 370)

GILES DRIVER versus JESSE SEWEL. The complainant has fully recovered the amount due him. 20 Mar 1857. (Pp. 370-371)

JAMES PAGE versus JOHN BETHEL TAYLOR. Compromise. 20 Mar 1857. (Pp. 371-372)

VINSON WILLIAMS versus JOHN W. WILLIAMS and M. M. BRIEN. The Clerk begs leave to report. 20 Mar 1857. (Pp. 372-373)

A. BONE and others versus B. YEARGAN and others. Final Decree. The defendants have paid to the complainant their debt and interest. 20 Mar 1857. (P. 373)

JOHN B. RODGERS versus WILLIAM GREEN and THOMAS LEEK. This cause is continued. 20 Mar 1857. (P. 374)

FELIX N. PATTERSON versus RILEY MEDLIN, Administrator of Richard Herrin, JACKSON HERRIN, and MARY DYER. The complainant's bill is dismissed. 20 Mar 1857. (P. 374)

JOHN MARTIN, Administrator, and wife and others versus WILLIAM CAMPBELL and others. Final Decree. Defendant William Campbell was chargeable as the Administrator of Reuben Hawkins for $1859.52. Complainant Martin as Administrator of Martha Butcher was entitled to one fifth of the same. Defendant Campbell in right of his wife was entitled to one fifth of said amount. The other three fifth's belongs to the heirs of Reuben Hawkins.

There were several minors and administrators entitled to said fund. Manson M. Brien has been counsel in said cause throughout this. It has been a very tedious and heavy duty. It would seem reasonable for him to receive $500. 20 Mar 1857. (Pp. 375-376)

SEBASTIAN WILLIAMS versus BRACKET ESTES and others. Complainant was a bona fide creditor of said Bracket Estes. The said Estes executed a deed of trust to the said Williams. Property is ordered to be sold to pay the debt. 20 Mar 1857. (Pp. 376-379)

GEORGE W. EASTHAM versus JAMES C. BAKER and J. M. WHITLEY and others. Final Decree. Defendant Baker's intestate, Robinson, in his life time received for timber etc. at various times as trustee of said Eastham. Whitley was a partner of the said Robinson. The said George W. Eastham recovers from the Administrator of the said Robinson deceased and John M. Whitley jointly. 20 Mar 1857. (Pp. 379-380)

SAMUEL L. TYREE versus JAMES M. BAKER and JOHN B. RODGERS and others. Decree. The complainant's bill is well takened and sustained. 20 Mar 1857. (Pp. 380-381)

A. M. SAVAGE, Administrator of Joseph Crowder, versus JEREMIAH COGGIN and others. 20 Mar 1857. (Pp. 381-383)

SUSAN PITMAN versus JOHN PITMAN. Decree. The bill is taken for confessed. Complainant and defendant intermarried several years since. Defendant has abandoned the said complainant and has gone beyond the limits of the State. Said Susan is one of the legal heirs of William B. Allen. The property from the estate is ordered to be settled upon her free from the debts of her husband. 20 Mar 1857. (Pp. 383-384)

W. J. GIVAN and others versus ABNER S. LEECH. Decree. The bill is taken for confessed. The house and lot in Liberty on the west side of the turnpike adjoining the store house of Daniel Smith is ordered to be sold. 20 Mar 1857. (P. 384)

J. L. DEARMAN versus JESSE SEWELL and others. The bill is taken for confessed. Sewell is indebted to the said Dearman, but it does not appear what amount. The Clerk is to make a report. 20 Mar 1857. (P. 385)

REBECCA GARRISON versus JAMES L. GARRISON. Complainant and defendant intermarried about fifteen years ago in this State. They have continued to live together until a short time before the filing of complainant's bill. They had six children as the issue of said marriage, to wit, Lafayette, Angelena, Eliza, Melissa, William Carroll, and Thomas Jefferson. Said defendant has been greatly guilty of divers acts of adultery since the said marriage and was otherwise a man of immoral and evil habits given to profanity and intoxication. The bonds of matrimony are dissolved. The complainant is restored to her maiden name of Rebecca Malone. 20 Mar 1857. (P. 387)

MASSEY PICKETT versus JOSHUA PICKETT and others. This cause is continued. 20 Mar 1857. (P. 387)

SAMPSON BETHEL versus HENRY McRAY and others. On 10 Jan 1857, the land mentioned in the pleadings was sold at public auction. Sampson Bethel became the purchaser. 20 Mar 1857. (Pp. 387-388)

THOMAS D. PRICE versus BRACKET ESTES. The bill is taken for confessed. Said Bracket Estes purchased of said Price some years since a tract of land in the 9th District about one and a half miles west of Smithville on the Stage Road. Price recovered a judgment against the said Estes on 10 Jul 1856. The land is ordered sold. 20 Mar 1857. (Pp. 358-359)

SHADE TRAMEL versus THOMAS MALONE. The said Tramel became the purchaser of the tract of land mentioned in the pleadings. 20 Mar 1857. (P. 389)

WILLIAM GREEN versus ROBERT GORDON and others. Decree confirming report of sale. 20 Mar 1857. (Pp. 389-390)

WILLIAM J. GOSSETT and WILLIAM BURTON versus JAMES F. FOSTER. Order dissolving injunction. 20 Mar 1857. (Pp. 390-391)

C. W. L. HALE versus WILLIAM BLACKBURN. Blackburn recovered a judgment against the complainant for $175. Afterwards, the said Hale sued the defendant in Circuit Court for damages and filed this bill to enjoin the defendant from the collection of the said $175. (P. 391)

A number of causes ordering overruling demurrer. (Pp. 392-394)

STEPHEN ATNIP versus JOSEPH ATNIP. It is in the interest of the parties that the land be sold. 20 Mar 1857. (P. 394)

JAMES T. HENDERSON versus ROBERT CANTRELL, CAROLINE WADE, EVALINE WADE, WILLIAM M. WADE, GEORGE WADE, LUELLA WADE, TIMOTHY M. WADE, AND JESSE SEWELL. Robert Cantrell and William M. Wade were partners with the privilege of repurchasing. The said Wade died, leaving the said widow and minors as his heirs. After the death of the said Wade, said Sewell, by his agent, repurchased the land from said Cantrell. Said Sewell is indebted to the said Henderson for $446.87. Complainant dismisses his bill as to the widow, Caroline Wade, and the minors. The land is ordered to be sold by the clerk. 20 Mar 1857. (P. 396)

GEORGE E. BAKER and others versus JOSEPH ATNIP and others. Decree. 20 Mar 1857. (P. 397)

L. B. FITE & COMPANY versus THOMAS HUNT and others. The defendant has been guilty of a contempt of court in violating the injunction. 20 Mar 1857. (P. 398)

THOMAS WHALEY, Clerk & Master, versus WILLIAM T. ISBELL. 20 Mar 1857. (P. 399)

Chancery Court met in the town of Smithville on the second day of Apr 1883, it being the first Monday in said month. W. G. Crowley, presiding. (P. 1)

In the matter of W. W. Wade, Clerk & Master. Be it remembered that heretofore, to wit, on the ___ day of Mar 1883, W. W. Wade, Clerk & Master of this Court, tendered his resignation. The resignation was to take effect Monday, the 19th of Mar 1883. The resignation is accepted by the Chancellor. (P. 1)

W. G. Crowley is appointed to fill the vacancy for the term of six years from this day. (The name is also written as M. A. Crowley.) (Pp. 1-6)

John B. Tubb is appointed as Deputy Clerk. 2 Apr 1883. (P. 6)

S. W. McCLELLAN Et Al versus THOMAS J. SNEED Et Al and ELLEN F. SNEED. Thomas F. Bowman, Administrator of Thomas J. Sneed, has agreed to waive the service of process and enter his appearance. 3 Apr 1883. (P. 7)

WILLIAM LINDSEY versus W. F. CALLICOT. This cause came for hearing upon motion of solicitor of Anne Callicot, Administrator of J. J. Callicot to be allowed to file her answer as a cross bill. 3 Apr 1883. (P. 8)

J. H. OVERALL versus P. L. REYNOLDS. Complainant has paid to defendant $100 on the judgment mentioned in the bill. The remainder of said judgment has been settled between parties. 3 Apr 1883. (Pp. 8-9)

A number of causes are continued. (Pp. 9-10)

JOHN E. ROBINSON Et Al versus JAMES A. BARRETT, Executor. The plaintiffs suggested the death of Caroline Barrett. Said Caroline has no administrator. Robert, Eugene, Charles, Ocea, Elom, and Earnest Barrett are her only children and heirs. The former order in this cause to take and state an account with defendant James A. Barrett is revised. 3 Apr 1883. (Pp. 10-11)

MOSES PACE and wife versus A. D. BAIN. There is a tract of land on which a lien was decreed. The clerk is to sell the land. 3 Apr 1883. (P. 11)

THOMAS J. SNEED, JR. versus W. B. STOKES Et Al. 3 Apr 1883. (P. 11)

J. L. COLVERT, Administrator, versus JAMES STALEY Et Al. A number of parties are made a part of this suit for the purpose of prosecuting claims against the estate of T. N. Christian. 3 Apr 1857. (P. 12)

A. T. WOOD versus J. A. WOOD. Certain property was attached in this cause belonging to the defendant. The land is ordered to be sold. 3 Apr 1883. (P. 12)

JAMES H. CAMERON next friend versus J. L. COLVERT, Administrator. 3 Apr 1883. (Pp. 12-13)

M. A. SCOTT next friend versus WILLIAM VICK, Administrator, and others. The complainants have further time to comply with the order. 3 Apr 1883. (P. 13)

JOSEPH RAULSTON versus C. M. RAULSTON Et Al. The parties agree to a compromise. 3 Apr 1883. (P. 13)

A. G. WILLIAMS versus M. A. CATHCART Et Al. The Clerk took an account with defendant Leroy Braswell as Administrator of Jane Biford. The administrator did not show that he made any distributions. 3 Apr 1883. (P. 14)

The Chancellor failed to appear today to hold the Court. Honorable H. H. Dillard appeared and presented a commission from the Governor of the State of Tennessee as Special Chancellor to hold this court. 4 Apr 1883. (Pp. 15-16)

J. H. OVERALL versus BERRY BALLENGER. The Clerk sold the (feat) boat to James H. Overall for $150. 4 Apr 1883. (P. 16)

A number of causes are continued. (P. 17)

WILLIAM WILDER Et Al versus J. T. CLAYBORN Et Al. Decree. The Chancellor is of the opinion and so decrees that the sale and purchase of the premises in controversy is null and void. Title is vested in the heirs of Moses Wilder as set out in the bill. 4 Apr 1883. (Pp. 18-19)

L. Y. DAVIS Et Al versus W. L. DRIVER Et Al. The death of M. J. Lewis is suggested, leaving an infant child named W. P. Lewis who it appears is a necessary party to this cause. He is ordered to appear before this court in Oct 1883. (P. 19)

GEORGE W. ALLEN and others versus S. P. ELLIOTT and others. Depositions are ordered suppressed. 4 Apr 1883. (P. 20)

NANCY DURHAM versus W. R. DURHAM. The bill is taken for confessed. 5 Apr 1883. (P. 21)

NANCY DURHAM versus W. R. DURHAM. A considerable amount of property has been attached. Complainant has no seperate property of her own. It is a proper cause in which to allow her alimony pending the litigation to pay counsel. 5 Apr 1883. (P. 21)

JANE HATHAWAY VERSUS JAMES H. WITT and others. The bill is taken for confessed. 5 Apr 1883. (Pp. 21-22)

W. B. STOKES versus ROBERT JOHNSON and wife. The depositions are not well taken. 5 Apr 1883. (P. 22)

R. B. FLOYD versus B. J. BETHEL. The bill is taken for confessed. 5 Apr 1883. (P. 22)

NANCY DURHAM versus W. R. DURHAM. The Clerk reports that $75 would be a reasonable fee for counsel. Defendant is allowed sixty days to pay the same. 5 Apr 1883. (P. 23)

S. W. McCLELLAN Et Al versus T. J. SNEED Et Al. Motion for the appointment of a guardian for the minor defendants. Petition of complainants that the defendants Horace Sneed, Joseph Sneed,

(Beauty) Williams, Robert Williams, Adolphus Williams, John Williams, Kate Lamb, Lou Lamb, and John Lamb are minors without guardian. P. T. Shores is appointed guardian. 5 Apr 1883. (P. 24)

MARY BRASWELL versus S. BRASWELL Et Al. Decree. The Clerk is to take proof and report as to the value in money of the dower interest of the complainant in the lands of William Braswell deceased. 5 Apr 1883. (Pp. 24-25)

ELI STALEY versus R. V. STALEY. The death of Eli Staley was suggested. William Moore is his administrator. 5 Apr 1883. (P. 25)

GEORGE W. PUCKETT versus GEORGE W. MEDLEY. Decree. The court is of the opinion that the conveyance of the 200 acre tract was not intended by the parties as an absolute sale, but was made to indemnify and secure the defendant in the event he had the debt to pay. 6 Apr 1883. (Pp. 26-27)

T. N. CHRISTIAN versus M. A. J. FERRELL. The death of complainant T. N. Christian was suggested. J. L. Colvert is his administrator. Rebecca Christian is the widow of the said T. N. Christian. William Christian, Thomas Christian, John Christian, James Christian, John Windham and wife Nancy of DeKalb County; James Staley and wife Etta of White County are the only children of the said T. N. Christian. 6 Apr 1883. (P. 28)

C. M. SCHURER Et Al versus M. M. BRIEN, SR. Et Al. The injunction should not be dissolved. 6 Apr 1883. (Pp. 28-29)

NANCY ADCOCK versus T. M. ADCOCK. Complainant is allowed to file an amended bill. 6 Apr 1883. (P. 29)

W. R. COGGIN versus E. A. COGGIN. The county tax is improperly taxed. The same is strickened out of the cost bill. 6 Apr 1883. (P. 29)

R. H. CATHCART and wife CHARITY versus WILLIAM SELLARS, Executor of Matthew Sellars. The cause is continued in order that the witnesses might be cross examined. 6 Apr 1883. (Pp. 31-32)

WEBB, CHEEK, & COMPANY versus J. S. DUNLAP Et Al. Decree. 6 Apr 1883. (P. 32)

JAMES H. CAMERON Et Al versus J. L. COLVERT, Administrator, Et Al. The Clerk reports that it is in the interest of the parties that the land be sold for distribution among the heirs. A portion of the heirs are minors. The lands on account of their condition cannot be rented for as much as the interest would be worth on the money. 6 Apr 1883. (Pp. 32-34)

P. C. BLUGHM versus W. C. HAYS Et Al. Order. 6 Apr 1883. (Pp. 34-35)

JOB TRAPP, Guardian, and others versus J. H. TRAMMELL Et Al. The Clerk will make a report at the next term of court. 6 Apr 1883. (P. 35)

C. H. HALL versus S. W. HALL. Sale of a tract of land to

W. L. Turney. 7 Apr 1883. (P. 36)

A number of causes are continued. (Pp. 36-37)

J. H. CANTRELL versus J. L. COLVERT Et Al. Final Decree.
Complainant announced that he was not ready for hearing on account of his title papers to the land in dispute not being on
file. 7 Apr 1883. (Pp. 38-39)

L. J. DAVIS, Widow of A. L. Davis, versus M. D. SMALLMAN
and other heirs of A. L. Davis. Complainant has filed the bill
to be endowed of the real estate of her husband A. L. Davis.
She elected to take a sum in gross in lieu of dower. This
cause being heard in connection with the cause of F. H. Robertson and wife against D. B. Davis Et Al now pending in this court.
Complainant is entitled to endowment from the lands sold in the
said cause of Robinson and wife to the extent of the interest of
A. L. Davis. 6 Apr 1883. (Pp. 39-40)

M. C. PARRISH versus FRANKLIN PARRISH. Complainant is a
citizen of DeKalb County. She has been a citizen for more than
two years. She and defendant were married to each other and
lived together as husband and wife. During said marriage, defendant failed to provide for her the necessities of life for the
several years. The bonds of matrimony are dissolved. 6 Apr
1883. (Pp. 40-41)

GEORGE W. DURHAM versus ELIZABETH DURHAM. The bill is
taken for confessed. The charge is sustained of an attempt to
poison complainant by defendant. The bonds of matrimony are
dissolved. 6 Apr 1883. (P. 41)

JAMES H. CAMERSON next friend versus J. L. COLVERT, Administrator Et Al. The lands are situated so that they cannot be
divided among the heirs without manifest injury to parties.
About 250 acres of the land is woodland with no improvements and
not valuable for cultivation. The home place including the
dwelling is worth $1000. 9 Apr 1883. (Pp. 42-43)

SOLOMON GOODMAN versus ELIZABETH GOODMAN. A sale was ordered to satisfy the lien which has not been complied with. 9
Apr 1883. (P. 44)

GEORGE W. PUCKETT versus GEORGE W. MEDLEY. The Master will
sell the land to the highest bidder. 9 Apr 1883. (P. 44)

JOHN TURNEY versus ISAAC TURNEY. The former report made
with the Administrator of Joseph Turney, the guardian of John
Turney and Parlee Turney has been lost or unintentionally mislaid and cannot be found. The court orders that the former order of reference be revived. 9 Apr 1883. (P. 45)

S. W. McCLELLAN Et Al versus T. J. SNEED Et Al. Decree.
In 1859 or 1860, Yancy Lamb and wife filed their bill in this
court against Thomas J. Sneed Et Al to recover the hire for
certain slaves then in possession of said Sneed which cause was
finally determined by the Supreme Court. In 1873, J. D. White
as Treasurer of Alexandria Chapter Royal Arch Masons recovered
against said Sneed. 9 Apr 1883. (Pp. 46-48)

M. J. WILLIAMS versus W. R. WILLIAMS Et Al. An report is to be given as to whether the lands mentioned in the pleadings can be equitably partitioned between the parties. 10 Apr 1883. (P. 49)

G. R. WEST versus W. J. GIVAN Et Al. All equities set forth in the bill are met. 10 Apr 1883. (Pp. 49-50)

T. W. WEST versus T. E. WEST. The Special Commissioner is to be paid $100 for his services. 10 Apr 1883. (P. 50)

LAFAYETTE GARRISON versus J. J. FORD and T. W. WADE. Defendants are enjoined from proceeding further with the sale of the lands. 10 Apr 1883. (P. 51)

JAMES H. CAMERON next friend versus J. L. COLVERT and others. The settlement made by R. V. Staley, Executrix of T. Staley is set aside. The Clerk will settle between the legatees of said T. Staley. 10 Apr 1883. (P. 52)

MARY HAIL Et Al versus E. A. COGGIN and others. The Court orders that cost bill be so retaxed as to strike out all the fees of witnesses. 10 Apr 1883. (P. 52)

J. W. INGE Et Al versus M. J. MALONE Et Al. Process has been served on John Reed and wife Matilda, Monroe Malone, James Fisher, Mary Fisher, Andrew Scruggs and wife Mary. 10 Apr 1883. (P. 53)

JAMES HOLLANDSWORTH versus WILLIAM VICK Et Al. B. M. Cantrell has performed services as guardian to the minoe heirs of Marget Fite and Mary Carnes. They have no funds. 10 Apr 1883. (P. 54)

GABE HERRON versus JACKSON HERRON Et Al. The death of Gabe Herron was suggested. The cause has not been revived. 10 Apr 1883. (P. 84)

JOSEPH CLARK Et Al versus A. FRAZIER Et Al. The receiver's report is made and confirmed. 10 Apr 1883. (Pp. 54-58)

W. W. WADE Et Al versus J. E. CLARK Et Al. T. A. Gold, J. R. Gold, J. E. Gold, W. D. Gold, F. M. Gold, J. G. Gold, and N. L. Gold pray to be made parties to this cause. The Court is of the opinion that said Golds should be made defendants. 10 Apr 1883. (Pp. 58-59)

M. M. BRIEN versus R. B. HENDRIXSON, JOHN PARKER, JOHN CURTIS, ISAAC W. OVERALL, ANDREW JACKSON OVERALL, and the heirs of Andrew Jackson Overall, to wit, J. M. and S. M. Overall, minors, SOPHIA OVERALL, J. M. OVERALL, and others. On 25 Jul 1842, there was granted by the State of Tennessee to defendant Andrew Jackson Overall and Isaac Overall by Grant No. 8796 400 acres. Said Andrew Jackson Overall and Isaac Overall sold to the said M. M. Brien the said tract of land. Said Brien went into immediate possession. The deed is lost or unintentionally mislayed. Brien is to be allowed to set up and establish his last deed. 10 Apr 1883. (Pp. 59-61)

GEORGE BRATTEN versus S. B. SPURLOCK and J. N. CAMPBELL.

10 Apr 1883. (Pp. 62-63)

J. W. HENDERSON versus WILLIAM FITE. The former Clerk has collected the purchase notes and cash judgments mentioned in this cause. 10 Apr 1883. (P. 64)

B. M. CANTRELL, Administrator, and others versus MICKEY CRIPS Et Al. The land was sold in Sep 1879. John B. Robinson became the purchaser. 10 Apr 1883. (Pp. 64-65)

F. B. NOLLNER versus JOHN E. CLARK Et Al. The Receiver insists he is entitled to a fee. 10 Apr 1883. (Pp. 65-66)

WILLIAM MANNERS Et Al versus T. N. CHRISTIAN Et Al. Since the filing of the bill, the defendant, T. N. Christian, has departed this life. James L. Colvert has been appointed administrator. This cause is revised against him. 10 Apr 1883. (P. 66)

C. M. SCHURER Et Al versus M. M. BRIEN Et Al. This is a proper cause for a reference. 10 Apr 1883. (Pp. 66-67)

T. E. WEST and others versus THOMAS W. WEST and J. B. ROBINSON. The decree is rescinded and for nothing. 10 Apr 1883. (P. 67)

W. W. WADE, Clerk & Master, versus Z. A. CULWELL Et Al. It is ordered that the cost of this cause be taxed as the other cost. 10 Apr 1883. (Pp. 67-68)

J. G. SQUIRES versus S. S. CRADDOCK Et Al. The Clerk is to report on the sale of a tract of land belonging to Stephen Sellers and located in the 4th District. 10 Apr 1883. (Pp. 68-69)

B. M. CANTRELL, Administrator, versus MICKEY CRIPS. M. J. Crips, C. Crips, John T. Crips, W. H. Crips, Nancy Edge, Daniel Crips, and Mickey Crips are minors except the said Mickey and she is not capable of acting for herself. This is a proper cause for a guardian. J. J. Ford is appointed guardian. 10 Apr 1883. (P. 69)

GEORGE W. ALLEN Et Al versus S. P. ELLIOTT. Complainant recovers of defendant. 10 Apr 1883. (Pp. 69-70)

JAMES HOLLANDSWORTH versus WILLIAM VICK Et Al. The house and lot mentioned in the pleading is ordered sold. James Hollandsworth was the highest bidder. 10 Apr 1883. The property is divested out of the heirs of Eli Vick and vested in the said Hollandsworth. 10 Apr 1883. (Pp. 70-71)

S. W. McCLELLAN Et Al versus T. J. SNEED Et Al. Petition of Ellen F. Sneed for a new hearing. Said Ellen F. Sneed is not able to appear in court on account of physical disability. 10 Apr 1883. (P. 72)

B. T. R. FOSTER Et Al versus MARY L. FOSTER Et Al. The former decree is set aside. The former order of sale is revived. The Master will sell the house and lot. 10 Apr 1883. (P. 72)

W. B. BRIDGES versus A. J. EDWARDS Et Al. It appears to the court that the answer of defendants and the deposition of John D. Bone is out of the file. The same is unintentionally lost or mislaid. The cause is continued. 10 Apr 1883. (P. 73)

I. ALEXANDER Et Al versus A. FRAZIER, Executor, Et Al. It was suggested that M. H. Pack is the husband and administrator of Martha Pack. The only children and heirs of the said Martha are Mary E., Helen L., Parlie F., and Cornelius C. Pack. Helen Alexander, wife of complainant Alexander, is dead. This suit has been revised in favor of the said Isaac Alexander as the Administrator of the said Helen Alexander. The said Helen left the following minor children, to wit, Henry, Maggie, Nancy, and Harrison Alexander. The cause is revised in the name of the said minor children. 10 Apr 1883. (Pp. 73-74)

TILMAN ADCOCK, Guardian, Et Al versus HIRAM CANTRELL Et Al. The land mentioned was sold to R. T. Frisby with a lien on it. The Clerk will advertize the land for sale. 10 Apr 1883. (P. 74)

GABRIEL HERRON versus JACKSON HERRON. The Clerk is to take an account. 10 Apr 1883. (P. 74)

WOOD versus J. B. PARRISH Et Al. Lela Sanders is a minor without guardian. B. M. Cantrell is appointed guardian. 10 Apr 1883. (P. 75)

JANE HATHAWAY versus JAMES H. HATHAWAY Et Al. Thomas Hathaway, Samuel Hathaway, and Tennie Hathaway are minors without guardian. B. M. Cantrell is appointed guardian. 10 Apr 1883. (P. 75)

R. B. FLOYD versus B. J. BETHEL. Complainant is the legal owner and is entitled to receive the amount of the balance of the note. 10 Apr 1883. (Pp. 76-77)

TANNER O'CANNON versus TENNESSEE O'CANNON. Defendant recovers of the complainant. 10 Apr 1883. (P. 77)

WEBB, CHEEK, & COMPANY versus J. S. DUNLAP. Report of the receiver to the present term of court. 10 Apr 1883. (P. 78)

A number of causes are continued. (Pp. 79-81)

WILLIAM H. MAGNESS versus W. G. ROWLAND. The defendant has failed to answer. The bill is taken for confessed. 10 Apr 1883. (P. 81)

JAMES GOODNER versus C. TURNER Et Al. The deed from James Goodner to William Eller was legally registered in the Register's Office on 9 Jun 1874 and before defendant C. Turner purchased the said land. 10 Apr 1883. (Pp. 82-83)

A number of causes are continued. (P. 84)

S. B. HARRIMAN and wife versus TILMAN CROOK and others. Defendant Crook had no title to the land he sold to complainants. Complainants have been ejected from the same. Defendant is insolvent. 10 Apr 1883. (P. 85)

41

WILLIAM H. MAGNESS versus W. G. ROWLAND. The bill is taken for confessed. J. P. Barry and wife executed a deed to said Rowland to the land mentioned in the bill. Said deed was dated 18 Sep 1878 retaining a lien on it. Rowland executed two notes. The note is due. The land was ordered sold. 10 Apr 1883. (Pp. 85-86)

SAM SMITH, Administrator of David Smith's, versus JOHN T. STOKES Et Al. Commissioners appointed to lay off and set apart to John T. Stokes out of the land mentioned in the pleadings. 10 Apr 1883. (P. 87)

M. C. VICK Et Al versus WILLIAM VICK Et Al. Complainants in the original bill, M. C. Vick and others were the wards of Eli Vick deceased. They are entitled to a tract of land left by Leonard Fite to his grandchildren, to wit, L. F. Moore, Peggy Jane Vick and others. Said deed is dated 27 Feb 1841. The widow, Amanda Vick, is entitled to all the rents from the Hollandsworth lot. Said Amanda is entitled to the homestead and dower. 10 Apr 1883. (Pp. 88-89)

P. M. MARTIN Et Al versus JOHN J. AUSTIN. The bill is taken for confessed. 10 Apr 1883. (Pp. 89-90)

GARR, SCOTT, & COMPANY versus T. W. FITTS Et Al. 10 Apr 1883. (Pp. 90-91)

JANE HATHAWAY versus J. H. WITT Et Al. Complainant is the owner of the mortgage. 10 Apr 1883. (Pp. 91-92)

SARAH PACK Et Al versus I. CANTRELL Et Al. Defendants Bartemus Pack, Elizabeth Pack, William Rhodes, and W. T. Shields have failed to plead answer. The bill is taken for confessed. 10 Apr 1883. (Pp. 93-94)

M. J. WILLIAMS versus W. R. WILLIAMS Et Al. It is in the interest of the parties that the land be sold. 10 Apr 1883. (Pp. 94-95)

J. E. ROBINSON Et Al versus J. A. BARRETT Et Al. J. A. Barrett, Administrator of his wife, agrees that this suit might be revived against him as administrator. The order entered at the present term directing the issuance of a sci fa against his children is rescinded. 10 Apr 1883. (Pp. 95-96)

J. M. FITE Et Al versus J. T. HOLLIS Et Al. 10 Apr 1883. (P. 96)

C. W. ANDERSON and wife versus HENRY ADCOCK Et Al. Defendant and his wife executed deeds in the manner prescribed by the statute to the land mentioned in the pleadings to complainant M. A. Anderson. The cause is dismissed. 10 Apr 1883. (P. 97)

WOOD, Administrator, versus J. B. PARISH Et Al. The estate is insolvent. 10 Apr 1883. (Pp. 97-98)

G. W. PUCKETT versus G. W. MEDLEY Et Al. The defendant prayed an appeal. 10 Apr 1883. (P. 98)

WILLIAM LINDSEY versus W. F. CALICOTT Et Al. The death of

defendant John J. Calicott has been suggested and proven. Said parties are his only heirs at law. The bill is revived against against Vera Calicott. B. M. Cantrell is appointed her guardian. 10 Apr 1883. (Pp. 98-99)

Court is adjourned until next term of court. (P. 99)

Chancery Court met in the town of Smithville on the 1st Monday in Oct, it being the 1st day of said month, 1883. This, being the time appointed by law for the Fifth Chancery Division to meet in the town of Smithville. The Honorable W. G. Crowley failed to appear. The Clerk proceeded to open court and hold an election to elect a Special Chancellor. T. J. Bradford was elected as Special Chancellor. The court then adjourned until 6 Nov 1883. (P. 100)

Chancery Court met in the town of Smithville on 6 Nov 1883, it being the first Tuesday after the 1st Monday in said month. H. W. McConnell, presiding. (P. 101)

A number of causes were continued. (Pp. 101-102)

HELEN SCHURER, Administrator of Charles Schurer, versus MARTIN FOUTCH and others. Final Decree. On 16 Oct 1866, complainant in the Circuit Court of DeKalb County obtained a judgment against Defendant Foutch for the sum of $368. Said debt was secured by a tract of land made by Defendant Foutch to Samuel Wafford on 25 Nov 1865. The land has been sold. 6 Nov 1883. (Pp. 102-103)

GABRIEL HERRON versus JACKSON HERRON. The commissioner is to take an account to determine what, if anything, is due from Jackson Herron to Gabriel Herron. 6 Nov 1883. (Pp. 103-106)

G. W. PUCKETT versus G. W. MEDLEY Et Al. A tract of land is ordered sold. 6 Nov 1883. (Pp. 106-107)

MARY FRAZIER versus J. B. FRAZIER. Final Decree. The court was to determine whether or not a partnership existed between defendant's intestate, A. L. Frazier, and complainant Mary Frazier. If so, what was the basis of the partnership. The court has determined that there was a partnership. The partnership began in 1872 or 1873. They were partners in the use of their land and the livestock owned by each. A. L. Frazier was to manage the business and the profits were to be equally divided. 6 Nov 1883. (Pp. 107-109)

MORGAN, THOMAS, & COMPANY versus OVERALL and HOLLANDSWORTH. Decree. 7 Nov 1883. (Pp. 109-110)

H. L. C. MOORE versus C. A. CANTRELL Et Al. Decree. 7 Nov 1883. (Pp. 110-111)

SARAH SHAW Et Al versus W. B. SHAW Et Al. The defendant shall be permitted to make defense to complainant's bill. 7 Nov 1883. (P. 111)

M. D. SMALLMAN, Administrator of A. L. Davis; L. J. DAVIS, J. L. DAVIS, MOLLIE E. DAVIS, ANNA L. DAVIS, ROBERT WHARTON and MARGARET T. WHARTON versus SAMUEL McHOOD and others. The allegations of the bill are sustained by the proof. The logs in the controvery belonged to the complainant. 7 Nov 1883. (Pp. 111-112)

J. E. ROBINSON Et Al versus J. A. BARRETT, Executor. James A. Barrett, Executor of N. Smith was on 2 Aug 1880 indebted to the heirs of the said deceased in the sum of $2358.74. 7 Nov 1883. (Pp. 112-114)

SARAH SHAW versus W. B. SHAW Et Al. The court is pleased to set aside the judgment. 7 Nov 1883. (P. 115)

JOHN C. HUGHES versus JAMES R. SMITH. Final Decree. Complainant recovers of the defendant. 7 Nov 1883. (Pp. 115-116)

ELI STALEY versus R. V. STALEY Et Al. Judgment in favor of Eli Staley against defendant R. V. Staley as Executor of T. Staley. 7 Nov 1883. (P. 116)

C. W. ANDERSON versus DAVID FISHER Et Al. The death of defendant Isaac Cantrell was suggested. Mary L. Cantrell and Sarah J. Moore of Warren County and Charlie A. Cantrell, William H. Cantrell, Martha L. Cantrell, Nancy A. Cantrell, Calvin B. Cantrell, Jr., Edna F. Cantrell, Emma F. Cantrell, Walter J. Cantrell, and Virginia Cantrell of DeKalb County are his heirs. 7 Nov 1883. (Pp. 116-117)

RICHARD M. DELONG Et Al versus DAVID DELONG Et Al. Final Decree. The Clerk is to pay over to complainant's solicitor the purchase money. 8 Nov 1883. (P. 117)

M. C. VICK Et Al versus WILLIAM VICK Et Al. The tract described in the deed from Leonard Fite to his grandchildren, L. F. Moore, Peggy Jane Vick, and others. The deed was for 235 acres in the 2nd District and was dated 27 Feb 1841. The land was sold to J. G. Squires. A note was executed with W. L. Vick and William Vick. 8 Nov 1883. (PP. 118-119)

P. H. HANKINS versus W. R. PARRISH Et Al. 8 Nov 1883. (P. 120)

H. DENTON and others versus SAM H. MALONE and others. Motion of complainants to have a guardian appointed for the minor defendants, James L. and Mary Fisher. T. J. Fisher was appointed guardian. H. Dycus was guardian for the minor defendant W. D. Hardcastle. 8 Nov 1883. (P. 121)

A. J. VANTREASE, Administrator, versus JAMES P. DOSS Et Al. A decree was rendered against said A. J. Vantrease. 8 Nov 1883. (Pp. 121-122)

C. B. CANTRELL Et Al versus C. D. SMALLMAN Et Al. This is a proper cause for a bill to be filed. 8 Nov 1883. (P. 123)

JOHN H. SAVAGE versus DAVID MALONE. The minor defendant, J. A. Dycus, and his guardian, W. D. Hardcastle, have been served by the Sheriff of Jackson County. No answer has been filed. Defendants, Mary L. Fisher and James N. Fisher are minors without guardian. They have been summoned by the Sheriff of Smith County. T. J. Fisher is their court appointed guardian. 8 Nov 1883.

(Pp. 123-124)

T. DUNN and wife versus H. P. KEMP and others. Decree. The petitioner and the other heirs of John Goodner are made defendants. They are allowed until March to file. 8 Nov 1883. (P. 124)

JOSEPH CLARK Et Al versus AARON FRAZIER Et Al. Counsel for complainants have been paid out of the funds. 8 Nov 1883. (Pp. 125-126)

WILLIAM WILDER Et Al versus J. F. CLAYBORN. The premises in controversy are not susceptible of a fair and equal division among the Wilder heirs. A sale is ordered. 8 Nov 1883. (Pp. 126-127)

THOMAS J. SNEED versus W. B. STOKES and others. The court is of the opinion that the paper written by C. W. L. Hale did not authorize Wade to sign his name to the injunction bond. 8 Nov 1883. (Pp. 127-128)

J. D. WHEELER Et Al versus T. W. EASON Et Al. Decree. Complainants are not entitled to the relief sought. 8 Nov 1883. (P. 128)

L. Y. DAVIS and others versus LAWRENCE DRIVER and others. The Clerk is to determine how much is due to each of the heirs of Giles Driver. 8 Nov 1883. (Pp. 129-130)

MARY L. FOSTER Et Al versus J. B. ROBINSON Et Al. Defendants Bettie Meacham, Mattie Foster, Charles Foster, Sidney Foster, Jesse Foster, Frierson Foster, Annie Foster, Fannie Foster, Sauky Foster, and Flora Foster are minors without guardian. A. Avant is appointed guardian. 8 Nov 1883. (Pp. 130-131)

B. N. HICKS versus B. B. TAYLOR Et Al. Complainant recovers of defendant. 8 Nov 1883. (P. 131)

WILLIAM LINDSLEY versus W. F. CALLICOTT. Final Decree. Complainant is indebted to defendants who are the administrators of J. J. Callicott. Defendant, W. F. Callicott, is indebted to complainant. 8 Nov 1883. (Pp. 132-134)

NANCY ADCOCK versus T. C. ADCOCK. Defendant has been guilty of adultery with Mat Parish, but not guilty of the cruel treatment as charged in complainant's bill. Complainant's bill is dismissed so far as it seeks relief upon the grounds of cruel treatment. But it is decreed that upon the grounds of adultery, the bonds of matrimony are dissolved. The custody of their child is to be decreed. 8 Nov 1883. (P. 135)

J. H. DENTON Et Al versus R. B. WEST Et Al. Decree. 10 Nov 1883. (P. 136)

WILLIAM H. MAGNESS VERSUS W. G. ROWLAND. Decree. A tract of land in the 1st District containing 65 acres was ordered sold. The said William H. Magness was the highest bidder. 10 Nov 1883. (Pp. 136-137)

Court adjourned until tomorrow morning. (P. 137)

R. C. NESMITH and M. D. SMALLMAN versus GEORGE W. WALTON. Decree. The bill is taken for confessed. There is a lien on a tract of land. A sale is ordered. 12 Nov 1883. (P. 138)

B. B. FLOYD versus B. J. BETHEL. Decree. T. W. Eason was the highest bidder for a tract of land. 12 Nov 1883. (Pp. 138-139)

JAMES GIBBS versus D. W. DINGES. Complainant recovers of Dinges. 14 Nov 1883. (P. 140)

A. T. FISHER Et Al versus C. J. WALKER. 14 Nov 1883. (Pp. 141-142)

J. A. MOSS versus R. S. LOVE, Administrator, Et Al. R. S. Love is the administrator of G. A. Love. S. F. Love is also the administrator. The estate is liable to the complainant. 14 Nov 1883. (Pp. 142-143)

(Page 144 is rescinded)

A. J. VANTREASE versus DANIEL SMITH Et Al. Complainant recovers. 14 Nov 1883. (P. 145)

LUCINDA TURNEY versus J. H. TURNEY and others. The Clerk will make a report as to what would be reasonable for Cantrell and Ford for their services. 14 Nov 1883. (P. 146)

J. C. JOHNSON versus WILLIAM TRUETT Et Al. The land mentioned in this bill belonged to the complainant. Defendant has commenced an action of damage in Circuit Court against the said Johnson. The suit in Circuit Court is perpetually enjoined. 14 Nov 1883. (Pp. 146-147)

CHARITY CATHCART Et Al versus WILLIAM SELLARS Executor, Et Al. Complainant Charity and her husband were parties to the bill filed on 11 Sep 1865 to sell the land and the estate of Mathew Sellars by her own consent. The bill of the complainant cannot be maintained. The Chancellor set aside the acts of the commissioners in 1863 as to negroes James and Clara. The charges of fraud in the bill are not sustained by the proof. 14 Nov 1883. (Pp. 147-149)

T. J. CRIPS and wife versus B. JENKINS Et Al. Report of the Clerk reporting the sale of the land of William M. Hall, Martha Hall, Joseph W. Hall, Julia Hall, and Jennie Bell Hall, heirs of Paralee Hall deceased. 14 Nov 1883. (Pp. 149-150)

SARAH HALL Et Al versus W. B. SHAW. 14 Nov 1883. (Pp. 150-151)

JOHN D. BONE, Administrator of A. L. Bone, versus JOHN RAMSEY. 14 Nov 1883. (P. 151)

JOHN H. SAVAGE versus DAVID MALONE Et Al. Complainant sold the land mentioned to Josiah W. Inge. There was a lien on the land. The said Inge has departed this life more than six months before the filing of this bill. No person can be found to administer the estate. If the notes are not paid, the Clerk is ordered to sell the land. 14 Nov 1883. (Pp. 152-154)

W. D. PRICHARD Et Al versus J. M. LOVE Et Al. Subpoena to
answer has been issued on J. M. Love, Susan Love, H. E. Love,
L. J. Magness, J. J. Hardcastle; E. A. Coggin, Administrator,
W. R. Coggin, S. H. Truett, W. B. Bartlett, James Turner, William
Turner, Jesse Hoggard, Milton Bartlett, Joseph Bartlett. De-
fendant H. E. Love is a minor without guardian. 14 Nov 1883.
(P. 154)

BENJAMIN ANDERSON versus E. J. BRATTEN Et Al. Complainant
recovers of Jordan Goggin, Administrator of E. J. Bratten, and
G. W. Turney. Defendant Matilda Bratten, wife of E. J. Bratten
is entitled to a house and lot. 14 Nov 1883. (Pp. 154-155)

J. D. WHEELER Et Al versus T. W. EASON Et Al. The heirs of
James Goodner deceased have no homestead rights in the lot in
dispute. 14 Nov 1883. (Pp. 155-156)

MARY BRASWELL Et Al versus SAMUEL BRASWELL Et Al. The fund
arising from the sale of the land of William Braswell in this
cause together with interest now amounts to the sum of $962.32.
Out of the sum is to be paid $315, the purchase money due the
estate of Sampson Braswell, leaving a balance of $647.32 out of
which the widow, Mary King, is to take dower. 14 Nov 1883. (Pp.
157-158)

T. N. CHRISTIAN versus M. A. J. FERRELL. Since the filing
of this bill, complainant T. N. Christian died. Si facias has
been issued and served upon the widow and children of the said
Christian, to wit, Rebecca Christian, William Christian, T. S.
Christian, John Christian, James Christian, John Windham and wife
Nancy, James Staley and wife Etta. 14 Nov 1883. (Pp. 159-160)

W. B. STOKES versus ROBERT and SARAH JOHNSON. About 11 Dec
1879, defendant Robert Johnson executed his note to Complainant
Stokes for $50. A mortgage deed was executed. A tract of land
will be sold to pay the mortgage. 14 Nov 1883. (P. 160)

J. E. ROBINSON versus M. H. ROBINSON. The bill is taken for
confessed. Defendant was indebted to complainant. It is ordered
that $160 .65 be paid out of the funds attached. 14 Nov 1883.
(P. 161)

T. A. TRACY versus RUFUS BETHEL Et Al. The Clerk is to
take proof and report back. 14 Nov 1883. (P. 161)

J. L. COLVERT, Administrator, versus JAMES STALEY Et Al.
The bill is taken for confessed. Defendants Thomas S. Christian,
John Christian, and James Christian are minors without guardian.
14 Nov 1883. (Pp. 162-163)

JAMES R. JONES versus JOSEPH H. LOVE, Administrator. It
was suggested that B. F. Winfree is dead. W. L. Hardcastle is
his administrator. 14 Nov 1883. (P. 163)

W. D. PRICHARD Et Al versus J. M. LOVE Et Al. The attachment is discharged and the injunction disallowed. 14 Nov 1883.
(Pp. 163-164)

E. A. COGGIN versus J. H. LOVE, Administrator of H. Love.
Decree ordering sale. 14 Nov 1883. (Pp. 164-165)

JOHN E. ROBINSON, Administrator, Et Al versus W. B. ROBIN-
SON Et Al. The Clerk is to make a report to sho the amount due
each heir of John Robinson deceased. 14 Nov 1883. (Pp. 165-
168)

JANE HATHAWAY versus JAMES H. WITT Et Al. John Haney became the purchaser of the tract of land mentioned in the proceedings. 14 Nov 1883. (Pp. 168-169)

JANE FOUTCH versus G. R. WEST Et Al. Judgment. 14 Nov
1883. (Pp. 170-172)

LUCINDA HILL versus T. W. FITTS Et Al. Decree. 14 Nov
1883. (Pp. 172-180)

GEORGE W. ALLEN Et Al versus S. P. ELLIOTT Et Al. Petition of John G. McKnight and the heirs of Polly Ann McFarland
to become parties to this suit. It appears to the court that
Defendant S. P. Elliott is entitled to three fifth's of the
dower lands of Sarah Allen. George W. Allen is entitled to
one twentieth of said land. Polly Ann McFarland's heirs are
entitled to one fifth of said land. L. B. Allen is entitled to
one twentieth of said lands. The heirs of Elizabeth Delta are
entitled to one twentieth of said land. The complainants and
heirs of William H. Allen recover of S. P. Elliott two fifth's
of said dower land. 14 Nov 1883. (Pp. 181-182)

W. E. BARTLETT Et Al versus R. S. ALCORN Et Al. Decree.
14 Nov 1883. (P. 183)

A number of causes are continued. (Pp. 183-186)

J. N. CARTWRIGHT, Executor of James Goodner, versus B. F.
BELL, Administrator, and E. TURNER. The parties enter into a
compromise. 14 Nov 1883. (Pp. 186-188)

J. L. COLVERT, Administrator, versus M. A. J. FERRELL.
14 Nov 1883. (Pp. 188-189)

LUCINDA HILL versus T. W. FITTS Et Al. The death of B. F.
Winfree was suggested. W. L. Hardcastle was his administrator.
This cause is revived in the name of the said Hardcastle. 14
Nov 1883. (P. 189)

A number of causes are rescinded. (Pp. 189-190)

J. N. CARTWRIGHT, Executor, versus B. F. BELL, Administrator, Et Al. The bill is dismissed for want of equity. 14 Nov
1883. (Pp. 191-192)

J. D. WHEELER Et Al versus T. W. EASON Et Al. Defendant
Eason is perpetually enjoined from prosecuting his suit. Complainant White Myres will be primarily liable for the court
costs. 14 Nov 1883. (Pp. 192-193)

J. H. OVERALL versus BERRY BALLENGER. A compromise is
entered into. 14 Nov 1883. (P. 193)

S. S. CRADDOCK and wife versus J. N. HAYES Et Al. 14 Nov
1883. (Pp. 193-194)

JANE FOUTCH versus G. R. WEST. 14 Nov 1883. (P. 194)

JAMES H. OVERALL versus BERRY BALLENGER. Judgment. A note was executed for a flat boat in this cause to W. W. Wade, former Clerk of this court. Said Wade moved the court for a judgment on said note. The former clerk sold a flat boat to J. H. Overall for which he executed his note. The amount is due. 14 Nov 1883. (P. 195)

J. H. CAMERON next friend versus R. C. STALEY. 14 Nov 1883. (Pp. 196-197)

JANE FOUTCH versus G. R. WEST Et Al. Judgment. 14 Nov 1883. (Pp. 198-199)

ERR WOOD, Administrator, versus J. B. PARISH Et Al. The Clerk gives his report on the estate of Wiley Sanders. 14 Nov 1883. (Pp. 200-202)

M. E. SMITH by next friend versus PALACE SMITH. All the funds in the hand of the Master coming to the complainant from the Vantrease estate are set apart for her seperate use free from the debts of her husband and will not be paid to her husband, Palace Smith, but to her. 14 Nov 1883. (P. 202)

W. G. CROWLEY Et Al versus J. M. LOVE Et Al. It is suggested that T. N. Christian, one of the defendants was dead. This cause is revived in the name of J. L. Colvert who is the administrator. 14 Nov 1883. (Pp. 204-205)

Chancery Court met in the town of Smithville on the first Tuesday after the second Monday, it being the 11th day of March 1884. H. W. McCONNELL, presiding. (P. 206)

DAVID MALONE Et Al versus M. J. MALONE Et Al. 14 Nov 1883. (Pp. 206-209)

Court adjourned until the 1st Tuesday after the second Monday in Jul 1884. (P. 209)

Chancery Court met in the town of Smithville on the first Monday in Apr 1884. W. G. Crowley, presiding. Court was opened in due form of law and this being the first Monday and the County Court being in session and entitled by law to the use of the courtroom on today, Court adjourned until tomorrow morning at eight o'clock. (P. 210)

J. H. CAMERON next friend versus J. L. COLVERT, Administrator. Defendants J. H. Cameron, Mary E. Cameron, Sr., Mary E. Cameron, Jr., and Lula V. Cameron have been served with process. 8 Apr 1884. (P. 210)

ELIJAH WARE Et Al versus THOMAS N. CLOSE Et Al. This cause is for the purpose of making the heirs of Elijah Self deceased parties to this suit. 8 Apr 1884. (P. 211)

W. B. STOKES versus ROBERT and SARAH JOHNSON. The land mentioned in the pleadings is divested out of the said Robert and Sarah Johnson and vested in W. B. Stokes. 8 Apr 1884. (Pp. 212-213)

NESMITH and SMALLMAN versus G. W. WALTON. The matter has been fully settled. 9 Apr 1884. (P. 214)

E. CLOSE Et Al versus T. N. CLOSE, Administrator, Et Al.
The other parties in this suit will have until June Rules 1884
to answer. 9 Apr 1884. (P. 214)

H. C. ROBINSON versus J. L. COLVERT, Administrator. Report
showing the rent funds and the amount collected. 9 Apr 1884.
(Pp. 214-218)

A number of causes are continued. (P. 218)

JOHN C. HUGHES versus JAMES R. SMITH. 9 Apr 1884. (P. 218)

Report of the Clerk & Master to the April Term of sale of
land. (Pp. 218-219)

M. LANCASTER versus JOHN T. STOKES. The Clerk will collect
the balance of the funds due. 9 Apr 1884. (P. 220)

W. E. BARTLETT Et Al versus R. S. ALCORN Et Al. All parties
in interest in this cause are properly before the court by personal service of process. 9 Apr 1884. (Pp. 220-221)

WILLIAM LINDSLEY versus W. F. CALICOTT Et Al. Report of
Clerk to sell the land. The sale of the Nicholas Smith Mills
and sixteen acres of land which the same is known and designated
in the division of Nicholas Smith land. 9 Apr 1884. (Pp. 221-
222)

DAVID SMITH, Executor, and heirs versus JOHN T. STOKES Et
Al. The decree of the Chancellor was not entered by oversight.
9 Apr 1884. It appears that by a former decree in this cause
that the title to the tract of land in controversy had been
divested out of the said John T. Stokes and vested in complainants, the heirs and devisees of David Smith deceased subject to
the right of homestead of said Stokes. 9 Apr 1884. (Pp. 222-
226)

F. M. FOUTCH and others versus T. J. ROLAND, Administrator,
Et Al. The court was pleased to so recodify the injunction in
this cause as to allow defendants Caroline, Maude, William, and
Mary Roland to use of the provisions on hand sufficient for their
support. It was manifestly to the interest of Mary Roland who
is a minor. The said William Roland is to be permitted to use
of the products of the farm. Thomas Roland is to proceed to rent
out the lands involved in this suit, reserving the house and
garden for the family. 10 Apr 1884. (P. 227)

MERCER & COFFEE versus GEORGE ALLEY and GEORGE D. BYBEE.
Supreme Court decree. 10 Apr 1884. (Pp. 227-228)

A number of causes are continued. (Pp. 229-230)

JOHN H. SAVAGE versus DAVID MALONE. Report of the sale of
land. 10 Apr 1884. (Pp. 230-231)

FANNIE TUBB Et Al versus HELEN SCHURER Et Al. Motion of
F. M. and C. M. Schurer to dissolve the injunction. 10 Apr
1884. (P. 231)

MARTHA THOMAS versus MADISON ALLEN and others. 10 Apr
1884. (P. 232)

E. A. COGGIN, Administrator, versus J. H. LANE and others. Report of sale by the commissioner. 11 Apr 1884. (Pp. 232-233)

J. H. CANTRELL versus TALITHA REEDER. Petition of Johnathan Johnson and Aaron Hughes to become party defendants. 11 Apr 1884. (P. 233)

A number of causes are continued. (Pp. 233-234)

H. L. C. MOORE versus C. A. CANTRELL. A compromise is agreed to. 11 Apr 1884. (P. 234)

ERR WOOD, Administrator, and others versus DRUCILLA SANDERS Et Al. B. M. Cantrell has performed services worth twenty-five dollars. 11 Apr 1884. (P. 235)

T. H. STARK and J. P. STARK versus A. H. THOMPSON Et Al. It appears to the court that J. J. Callicott is dead. The suit is dismissed as to him. The other defendants, A. H. Thompson, Etta Thompson, Alfred Smith, and Penelope Smith are properly brought before the court by service of process. The bill is taken for confessed. 11 Apr 1884. (Pp. 236-237)

M. C. VICK Et Al versus WILLIAM VICK, Administrator, and AMANDA VICK. 11 Apr 1884. (Pp. 237-239)

J. H. TURNEY Et Al versus LUCINDA TURNEY Et Al. Report allowing Joseph Clark a fee for services rendered by him since the sale of the land. 11 Apr 1884. (Pp. 239-240)

LETHA McCREA versus JOSEPH MITCHEL Et Al. A compromise is agreed to. George McCrea paid to Joseph Mitchell the amount of his said judgment. 11 Apr 1884. (P. 240)

WILLIAM H. MAGNESS versus G. R. WEST. The cause is continued. 11 Apr 1884. (P. 241)

MARTHA E. DOLLAR versus D. C. DOLLAR. Final Decree. The bill is taken for confessed. The defendant was not to be found in DeKalb County. Complainant and defendant intermarried in DeKalb County about the time charged. The complainant has resided and been a citizen of DeKalb County for more than two whole years before this bill was filed. Parties have no property of any description. Complainant has one child, the issue of said marriage. The defendant has abandoned the complainant and her child for the last four years. The bonds of matrimony are dissolved. Complainant is given custody of her child. 12 Apr 1884. (Pp. 242-243)

JACOB ADAMS and others versus M. A. CATHCART and others. Decree. The Clerk will make a report. 12 Apr 1884. (Pp. 243-244)

W. T. ROBINSON Et Al versus ANN H. J. CALLICOTT Et Al. A subpoena was ordered on Vera Callicott more than five days before the meeting of this term. She is a minor without guardian. T. W. Wade is appointed guardian. The administration of the Estate of J. J. Callicott is transfered from the County Court of Davidson County to this court to be here fully wound up. 12 Apr 1884. (P. 245)

F. D. HARRIS, Executor, Et Al versus A. T. PHILLIPS. The Clerk is to take an account among the several heirs of A. Martin deceased so as to show the amount due each heir and to show whether F. D. Warren, Executor, is entitled to any further compensation for services as executor. 12 Apr 1884. (Pp. 246-247)

JOHN B. ROBINSON, Administrator, versus G. W. HATHAWAY. There has been a partial settlement with Robinson. 12 Apr 1884. (P. 248)

W. T. ROBINSON Et Al versus ANN J. CALLICOTT Et Al. The said Ann J. is to be permitted to file her answer to the bill. 12 Apr 1884. (Pp. 248-249)

WILLIAM H. MAGNESS versus J. WHITE. The complainant demanded a jury to try certain issues of facts. He charged that White failed to charge himself with $2000 for goods and other effects and money belonging to the firm of MAGNESS & WHITE. 12 Apr 1884. (Pp. 249-254)

S. S. CRADDOCK and wife versus M. SANDLIN and others. Final Decree. The bill is taken for confessed. Complainants S. S. Craddock and wife, H. M., sold to defendant Sandlin the tract of land mentioned in the pleadings and lying in District No. 2, now District No. 19 and containing sixteen acres. There is a lien on the land. The Clerk is ordered to sell the land. 14 Apr 1884. (Pp. 254-255)

C. T. BURTON Et Al versus THOMAS MAYNARD Et Al. The bill is taken for confessed. 14 Apr 1884. (P. 256)

J. E. ROBINSON, Administrator, versus W. B. ROBINSON Et Al. The other four heirs are entitled to $183.78. William Reynolds and John Dulaney are entitled to one half each. 14 Apr 1884. (P. 257)

A number of causes are continued. (P. 258)

J. H. CAMERON next friend versus R. V. STALEY and others. 14 Apr 1884. (Pp. 258-259)

B. F. WINFREE versus T. W. FITTS. Each party is allowed to take further proof. 14 Apr 1884. (P. 259)

M. B. BRIDGES versus JOHN D. BONE Et Al. Defendants are perpetually enjoined from any trespassing upon the premises of the complainant. Complainant recovers fifty dollars in consequence of the trespass. 14 Apr 1884. (P. 260)

Z. H. DENTON Et Al versus B. B. WEST Et Al. Application for a change of venue to Woodbury. Attorney B. M. Webb, making oath, stated that His Honor W. G. Crowley is incompetent in this cause to preside to hear the cause for he has given counsel against complainants about the matter. He is one of the trustees of Pure Fountain College who concurred with defendants in the alleged misappropriating a school fund. 14 Apr 1884. (Pp. 261-262)

ERR WOOD, Administrator, versus J. B. PARRISH Et Al. 14 Apr 1884. (Pp. 262-264)

S. W. McCLELLAN versus T. J. SNEED Et Al. The Clerk was directed to sell the real estate mentioned in the pleadings, to wit, a house and lot in Alexandria. The land was sold. 14 Apr 1884. (Pp. 264-265)

T. E. WEST Et Al versus J. J. FORD. The case is compromised. 14 Apr 1884. (Pp. 265-266)

M. W. WILDER Et Al versus J. T. CLAYBORN Et Al. A report of the sale of the land was made. 14 Apr 1884. (P. 266)

J. J. FORD versus JOHN B. ROBINSON. All the equities in the bill are fully met. 14 Apr 1884. (P. 267)

GRIBBLE & WEBB versus W. B. STONE Et Al. The bill is taken for confessed. 14 Apr 1884. (P. 268)

A number of causes are continued. (Pp. 268-269)

H. L. C. MOORE versus C. A. CANTRELL. Application of complainants to have a receiver appointed to take charge of and rent out the land in controversy. 14 Apr 1884. (Pp. 269-270)

B. N. HICKS versus B. B. TAYLOR Et Al. A decree directing the sale of the land mentioned in the pleading. 14 Apr 1884. (Pp. 271-272)

T. A. TRACY versus RUFUS BETHEL. The bill is taken for confessed. 14 Apr 1884. (Pp. 273-275)

J. J. PEDIGO versus A. B. STALEY and wife. The bill is taken for confessed. 14 Apr 1884. (Pp. 275-276)

J. L. COLVERT, Administrator, versus JAMES STALEY Et Al. Defendants James Staley and wife, Etta, have entered their appearance by their lawyer. The Clerk is to take an account and among other things state what real estate that T. N. Christian died seized and possessed of. 14 Apr 1884. (Pp. 276-277)

Court adjounred until the first Monday in Jul 1884 at which time a special term of this court will be held. 14 Apr 1884. (P. 277)

Chancery Court met in the town of Smithville on the first Monday in Jul 1884, it being the eighth day of the month. W. G. Crowley, presiding. (P. 278)

T. DRIVER and wife versus H. P. KEMP and others. H. P. Kent, Cintha Kemp, James Kemp, William Kemp, and the other unknown heirs of H. P. Kemp have been served with process. The bill is taken for confessed. Bradford Kemp and Ellen Kemp, heirs of James Kemp, are minors without guardian. M. D. Smallman is appointed guardian. 8 Jul 1884. (Pp. 278-279)

J. L. COLVERT, Administrator, versus M. A. J. FERRELL. Final Decree. J. L. Colvert, Administrator of T. N. Christian, became the purchaser of a tract of land. 8 Jul 1884. (Pp. 279-280)

E. A. BRESHEARS versus JOHN SCURLOCK Et Al. The Sheriffs of Trousdale and Wilson County are ordered to serve James Scurlock.

8 Jul 1884. (F. 281)

L. GARRISON versus J. J. FORD. All the papers on file have been lost or mislaid and could not be found. 8 Jul 1884. (P. 282)

B. F. WINFREE versus T. W. FITTS. Final Decree. The report shows that T. W. Fitts is entitled to a further credit on the note mentioned in the pleading. 8 Jul 1884. (Pp. 282-287)

A number of causes are continued. (Pp. 287-289)

E. S. CLOSE and W. L. CLOSE versus T. N. CLOSE, Administrator. James White and wife are necessary parties to this cause. They are non residents of Tennessee. The bill is taken for confessed. 8 Jul 1884. (Pp. 289-290)

G. DRIVER and wife versus H. P. KEMP Et Al. The Clerk is to take proof as to whether the tract of land described in the pleadings can be partitioned between the several heirs without injury to the respective interest in the same. 9 Jul 1884. (P. 291)

J. H. CAMERON next friend versus J. L. COLVERT, Administrator. 10 Jul 1884. (Pp. 292-298)

M. C. LEWIS, Administrator, versus WILLIAM FRANCIS Et Al. Defendants William Francis, Mary Ann Francis, Tillman Haney, John Haney, Nancy E. Haney, Stanton Haney, Levi Haney, Sarah Haney, and Plummer Lewis have been served. The bill is taken for confessed. The said Plummer Lewis is a minor without guardian. James Clark is appointed guardian. 10 Jul 1884. (Pp. 298-299)

A number of causes are continued. (Pp. 299-300)

J. L. COLVERT Et Al versus JOHN CANTRELL. Decree. The Clerk is to take proof as to whether the land mentioned in the pleadings can be partitioned without manifest injury to the several interested parties. It appears to the court that the land cannot be partitioned. The land is ordered sold. 10 Jul 1884. (Pp. 300-302)

McADO JENKINS Et Al versus OBEDIAH JENKINS Et Al. McAdo Jenkins, James Jenkins, M. J. Jenkins, and Sarah Jenkins recovered a judgment against Joseph Clark. 10 Jul 1884. (Pp. 302-303)

C. T. BURTON versus F. MAYNARD Et Al. This is a proper cause for an account. 10 Jul 1884. (Pp. 303-304)

B. M. CANTRELL, Administrator, Et Al versus MICKEY CRIPS Et Al. The Clerk was directed to take and state an account and settlement with B. M. Cantrell, Administrator of the Estate of John L. Cripps deceased and at the same time to adjudicate the claims filed against said decease's estate. 10 Jul 1884. (Pp. 304-307)

A number of causes are continued. (Pp. 307-308)

L. B. RHODES next friend versus J. B. FRAZIER Et Al. 10 Jul 1884. (P. 309)

J. J. PEDIGO versus O. B. STALEY Et Al. J. J. Pedigo was the purchaser of a town lot in the 9th District. The land was sold for a debt. 10 Jul 1884. (Pp. 309-310)

J. J. VANTREASE Et Al versus J. D. BONE, Administrator, Et Al. The Master is to take proof about the amound due from the Estate of N. Vantrease to complainants, if anything, and also the amount due to complainants, if anything, from the Estate of Elizabeth Vantrease, the widow of the said Nicholas Vantrease. 10 Jul 1884. (P. 311)

F. M. FOUTCH and wife versus T. J. ROWLAND Et Al. This hearing came before J. B. Robinson, Special Chancellor, who was duly qualified, according to law, by reason of the incompetency of W. G. Crowley who was incompetent by relationship within the sixth degree. Defendants Caroline Rowland, Mark Rowland, Mary Rowland, and W. E. Rowland filed an original bill, but diligent search has been made for said bill and the same is lost or unintentionally mislaid. It appears to the court that Mary Rowland is a minor without guardian. J. W. Clark is appointed as her guardian. 10 Jul 1884. (Pp. 311-312)

J. J. FORD versus H. B. SMITH. Commissioners are appointed to set apart a homestead of $1000 in value, including the mansion house and set out in renting the boundaries of it, if it can be done. They will report to the next term of court. 11 Jul 1884. (Pp. 313-314)

CANTRELL & FORD versus JASPER RUYLE Et Al. Defendant recovers a judgment against the Administrator of Joseph Turney. 11 Jul 1884. (Pp. 314-315)

W. T. ROBINSON Et Al versus ANN H. J. CALLICOTT, Administratrix, Et Al. Defendant W. F. Callicott is a non resident of the State of Tennessee. Process cannot be served on him. The bill is taken for confessed. 11 Jul 1884. (P. 315)

J. H. HUGHES versus H. L. S. MAXWELL Et Al. Final Decree. Defendants are liable to complainant. 11 Jul 1884. (Pp. 315-317)

J. L. STALEY, Administrator, Et Al versus JAMES STALEY Et Al. The commissioner has failed to make the report pertaining to the estate of T. N. Christian. 11 Jul 1884. (Pp. 317-318)

R. E. ROBINSON versus C. E. PULLEN Et Al. Decree. Application of complainants to have a receiver appointed to take charge of the property attached. 11 Jul 1884. (P. 318)

L. B. RHODES next friend versus J. B. FRAZIER. Decree. Complainant obtained permission from the court to file the last will and testament of Henry Frazier as proof that Martha Rhody, the widow of A. L. Frazier, is entitled to dower. The several tracts of land willed to the said A. L. Frazier and defendant J. R. Frazier, willed to them by their father Henry Frazier, to be held by them as tenants in common until the said A. L. Frazier should become of age or marry. Said A. L. had become of age. 11 Jul 1884. (Pp. 318-321)

E. MAYNARD versus NANCY E. MAYNARD. The court dismisses the original bill, but declines to dismiss the cross bill. 12 Jul 1884. (P. 322)

GEORGE W. ALLEN Et Al versus S. P. ELLIOTT Et Al. Commissioners appointed to divide the dower land. The interest that the parties to this suit have in Lot No. 1 is divested out of them and vested in defendant S. P. Elliott. 12 Jul 1884. (Pp. 328)

C. B. CANTRELL Et Al versus M. D. SMALLMAN Et Al. The court was pleased to overrule the demurrer. 12 Jul 1884. (Pp. 328-329)

E. MAYNARD versus A. E. MAYNARD. The bill is taken for confessed. 12 Jul 1884. (P. 330)

B. M. CANTRELL versus MICKEY CRIPS Et Al. Decree. There is yet two tracts of land belonging to the estate that are yet to be sold. They are ordered to be sold at the Courthouse. 12 Jul 1884. (Pp. 330-331)

R. E. ROBINSON versus O. E. PULLEN. The Clerk was appointed receiver to take charge of the house and lot. 12 Jul 1884. (P. 331)

ANDREW TAYLOR versus B. R. PAGE. Defendant leased the land to complainant for five years. Said lease was not reduced to writing. Complainant had taken possession and made permanent improvements on said land under the contract of lease. Defendant had rescinded said contract and had taken possession of the said land before the bill in this cause was filed. The court is of the opinion that there is a proper cause for an account charging the defendant with the value of the improvements. 12 Jul 1884. (Pp. 331-332)

P. H. HANKINS versus W. R. PARISH. The court is to determine whether it is in the interest of the minor defendant, C. A. Parish, to have the compromise confirmed. 12 Jul 1884. (Pp. 332-335)

A number of causes are consolidated. (Pp. 336-337)

D. W. DINGES versus T. WEST. Defendants will be required to answer the amendment. 12 Jul 1884. (Pp. 337-338)

JANE BRITTON Et Al versus SALLIE BONE Et Al. Defendant owned a tract of land in the 1st District. Defendants have until Oct 1884 to file their answer. 12 Jul 1884. (Pp. 338-339)

GEORGE W. ALLEN and others versus S. P. ELLIOTT Et Al. Petition filed for hearing by L. B. Allen, the Ditto heirs, the McFarland heirs, and the May heirs. The court is pleased to announce that the decision pertaining to rents, etc. is set aside. The Clerk is to determine what improvements were put on the dower land by defendant S. P. Elliott since the death of the widow Allen in 1878. Defendant Elliott is only entitled to the betterments. 12 Jul 1884. (P. 339)

W. G. CROWLEY Et Al versus W. W. WADE. This cause is re-

ferred to Circuit Court for hearing. It appears that the Chancellor is incompetent to determine the same by being a party.
12 Jul 1884. (Pp. 339-340)

J. E. ROBINSON Et Al versus W. B. ROBINSON Et Al. Said Wade is charged with all the funds in his hands belonging to the heirs of the Robinson Estate. The incompetency of the court is by consent of all the parties waived. 12 Jul 1884. (P. 340)

JACOB ADAMS versus M. A. CATHCART Et Al. The court is pleased to disallow the plea filed at this state of the cause.
12 Jul 1884. (P. 341)

B. F. WINFREY versus T. W. FITTS. Defendant recovers of
W. L. Hardcastle, the administrator of B. F. Winfrey. 12 Jul 1884. (Pp. 341-342)

W. C. LEWIS versus WILLIAM FRANCIS and others. A. Avant, guardian for the Haney minors, is allowed time to make defense to complainant's bill. A survey of the lands is necessary. 12 Jul 1884. (P. 342)

A. M. C. ROBINSON versus HELEN SCHURER. Defendant makes motion to dismiss the bill as to defendants Charles Schurer and F. M. Schurer for want of equity on the face of the bill. 12 Jul 1884. (P. 342)

BENJAMIN ANDERSON versus C. J. BRATTEN Et Al. It is suggested that the Chancellor was incompetent on account of relationship to hear the motion. P. T. Shores was elected to act as Special Chancellor. 12 Jul 1884. (Pp. 343-345)

JACOB ADAMS Et Al versus SAMUEL BRASWELL, Administrator. The Master is to take and state an account of the proceeds of the land sold. He will determine the amount due to the Estate of Sampson Braswell. 12 Jul 1884. (P. 345)

WILLIAM WILDER Et Al versus J. T. CLAYBORN Et Al. The sale of the land to J. W. Scott is confirmed. 12 Jul 1884. (Pp. 345-349)

B. F. WINFREE versus T. W. FITTS. A hearing was held on the merits. 12 Jul 1884. (P. 349)

A. J. VANTREASE and others versus JAMES P. DOSS and others. Consolidated causes. The cause is continued. 12 Jul 1884. (P. 350)

SARAH JOHNSON versus JOHN JOHNSON. Each party is to retain the bed and furniture that each now has in possession. The court is to sell the cow and calf. 14 Jul 1884. (P. 351)

FRANCIS TURNER versus M. M. BRIEN. The Clerk is ordered to carry all his papers before him at next term. When he determines the cause, he is to make entry on the Minutes and have the same signed. 14 Jul 1884. (P. 352)

NANCY MALONE versus S. MALONE. Chancellor Crowley was incompetent to try this cause on account of relationship. A. P. Smith was elected as Special Chancellor. The bonds of matrimony are dissolved. Complainant is restored to her maiden name of

Mary Clayborn. (?Nancy or Mary) 14 Jul 1884. (P. 353)

W. G. CROWLEY Et Al versus W. W. WADE Et Al. This cause will be transferred to Circuit Court. 14 Jul 1884. (P. 354)

J. H. CAMERON next friend versus J. L. COLVERT, Administrator Et Al. The Clerk sold a portion of the lands in this cause to J. A. Nesmith for which he executed a note. The note is due. 14 Jul 1884. (Pp. 354-360)

T. DRIVER and wife versus H. P. KEMP Et Al. The land cannot be partitioned without manifest injury to the several heirs. The Clerk is to sell the land. 14 Jul 1884. (Pp. 360-361)

A. S. McCLELLAN versus GEORGE CURTIS Et Al. Decree. A compromise has been reached. 14 Jul 1884. (P. 361)

SARAH E. JOHNSON versus JOHN JOHNSON. The bill is dismissed. 14 Jul 1884. (P. 362)

M. A. CROWLEY, Clerk & Master, versus C. S. FRAZIER, Sheriff. On account of relationship, the regular Chancellor was incompetent to hear the motion. John B. Robinson was appointed Special Chancellor. 14 Jul 1884. (Pp. 362-363)

R. E. ROBINSON versus C. E. PULLEN. A attachment has been issued from this court to be levied on the store house and stock of goods, groceries, etc. The complainant, Mary A. Pullen by her next friend filed her bill asking, among other things, to enjoin said sale. Judge Robert Cantrell granted an injunction to restrain the sale. 14 Jul 1884. (P. 364)

G. R. WEST versus JANE FOUTCH. This suit was heard in Circuit Court because of the incompetency of the Chancellor to hear the cause. The injunction is dissolved. 11 Jul 1884. (P. 365)

Court adjourned until the first Tuesday after the second Monday in Nov 1884. (P. 365)

(Page 366 is marked out)

Chancery Court met in Smithville on the first Monday in Oct 1884, it being the sixth day of the month. W. G. Crowley, presiding. (P. 367)

A number of causes are continued. (Pp. 367-368)

MARY BRASWELL Et Al versus SAMUEL BRASWELL Et Al. Decree The Clerk is to give a report. 7 Oct 1884. (P. 368)

WILLIAM H. MAGNESS versus A. M. C. ROBINSON. This cause is transferred from the Chancery Court of DeKalb County to the Chancery Court of Cannon County. 7 Oct 1884. (Pp. 368-369)

WILLIAM H. MAGNESS versus G. R. WEST. Defendant is justly indebted to the complainant on a promissory note. A tract of land is ordered to be sold. 7 Oct 1884. (P. 369)

S. W. McCLELLAN versus C. L. BARTON Et Al. A sale of the property attached is ordered. 7 Oct 1884. (P. 370)

T. DRIVER Et Al versus H. P. KEMP Et Al. Decree. 7 Oct 1884. (P. 370)

M. A. SCOTT by next friend versus W. VICK, Administrator of
E. Vick. The Clerk is to take proof and report back. 7 Oct
1884. (P. 372)

J. J. FORD versus H. B. SMITH. 8 Oct 1884. (Pp. 372-374)

A. TAYLOR versus BARNEY R. PAGE. Final Decree. The kind
of improvements placed upon the land was the building of a dwelling house, smoke house, stables, making rails, clearing ground,
and making a road. Complainants occupied and had possession of
said land for about sixteen months. Complainant recovers from
the defendant. 8 Oct 1884. (Pp. 374-376)

SAMUEL BRASWELL and others versus WILLIAM BRASWELL and
others. It appears to the court that William Braswell and Samuel
Braswell were advanced more than their part of the Sampson Braswell Estate. The funds should be distributed among Leroy Braswell, Samuel Braswell, Nicy Cubbins, Jacob Adams, Administrator
of his wife Lucinda. 8 Oct 1884. (Pp. 377-378)

JOHN B. ROBINSON, Administrator, Et Al versus G. W. HATHA-
WAY. 8 Oct 1884. (Pp. 378-379)

J. J. FORD versus JAMES H. BLACKBURN Et Al. Appointment
of a receiver to take charge of the house and lot in controversy.
8 Oct 1884. (Pp. 380-381)

M. A. PULLEN by next friend versus R. E. ROBINSON Et Al.
It appears to the court that C. E. Pullen has absconded and gone
to parts unknown and cannot be served with process. The bill
is taken for confessed. 8 Oct 1884. (P. 381)

S. W. McCLELLAN versus C. L. BARTON Et Al. 8 Oct 1884. (P.
382)

W. E. BARTLETT Et Al versus R. S. ALCORN Et Al. The papers
in this cause have been mislaid. 8 Oct 1884. (P. 383)

WEBB, CHEEK, & COMPANY versus J. S. DUNLAP Et Al. Complainants dismissed their original cause. 8 Oct 1884. (Pp. 383-
384)

SALLIE A. MAGNESS by next friend versus B. M. CANTRELL,
Administrator, Et Al. The bill is taken for confessed. The
Clerk will take proof and report. The report will show the ages
of the three children of R. M. Magness deceased, the financial
and social standing of the estate. 9 Oct 1884. (P. 384)

A. C. GOFF versus MARY SMITH, alias Mary Goff. The contract
of marriage and the marriage of complainant and defendant is
void because the same was obtained through fraud. Defendant is
restored to her name before said void marriage, to wit, Mary
Smith. 9 Oct 1884. (P. 385)

N. E. MAYNARD versus E. MAYNARD. The cause is continued.
9 Oct 1884. (P. 386)

SALLIE A. MAGNESS by next friend versus B. M. CANTRELL,
Administrator, Et Al. R. M. Magness died a few months since,
leaving complainant, Sallie A. Magness, his widow. The three

other complainants, to wit, Robert, Mattie, and Olah D. Magness
are his only children and heirs. They are minors without guardian. Said children occupy a high place in society and have
been raised well and well educated for their ages. They have
no estate or but little estate outside of a life policy in the
Etna Life Insurance Company for $225, payable to them and their
mother, Sallie A. Magness. It is in the interest of the children that they be made wards of this court. 9 Oct 1884. (Pp.
386-387)

J. J. FORD versus JAMES C. BLACKBURN Et Al. The bill is
taken for confessed against the defendants. 9 Oct 1884. (Pp.
387-388)

J. H. TURNEY Et Al versus LUCINDA TURNEY. It is agreed
that the parties represented are to be paid out of the funds
due the children of Isaac Turney deceased. 9 Oct 1884. (P.
388)

GARR, SCOTT, & COMPANY versus T. W. FITTS Et Al. Report
of sale. 10 Oct 1884. (Pp. 389-390)

SARAH HILDRETH versus JOHN HILDRETH. On account of the
disability of the regular Chancellor, W. G. Crowley, A. P.
Smith was named Special Chancellor. The bill is taken for confessed. Complainant and defendant have lived together as husband and wife in the State for more than two years next. The
defendant has abandoned complainant and has failed to provide
for her. The bonds of matrimony are dissolved. Complainant
is restored to her maiden name of Sarah Johnson. 10 Oct 1884.
(P. 391)

J. H. CAMERON by next friend versus J. L. COLVERT, Administrator, Et Al. Decree. Sale of a tract of land. 10 Oct 1884.
(Pp. 392-395)

W. D. PRICHARD Et Al versus J. M. LOVE Et Al. The claim
of the complainant has been settled. 10 Oct 1884. (P. 396)

J. H. CAMERON by next friend versus J. L. COLVERT. 10
Oct 1884. (Pp. 396-398)

JOHN S. PACK versus JOHNATHAN HALL Et Al. Report of sale.
10 Oct 1884. (Pp. 398-399)

HENRY ALLEN versus A. L. SHERRILL Et Al. The Clerk is
appointed receiver to take charge of the oxen in controversy.
The are to be sold at the Courthouse. 10 Oct 1884. (P. 399)

C. T. BURTON Et Al versus T. MAYNARD Et Al. 10 Oct 1884.
(Pp. 399-402)

J. L. COLVERT, Administrator, Et Al versus JAMES STALEY
Et Al. B. M. Cantrell was appointed Special Chancellor to hear
the cause. 10 Oct 1884. T. N. Christian deceased conveyed in
his lifetime to his wife and children his property. Rebecca
Christian is the widow of said T. N. Christian. James Christian,
John Christian, and Thomas Christian are his children. (Pp.
402-414)

GRIBBLE & WEBB versus W. B. STONE Et Al. Sale of the land mentioned in the proceedings. 10 Oct 1884. (Pp. 414-415)

WILLIAM LINDSLEY versus W. F. CALLICOTT. The Clerk the real estate to N. M. Robinson for which he executed a note. The Clerk is ordered to recover from the said Robinson and his security. 10 Oct 1884. (P. 416)

J. M. FITE Et Al versus J. T. HOLLIS Et Al. Sale of a tract of land. 10 Oct 1884. (P. 417)

G. W. ALLEN versus S. P. ELLIOTT Et Al. 10 Oct 1884. (Pp. 417-418)

Chancery Court met in Smithville on the first Tuesday after the second Monday in Jul 1885. (P. 419)

J. M. FITE Et Al versus J. T. HOLLIS Et Al. John H. Savage was a party to the suit and is entitled to one fourth of the fund. No account has been made to any party. Jul 1885. (Pp. 419-420)

A. J. VANTREASE Et Al versus J. P. DOSS Et Al. D. B. Hayes, Guardian of Robert Vantrease recovers of the former Clerk and Master W. W. Wade. Jul 1885. (P. 420)

CHANCERY COURT MINUTES BOOK APR 1885-DEC 1887

Chancery Court met in the town of Smithville on the sixth day of Apr, it being the first Monday in said month. W. G. Crowley, presiding. (P. 1)

R. E. ROBINSON versus C. E. PULLEN. It is ordered by the court that M. A. Crowley, Clerk & Master, for the use of the parties recover of R. B. West and his security. 6 Apr 1885. (Pp. 1-9)

G. W. PUCKETT versus G. W. MEDLEY. Judgment. The Clerk is to recover of T. C. Ervin and his securities. 6 Apr 1885. (Pp. 9-10)

J. H. HUGHES versus H. L. S. MAXWELL. Decree. The Clerk will sell the tract of land mentioned in the pleading. 7 Apr 1885. (P. 10)

JOB TRAPP, Guardian, Et Al versus J. H. TRAMELL Et Al. Judgment. The said Tramell recovers. 7 Apr 1885. (P. 11)

A number of causes are continued. 7 Apr 1885. (Pp. 11-12)

WILLIAM WILDER Et Al versus J. T. CLAYBORN Et Al. J. W. Scott appeared in court and directed that his bid be transferred to his son, E. Y. Scott. 7 Apr 1885. (P. 12)

WILLIAM MAYNARD versus W. C. JOHNSON. Decree. 7 Apr 1885. (P. 14)

MARY BALLARD versus J. J. FORD. A compromise has been reached. 7 Apr 1885. (P. 14)

ANDREW SMITH Et Al versus LEROY BRASWELL Et Al. Decree. Leroy Braswell was the guardian to Mary J. Smith, Leroy Cubbin, Alace Shehan, Jacob Adams, and George Cathcart. On 20 Jan 1879, Leroy Braswell, Guardian aforesaid, made a settlement in County Cort showing a balance of $45.95 due to each of said wards, namely, Mary J. Smith, formerly Mary J. Cubbin, and Alace Shehane. Andrew Smith as next friend of Alace Shehan Alace Shehane recovers of Mathew Cathcart as Administrator of Leroy Braswell deceased and others. Andrew Smith and his wife, Mary J. Smith recover of Mathew Cathcart, Administrator. 7 Apr 1885. (P. 15)

A number of causes are continued. (Pp. 15-16)

F. H. ROBERTSON and wife versus D. B. DAVIS. Decree. The appearance in open court of Elizabeth Davis, Administratrix, The death of O. W. Davis has been suggested. Elizabeth Davis is his administrator. 7 Apr 1885. (P. 16)

SARAH SHAW Et Al versus E. B. SHAW Et Al. Decree. 7 Apr 1885. (P. 17)

JACOB ADAMS versus J. R. FUSON Et Al. Decree. Petition of complainant to have a receiver appointed. 7 Apr 1885. (Pp. 17-18)

J. R. FUSON Et Al versus J. T. HOLLIS Et Al. Decree. The Clerk is to take an account between John B. Robinson, former

J. R. FUSON Et Al versus J. T. HOLLIS Et Al. Decree. The Clerk is to state an account between John B. Robinson, former Clerk & Master, and the heirs of Sampson Braswell deceased and show how much money belonging to the estate and heirs of the said Sampson Braswell went into said Robinson's hands. 8 Apr 1885. (P. 19)

JACOB ADAMS, Guardian. Ex Parte. In Apr, 1882, the Clerk sold to Wiley Eastridge 25 acres. The land was bounded south by the heirs of Lee Braswell. 8 Apr 1885. (Pp. 19-20)

T. DRIVER and wife versus H. P. KEMP Et Al. Decree. Report of the sale of a tract of land. F. L. Foutch was the purchaster. 8 Apr 1885. (Pp. 20-22)

G. W. ALLEN Et Al versus S. P. ELLIOTT. Decree. The Clerk is to take proof and report the value of the rents of the dower land since the year 1878 up to 1884. The Clerk reported that no improvements have been put on the dower land to enhance its value since the death of the Widow Allen in 1878. J. M. Allen gavehis deposition. 8 Apr 1885. (Pp. 22-23)

FANNIE TUBB Et Al versus HELEN SCHURER Et Al. Decree. 8 Apr 1885. (P. 24)

A number of causes are continued. 8 Apr 1885. (Pp. 24-26)

WILLIAM R. TALLEY versus C. H. J. TALLEY. Decree. The bill is taken for confessed. Defendant is guilty of adultery as charged. The bonds of matrimony are dissolved. 8 Apr 1885. (P. 27)

B. T. R. FOSTER Et Al versus M. L. FOSTER Et Al. The said B. T. R. Foster is dead and without administrator on his estate. He left no property subject to execution. E. T. Foster is security for the prosecution of the first cause. 8 Apr 1885. (Pp. 27-28)

W. H. MAGNESS versus G. R. WEST. Decree. The Clerk is directed to sell a tract of land. The land was sold to the said W. H. Magness. 8 Apr 1885. (Pp. 28-29)

J. J. FORD versus JOHN B. ROBINSON Et Al. Complainant Ford paid to defendant T. W. West $216. Complainant Ford recovers of defendant T. W. West. 8 Apr 1885. (P. 30)

T. DRIVER and wife versus H. P. KEMP Et Al. Decree. Motion of solicitor J. J. Ford to have a fee allowed out of the funds arising from the sale of the lands mentioned. 8 Apr 1885. (Pp. 30-31)

WASHINGTON BRYANT versus T. K. DAVID Et Al. The demurrer is overruled. 9 Apr 1885. (P. 31)

MARTHA THOMAS versus M. M. ALLEN, Executor, Et Al. Decree. The costs of this cause are to be paid by the Executor out of the first money hereafter coming into their hands due or to become due the Estate of A. Allen for which cost the Executor will have credit. 9 Apr 1885. (Pp. 31-32)

M. T. ROBINSON Et Al versus ANN H. J. CALLICOTT Et Al. The lands of which N. Smith died seized and possessed were heretofore sold under proceedings of this court. Lot No. 3 was purchased by William Robinson and others. He executed a note. On 11 Feb 1879, Ann H. J. Callicott who was the wife of J. J. Callicott and daughter of said N. Smith and an heir in his estate agreed to apply a portion of her share in said fund to the payment of certain debts of her said husband to the executor of her father. She was under the mistakened impression that her said husband was the purchaser of one half of said lot. 9 Apr 1885. (Pp. 32-33)

E. W. CLOSE Et Al versus T. N. CLOSE Et Al. The complainants dismiss their suit as far an any question of incapacity of J. S. Close to make contracts or as to the imbecility of said J. S. Close. 9 Apr 1885. (P. 34)

A number of causes are continued. (Pp. 34-35)

VICTORIA LINDER versus WILLIAM LINDER. The bill is taken for confessed. The allegations are sustained. The bonds of matrimony are dissolved. The said Victoria Linder is restored to her maiden name of Victoria Thompson. The defendant is not the owner of any property. Title to the property belongs to Minerva Mangrum and her husband Joseph Mangrum. The injunction is dissolved. 9 Apr 1885. (Pp. 35-36)

F. H. ROBERTSON and wife versus D. B. DAVIS Et Al. Decree. The Clerk is to make a report and present to the court. 9 Apr 1885. (Pp. 36-37)

A number of causes are continued. (Pp. 38-39)

R. J. CHRISTIAN versus J. L. COLVERT, Administrator. Move to suspend the sale of the house and lot known as the T. N. Christian homeplace. 9 Apr 1885. (P. 39)

A number of causes are continued. (Pp. 40-41)

W. J. HOLLIS versus R. C. HAYS. The settlements made by defendant R. C. Hays, Executor of W. J. Isbell and S. M. Isbell are set aside. The Clerk will report back. 10 Apr 1885. (Pp. 41-42)

JACOB ADAMS versus J. R. FUSTON Et Al. The parole sale of the lands mentioned in the pleadings by complainant to defendant is rescinded. 10 Apr 1885. (Pp. 42-43)

W. C. LEWIS, Administrator, versus WILLIAM FRANCIS Et Al. 10 Apr 1885. (P. 43)

WILLIAM McDOWELL versus MARY McDOWELL. The bill is taken for confessed. A hearing is set. 10 Apr 1885. (P. 44)

R. T. FRISBY versus T. ADCOCK Et Al. The bill is taken for confessed. Cleopatra Cantrell, T. P. Cantrell, Eliza J. Cantrell, Moses H. Cantrell, Samantha Cantrell, and Bela Dona Cantrell are minors without guardian. B. M. Cantrell is appointed as guardian. 11 Apr 1885. (Pp. 45-46)

NANCY E. MAYNARD versus E. MAYNARD. 11 Apr 1885. (P. 46)

T. N. SMITH and wife versus H. C. TAYLOR Et Al. The bill is taken for confessed. Defendants James Morgan, Elizabeth Taylor, Martha Morgan, Mary Taylor, and David Taylor are non residents of the State of Tennessee. Motion made to have a guardian for the minor defendants Martha Morgan, Mary Taylor, and David Taylor. B. M. Cantrell is appointed as guardian. 11 Apr 1885. (P. 47)

J. M. VANTREASE versus A. J. VANTREASE. The cause is continued. 11 Apr 1885. (P. 47)

G. W. PUCKETT versus G. W. MEDLEY Et Al. Sale of a tract of land. 11 Apr 1885. (P. 48)

J. H. HUGHES versus H. L. MAXWELL Et Al. The order for reopening the bids is rescinded. 11 Apr 1885. (P. 49)

J. H. TURNEY Et Al versus LUCINDA TURNEY Et Al. 11 Apr 1885. (Pp. 50-53)

C. B. CANTRELL versus M. D. SMALLMAN, Trustee, Et Al. Decree. 11 Apr 1885. (Pp. 53-54)

JOHN F. LUCKEY versus JOHN D. BONE, Administrator, and M. D. BONE deceased. The parties reach a compromise. The defendant agrees to deliver up the note that he holds. 11 Apr 1885. (Pp. 54-56)

DOBSON JOHNSON versus MONROE NEAL Et Al. The bill is taken for confessed. Charles Cooper has been dead for more than six months leaving property in DeKalb County. No one has qualified as administrator. B. M. Cantrell is appointed as administrator. 11 Apr 1885. (P. 57)

JOHN MARTIN, Executor of John Martin, Et Al versus W. C. MARTIN Et Al. Complainant John Martin is dead, his death having been suggested at a former term of court. John H. Savage has been appointed as administrator. The Clerk is to report the amount due John Martin under former decrees from the estate of his father John Martin. Also, the amount due from M. B. Martin. 11 Apr 1885. (Pp. 57-58)

NANCY E. WARREN versus SQUIRE WARREN. Complainant and defendants were citizens of DeKalb County for two whole years next before filing this bill. They had married each other as husband and wife. The defendant has been guilty of offering cruel and inhuman treatment to the complainant. However, these charges were not sustained by the cross bill. The bonds of matrimony are dissolved. 11 Apr 1885. (Pp. 59-60)

JAMES HICKMAN versus H. P. KEMP Et Al. Some of the defendants are non residents. The bill is taken for confessed. 11 Apr 1885. (P. 61)

T. C. ERVIN versus ELLA ERVIN. The cause is continued until next term of court. 11 Apr 1885. (P. 61)

NANCY E. MAYNARD versus EZEKIEL MAYNARD. Parties were intermarried. Defendant has been guilty of cruel and inhuman treatment toward complainant. The bonds of matrimony are dissolved. She is restored to her maiden name of Nancy Elizabeth Bass.

11 Apr 1885. (Pp. 61-62)

JEFFERSON ALCORN versus SARAH ALCORN. This cause is ordered continued until next term of court. Defendant recovers of complainant the cost of this cause. 11 Apr 1885. (P. 62)

A number of causes are continued. (Pp. 63-64)

J. C. WATSON Et Al versus E. MAYNARD Et Al. The court is of opinion and so decrees that the property mentioned in the deed from E. Maynard to his first wife, M. A. Maynard, and her children which deed is exhibited with the bill of J. C. Watson Et Al with the increases and profits of said property. The said J. C. Watson was by order of the court appointed receiver in this cause. It is ordered that he turn over to E. Maynard, Trustee for said children, all property in his hands. 13 Apr 1885. (P. 65)

G. W. ALLEN Et Al versus S. P. ELLIOTT Et Al. The land, decreed to be sold, was sold to W. A. Johnson. 13 Apr 1885. (Pp. 66-67)

WILLIAM MAYNARD versus W. C. JOHNSON. Complainant's bill is dismissed. 13 Apr 1885. (P. 67)

RUTH BATES versus GEORGE BATES. Complainant is entitled to the relief sought. The bonds of matrimony are dissolved. The said Ruth Bates is restored to her maiden name of Ruth Johnson. Complainant recovers of defendant the sum of $100 in alimony. 13 Apr 1885. (P. 67)

C. T. BURTON Et Al versus THOMAS MAYNARD Et Al. Sale of 125 acres. 13 Apr 1885. (Pp. 68-69)

WILLIAM McDOWELL versus MARY McDOWELL. The defendant was guilty of adultery. The bonds of matrimony are dissolved. 13 Apr 1885. (Pp. 69-70)

SOLOMON GOODMAN versus ELIZABETH GOODMAN. Sale of a tract of land to Allen and Tubbs. 13 Apr 1885. (P. 70)

A number of causes are continued. (Pp. 71-72)

HENRY ALLEN versus A. L. SHERRILL. Defendant Harry Allen has agreed that complainant is entitled to the note given by defendant Sherrill for the oxen. 14 Apr 1885. (P. 73)

M. A. PULLEN by next friend versus R. E. ROBINSON Et Al. Defendant R. E. Robinson agrees that the complainant, M. A. Pullen, may have out of the funds now in the hands of the Clerk arising from the sale of the goods. 14 Apr 1885. (Pp. 74-75)

MARY BRASWELL Et Al versus SAMUEL BRASWELL Et Al. The Clerk is to make a report. 14 Apr 1885. (Pp. 75-76)

R. E. ROBINSON versus C. E. PULLEN. Complainant is entitled to have the funds in the hands of the receiver. 14 Apr 1885. (Pp. 76-77)

J. J. FORD versus H. B. SMITH Et Al. The bill is taken for confessed. 14 Apr 1885. (Pp. 78-79)

F. H. ROBERTSON and wife versus D. B. DAVIS and others. The title to 169½ acres is divested out of Wesley Johnson and vested in Samuel Whitley. 14 Apr 1885. (P. 79)

S. S. CRADDOCK and wife versus J. N. HAYES Et Al. There is yet due on the notes of defendant Hayes. A tract of land is ordered sold. 14 Apr 1885. (P. 80)

W. J. JONES versus JAMES L. COLVERT, Administrator. Demurrer of J. L. Colvert, Administrator of T. N. Christian. 14 Apr 1885. (Pp. 81-82)

J. H. CAMERON next friend versus J. L. COLVERT. 14 Apr 1885. (Pp. 82-84)

E. S. CLOSE Et Al versus T. M. CLOSE Et Al. It is a proper for the Master to make a settlement with the several heirs to the amount they have received from their father, J. S. Close, in land or otherwise and also with T. N. Close, the administrator. 15 Apr 1885. (Pp. 84-85)

J. J. FORD versus H. B. SMITH and M. C. MARCUM. Decree. 15 Apr 1885. (P. 86)

J. E. ROBINSON Et Al versus W. B. ROBINSON Et Al. The Clerk makes his report. 15 Apr 1885. (Pp. 87-90)

The Clerk & Master will enroll in a book kept for the purpose all pleadings and exhibits upon the filing thereof. 15 Apr 1885. (P. 91)

MARY BRASWELL Et Al versus SAMUEL BRASWELL Et Al. Decree. 15 Apr 1885. (P. 92)

Chancery Court met in the town of Smithville on the first Monday in July, it being the sixth day of said month, 1885. (P. 93)

CLERK & MASTER versus C. S. FRAZIER, Sheriff. 7 Jul 1885. (Pp. 94-95)

J. B. FRAZIER versus W. H. BROWN, Cashier. The injunction is granted. 6 Jul 1885. (Pp. 96-97)

THOMAS GRACE versus J. L. GRACE. The bill is taken for confessed. 7 Jul 1885. (P. 98)

W. A. JONES Et Al versus JOHN TURNER Et Al. The bill is taken for confessed against John Turner and Hannah Turner. 7 Jul 1885. (Pp. 98-99)

W. A. JONES, J. M. JONES, T. J. JONES, J. C. JONES, W. E. JONES, WILLIAM TURNER and wife SARAH, JOSEPH WEBB and wife FANNIE versus JOHN TURNER and wife HANNAH, (THULA) JONES, JULUS JONES, and J. R. MOORE, Guardian. It is agreed to the division of the land of John Jones deceased. John Jones died about eight years ago leaving complainants except William Turner and Joseph Webb and one Alex Jones now dead as his only children and heirs. At his death, he owned 150 acres in the 8th District. Since his death, his widow died never having claimed homestead or dower. 7 Jul 1885. (Pp. 99-101)

WILLIAM B. WOOD and wife versus G. W. WOOD. The court is pleased to overrule and disallow said demurrer. 7 Jul 1885. (P. 102)

JANE MILSTED versus JOHN MILSTED. The bill is taken for confessed. Complainant is a lady of good character. Defendant has failed and refused to provide for her. He maliciously deserted her without justy cause for more than seven years. Complainant is restored to all the rights of an unmarried woman. Defendant to pay the costs. 7 Jul 1885. (P. 103)

B. A. EMERY versus J. C. EMERY. The bill is taken for confessed. Complainant is a lady of good character. Defendant has failed to provide for her and deserted her without just cause. Complainant is restored to all the rights and privileges of a single woman. Her name is changed to Bettie Gilbert, her maiden name. 7 Jul 1885. (P. 103)

Chancery Court met in the town of Smithville on the first Monday, it being the fifth day of Oct 1885. W. G. Crowley, presiding. (P. 104)

SANFORD MANN Et Al versus J. L. BOWMAN. Decree. 6 Oct 1885. (P. 104)

OLIVIA YORK versus ISAAC YORK. Complainant has dismissed her bill. 6 Oct 1885. (P. 105)

C. W. ANDERSON versus C. B. CANTRELL. It appears to the court that the heirs of Isaac Cantrell viz. Charles A. Cantrell, William H. Cantrell, Martha L. Cantrell, Robert H. Cantrell, Mary A. Cantrell, Calvin B. Cantrell, Jr., Edner F. Cantrell, Emma F. Cantrell, Walter J. Cantrell, and Virginia Cantrell are minors without guardian. B. G. Adcock is appointed as guardian. 6 Oct 1885. (P. 105)

NANCY E. WARREN versus SQUIRE WARREN. 6 Oct 1885. (P. 106)

E. A. BRESHEARS versus I. JOHNSON. The death of complainant E. Ā. Breshears since last term of court is suggested. 6 Oct 1885. (P. 106)

JOHN T STOKES versus W. B. ROBINSON Et Al. It appears to the court from the written transfer of John T. Stokes and wife, E. P. Stokes that they bought ten acres of land and then transferred their bid to R. W. Mason. 7 Oct 1885. (Pp. 107-108)

J. H. SAVAGE Et Al versus J. K. FISHER Et Al. This is a proper case for a receiver. 7 Oct 1885. (Pp. 108-109)

J. J. FORD versus JAMES H. BLACKBURN Et Al. Defendant Dinges is to take possession of the house and land. 7 Oct 1885. 7 Oct 1885. (Pp. 110-111)

J. M. MALONE next friend versus JACOB ADAMSON. The Clerk will take an account with Jacob Adamson as Guardian of Polly Adamson. 7 Oct 1885. (P. 111)

W. H. BAKER versus F. P. FISHER Et Al. This cause is dismissed. 7 Oct 1885. (P. 111)

C. M. SCHURER Et Al versus M. M. BRIEN Et Al. The death of the complainant in the original bill was suggested. J. A. Donnell is the administrator of said deceased. 7 Oct 1885. (P. 112)

G. W. ALLEN Et Al versus S. P. ELLIOTT. S. P. Elliott has since 1878 put and caused to be put on said dower improvements. 7 Oct 1885. (Pp. 112-114)

SARAH PACK versus ISAAC CANTRELL Et Al. Defendant is entitled to be reimbursed the amount of money paid by him to complainant with interest. 7 Oct 1885. (Pp. 114-115)

A number of causes are continued or dismissed. (Pp. 115-117)

J. M. LORING Et Al versus JOHN MARTIN Et Al. Sale of a tract of land. 7 Oct 1885. (Pp. 117-118)

SARAH SHAW Et Al versus W. B. SHAW Et Al. The bill is taken for confessed as to Sarah Shaw, H. C. Shaw, H. C. Eastham, E. C. Murry and wife Nannie, Joseph M. Shaw, Thomas Hopkins, W. B. Shaw, N. B. Bozarth, and N. G. Tyree. 7 Oct 1885. (P. 118)

J. M. VANTREASE versus A. J. VANTREASE. The Clerk is to report to the next term of court. 8 Oct 1885. (Pp. 119-120)

NANCY E. WARREN versus SQUIRE WARREN. Sale of a tract of land. 8 Oct 1885. (P. 120)

F. M. FOUTCH and wife versus T. M. ROWLAND, Administrator. A compromise has been reached in the case of Francis Foutch and wife versus Thomas Rowland and others. The suit is dismissed. 8 Oct 1885. (Pp. 120-121)

M. A. SCOTT next friend versus WILLIAM VICK, Administrator. Complainant Anna J. Scott is of full age. The cause is dismissed. 8 Oct 1885. (P. 121)

C. W. ANDERSON versus DAVID FUSTON Et Al. Motion of complainant to revive the cause against the heirs of Starky Cotton, to wit, William F. Cotton, Rubin Cotton, Thomas Cotton, Sallie Cotton, L. Chysm, Jane Cotton, W. C. Cotton, James Cotton, and Mat Cotton, each of whom are of full age. The bill is taken for confessed. 8 Oct 1885. (P. 122)

POLLY CAPSHAW versus A. B. HATHAWAY. This cause is continued. 8 Oct 1885. (P. 123)

C. H. ANDERSON versus DAVID FISHER Et Al. The Clerk will report whether Starkey Cotton was paid for the land or not. 8 Oct 1885. (Pp. 123-124)

JOHN C. HALCUM, MALVINA HALCUM, MALINDA HALCUM, B. H. WOMACK, Administrator of J. R. Halcum, and THOMAS H. HALCUM versus B. S. ST. JOHNS and wife DELILAH, formerly Williams, H. M. McDOUGAL and husband GUNTA, ABNER ST. JOHN, ADENA ST. JOHN, JOHN A. WILLIAMS, JOHN SCURLOCK and wife PALITHA, ALEXANDER HILDRETH and wife ALZENA, W. W. HERNDON and wife MARGARET, JAMES C. WILLIAMS, JAMES ST. JOHN, and MINERVA ST. JOHN. Complainants are the administrators, husband, and distributees of Jeptha Halcum.

Defendants are the administrator, heirs, and distributees of
Harden Williams deceased. J. R. Halcum in his lifetime sold
to Harden Williams a tract of land containing 300 acres. 8
Oct 1885. (Pp. 124-126)

W. B. PRICHARD Et Al versus J. M. LOVE Et Al. 8 Oct 1885.
(Pp. 126-127)

W. T. ROBINSON Et Al versus A. H. J. CALIICOTT, Adminis=
trator, Et Al. Report. 8 Oct 1885. (Pp. 127-130)

C. C. ODUM and wife versus CHARLIE DODD Et Al. Said defendant cannot be found in Wilson County, the place of his last
residence. His whereabouts is unknown. He is a non resident
of Tennessee. The bill is taken for confessed. 8 Oct 1885.
(P. 131)

L. F. GARRISON versus J. J. FORD. There was no fraud
practiced in obtaining the decree. 9 Oct 1885. (Pp. 131-132)

S. W. McCLELLAN versus C. L. BARTON Et Al. Complainant is
entitled to recover of defendant Barton. 9 Oct 1885. (P. 133)

J. T. QUARLES VERSUS F. E. BEARD. The demurrer is well
taken. 9 Oct 1885. (Pp. 133-134)

THOMAS GRACE versus J. L. GRACE. The bill is taken for confessed. Complainant and defendant were married in DeKalb County
in Apr 1882. Complainant and defendant have two children, one
a boy named Walter L. Grace, and the other a girl named Sarah
Dell Grace. They are now living with complainant. The defendant abandoned complainant and has since time wholly refused to
provide for her and said children. The bonds of matrimony are
dissolved. Complainant is given custody of the children. 9 Oct
1885. (P. 134)

A number of causes are continued. (Pp. 135-136)

REBECCA CHRISTIAN Et Al versus WILLIAM H. MAGNESS Et Al.
9 Oct 1885. (Pp. 136-137)

JAMES P. TUBB versus M. M. BRIEN. 9 Oct 1885. Report.
(Pp. 137-139)

JOHN A. MOSS versus R. S. LOVE, Administrator. The Clerk
is to report the amount of damage, if any, done the estate of
H. Love by the complainant wrongfully injoining defendant J. H.
Love in the administration of the estate of H. Love deceased.
9 Oct 1885. (Pp. 139-140)

W. L. B. LAWRENCE and JOHN M. LAWRENCE versus LOUIS B.
THOMPSON and others. Louis B. Thompson confessed judgment in
favor of John H. Savage for $140. 9 Oct 1885. (Pp. 140-141)

G. R. WEST and others versus T. W. WEST and others. 9
Oct 1885. (Pp. 141-142)

THOMAS W. WEST versus T. E. WEST. Commissioners are to
take and state an account and settlement of all matters in controversy upon the basis of the decree of the Chancellor. 9
Oct 1885. (P. 142)

W. C. LEWIS, Administrator, versus WILLIAM FRANCIS Et Al. Sale of a tract of land to P. T. Shores. 9 Oct 1885. (Pp. 143-144)

MARION TRAPP Et Al versus J. T. TRAPP Et Al. It was suggested to the court that defendant Amanda Atnip died in DeKalb County since this term of court commenced, leaving her only children and heirs living in DeKalb County. All are minors without guardian. They are Harrison Atnip, 18; Hamp Atnip, 16; Josie Atnip, 13; and Rebecca Atnip, 9 or 10. 10 Oct 1885. (P. 145)

DORA HATHAWAY versus MALINDA TAYLOR Et Al. The death of complainant is suggested. 10 Oct 1885. (P. 145)

J. M. MALONE next friend versus JACOB ADAMSON Et Al. 10 Oct 1885. (Pp. 145-146)

ELIZABETH ARNOLD versus JAMES ARNOLD. Final Decree. Complainant and defendant have been citizens of DeKalb County for more than two years next before filing this bill. They intermarried with each other about 15 Aug 1884 and lived together as husband and wife about four months. Defendant without cause abandoned complainant and refused and failed to provide for her in any manner. Complainant is fully divorced. She is restored to her maiden name of Elizabeth Hill. 10 Oct 1885. (P. 146)

MARY ISABEL SMITH versus J. B. SMITH. Defendant and complainant have been citizens of DeKalb County for more than two years next. They intermarried about the 28th of Dec 1882. The complainant is guilty of cruel and inhuman treatment toward the defendant. He is guilty of slandering the complainant. Complainant is a woman of good character and she was not guilty of any of the slanderous charges made against her particularly upon the subject of chastity. Complainant is fully divorced from the defendant and is restored to her maiden name of Mary Isabel Mullican. It appears to the court that the defendant has or is about to fraudulently dispose of his property. He is the owner of a roane mare. At attachment is ordered. Complainant has filed her bill as a pauper. The defendant is perpetually enjoined from molesting complainant in any manner. 10 Oct 1885. (Pp. 146-147)

MARTHA CARTER versus JOHN R. CARTER. The bill is taken for confessed. The allegations in complainant's bill are fully made out. The bonds of matrimony are dissolved. Complainant is to have all the property attached for alimony. 10 Oct 1885. (P. 148)

T. DRIVER and wife versus H. P. KEMP Et Al. 10 Oct 1885. (P. 149)

J. H. CAMERON next friend versus J. L. COLVERT, Administrator, Et Al. 10 Oct 1885. (Pp. 150-152)

GILLY DEWEESE versus ISAAC DEWEESE. This cause is dismissed. 10 Oct 1885. (P. 153)

MARY I. SMITH versus J. B. SMITH. 10 Oct 1885. (P. 154)

C. B. CANTRELL Et Al versus M. D. SMALLMAN Et Al. Decree. The homestead or dower tract set apart to Jennie Cantrell shall become vacant by death or otherwise of said Jennie Cantrell. 12 Oct 1885. (Pp. 155-156)

JEFFERSON ALCORN versus SARAH ALCORN. Complainant and defendant were married together in DeKalb County and had been citizens of the State of Tennessee for two years next before the filing of said bill. At the time of said marriage, the defendant was pregnant with child by some other man than complainant. Complainant was ignorant of that fact until three weeks after said marriage, that being the first time defendant or anyone else had informed him of said pregnancy. The bonds of matrimony are dissolved. 12 Oct 1885. (Pp. 156-157)

JACOB ADAMS versus J. R. FUSON. 12 Oct 1885. (Pp. 157-158)

MARTHA FOUTCH versus ELIJAH FOUTCH. The former order of sale is revived. 12 Oct 1885. (P. 158)

E. S. CLOSE Et Al versus T. N. CLOSE, Administrator, Et Al. Petition of complainant to review and set aside the decree dismissing the bill as to the charge of imbecility and undue influence of John Close deceased. 12 Oct 1885. (Pp. 158-159)

JAMES McMILLEN and wife versus SIMEON ADAMSON Et Al. Sale of a tract of land. 12 Oct 1885. (P. 159)

S. W. McCLELLAN versus C. L. BARTON Et Al. 12 Oct 1885. (Pp. 159-160)

W. B. FARLER Et Al versus JERRY FISHER HALE. Motion of the complainant to have a receiver to take charge of the land. 12 Oct 1885. (P. 161)

MARY B. BOZARTH Et Al versus WILLIAM BOZARTH Et Al. The deed executed by James H. Bozarth on 21 Aug 1878 to defendant William Bozarth to a tract of 75 acres was executed without consideration and should be set aside. It is not necessary that complainant Mary B. Bozarth, the widow of James H. Bozarth, to join in said conveyance. Complainant as the widow and heir of the said James H. Bozarth recovers of the defendant. 12 Oct 1885. (Pp. 162-163)

JAMES H. CAMERON next friend versus J. L. COLVERT, Administrator. Consolidated causes. 12 Oct 1885. (Pp. 163-169)

MOSES PACK versus A. D. BAIN. Sale of a tract of land. 12 Oct 1885. (P. 169)

W. D. PRICHARD Et Al versus J. M. LOVE Et Al. Decree. 12 Oct 1885. (Pp. 170-172)

Chancery Court met in the town of Smithville on the first Tuesday after the second Monday, it being the tenth day of Nov 1885. M. D. Smallman, Special Chancellor, presiding. (P. 173)

J. B. ROBINSON and wife versus J. W. FOUTCH. 12 Oct 1885. (Pp. 173-174)

W. G. CROWLEY versus ADAM CROWDER. Complainant's bill is dismissed. 10 Nov 1885. (Pp. 174-175)

Chancery Court met in the town of Smithville on the first Tuesday after the second Monday, it being the ninth day of Nov 1886. M. D. Smallman, presiding. (P. 176)

MARION TRAPP Et Al versus J. T. TRAPP, Administrator, Et Al. The death of Nancy O. Cantrell is suggested. It appears to the court that said Nancy O. Cantrell is dead and that she left the following children, to wit, Thomas Shields and wife Frances A., G. W. Denton and wife A. F., and G. H. Atnip of DeKalb County; J. B. Atnip of Coffee County; Sophia A. Atnip, T. L. Cantrell, E. T. Cantrell, and Zollie H. Cantrell of Davidson County, the last three are minors without guardian. 19 Nov 1886. (P. 177)

Chancery County met in the town of Smithville on the first Monday, it being the fifth day of Apr 1886. W. G. Crowley, presiding. (P. 178)

FRANCES TURNER Et Al versus M. M. BRIEN Et Al. Report of the Clerk. (Pp. 178-181)

JOHN D. BANE, Administrator, and MATTIE N. WOOD in her own right versus JAMES T. QUARLES Et Al. A compromise is agreed upon. 6 Apr 1886. (Pp. 181-183)

J. B. MOORE next friend versus J. T. TRAPP and others. It appears that J. T. Trapp as Executor of the estate of J. J. Pedigo has in his hands money and effects going to J. D. Pedigo amounting to about $700. The said J. D. Pedigo has a desire to purchase a tract of land in Putnam County valued at $600. Said J. T. Trapp has advanced to Rowland Pedigo a sum of money for the purchase of land. It is in the interest of the said J. D. Pedigo and Rowland Pedigo that they be allowed to receive their interest in the money now in the hands of the said J. T. Trapp. 6 Apr 1886. (Pp. 183-184)

J. B. MOORE versus J. T. TRAPP Et Al. It appears that Rowland and J. D. Pedigo are minors without guardian. H. J. Goodson is appointed their guardian. 6 Apr 1886. (P. 185)

GILBERT CLARK versus W. B. PRESTON. Defendants have been served with process. The bill is taken for confessed and set for hearing. 6 Apr 1886. (P. 185)

A number of causes are continued. (P. 186)

(Pages 187 and 188 are blank)

Chancery Court met in the town of Smithville. It appears from the record that on 23 Mar 1883, M. A. Crowley was appointed Clerk & Master to fill a vacancy created by the resignation of W. W. Wade. Crowley has since held office without any other appointment. The said Crowley is now offering his resignation under said appointment. The Chancellor accepts his resignation. The said M. A. Crowley desires to hold said office under a new appointment. The said M. A. Crowley is hereby appointed to fill the facancy. 18 Aug 1886. (Pp. 189-192)

(Pages 193 and 194 are blank)

Chancery Court met in the town of Smithville on the third Monday in Feb, it being the 21st day of said month 1887. W. W. Wade, presiding. (P. 195)

C. W. ANDERSON versus DAVID FISHER Et Al. B. G. Adcock was appointed guardian for the minor heirs of Isaac Cantrell. It appears that ten dollars is a reasonable fee for his services. 21 Feb 1887. (P. 195)

J. M. MALONE next friend versus JACOB ADAMSON, Guardian. The parties have entered into a compromise. 21 Feb 1887. (Pp. 195-197)

J. H. TRAMMEL versus WILLIAM TURANTINE. 21 Feb 1887. (P. 197)

A. and J. TURANTINE versus S. MANN Et Al. The bill is dismissed. 21 Feb 1887. (P. 197)

J. D. PHILLIPS Et Al versus PURE FOUNTAIN COLLEGE Et Al. The court is pleased to allow the amended bill to be filed. 21 Feb 1887. (P. 198)

J. ALCORN versus HORACE ATNIP. The demurrer was not well taken. 21 Feb 1887. (Pp. 198-199)

H. M. FITE, Administrator, versus C. E. PULLEN and wife. The deposition of W. V. Herald has been mislaid or lost. Leave is granted to Mrs. M. A. Pullen to retake the deposition. 21 Feb 1887. (P. 199)

ALLEN WRIGHT versus J. R. TURNER Et Al. Defendants J. R. Turner, Lean Turner, and Thomas K. David are justly indebted to complainant. 21 Feb 1887. (Pp. 200-201)

W. L. HARDCASTLE, Administrator, versus JOHN WINDHAM Et Al. Application of John Windham and wife Nancy; James Staley and wife Henrietta; William F. Christian; and Thomas S. Christian to file their answer. Motion to dissolve the injunction. 21 Feb 1887. (Pp. 202-203)

A number of causes are continued. (Pp. 203-207)

DORA A. HATHAWAY versus MALINDA TAYLOR Et Al. It appears that complainant is dead and her death has been proven fore more than two terms. There has been no revivor of the cause. Webb & Avant assert a lien for their fees on the lands recovered in the cause. 21 Feb 1887. (P. 207)

A number of causes are continued. (Pp. 208-210)

J. L. COLVERT Et Al versus JAMES STALEY Et Al. It appears to the court that Rebecca Christian had paid the taxes on the land mentioned in the pleadings for the year 1882. The said J. L. Colvert as administrator is to reemburse the said Rebecca. 21 Feb 1887. (P. 210)

T. FRISBY versus T. ADCOCK Et Al. The rights of Hiram Cantrell and others to a tract of land is divested out of them

74

and vested in Thomas Frisby. 22 Feb 1887. (P. 211)

W. L. HARDCASTLE, Administrator, versus JOHN WINDHAM Et Al. The court is pleased to modify the injunction. 22 Feb 1887. (P. 212)

J. H. CAMERON next friend versus J. L. COLVERT Et Al. The Clerk is ordered to make to E. D. Staley a deed to the land mentioned in the pleadings. 22 Feb 1887. (P. 214)

JOHN LYLES versus H. L. MAXWELL Et Al. This cause is dismissed as to said defendant and the attachment. 22 Feb 1887. (P. 215)

MARY A. RIGSBY versus J. D. RIGSBY. Application of the complainant to have alimony decreed pending this litigation. 22 Feb 1887. (P. 216)

JAMES VAUGHN Et Al versus B. M. CANTRELL Et Al. Motion to appoint a guardian for Rutha A. Vaughn, Leroy J. Vaughn, Perry G. Vaughn, and Malissa E. Vaughn who are minors without guardian. P. T. Shores was appointed guardian. 22 Feb 1887. (P. 217)

WILLIAM VANDERGRIFF and JOHN W. VANDERGRIFF versus S. W. McCLENNAN Et Al. Defendants recover of the complainants. 22 Feb 1887. (P. 217)

SARAH SHAW Et Al versus W. B. SHAW Et Al. The bill is taken for confessed. The Clerk is to make a report to the court. 22 Feb 1887. (Pp. 217-218)

J. J. FORD versus J. H. CARTWRIGHT. J. H. Cartwright is executor for James Goodner deceased. Said Ford is his surety. 22 Feb 1887. (Pp. 218-219)

GULY DURSE versus ISAAC DURSE. The charge in the complainant's bill is that the defendant has abandoned the complainant and refused to provide for her is fully sustained. The bonds of matrimony are dissolved. The property mentioned in the cause is decreed to the complainant for alimony. 22 Feb 1887. (Pp. 220-221)

JACOB ADAMS versus J. R. FUSON. 22 Feb 1887. (Pp. 221-222)

A number of causes are continued. (P. 223)

C. F. BURTON Et Al versus T. MAYNARD Et Al. 23 Feb 1887. (Pp. 223-224)

JOHN H. TRAMMEL versus WILSON TURANTINE. The demurrer is sustained. 23 Feb 1887. (P. 225)

T. C. HARPER Et Al versus S. H. SMITH Et Al. Motion by complainant for a rule on complainant to give other and better security. 23 Feb 1887. (Pp. 226-227)

WILLIAM CLARK Et Al versus E. L. MEGGERSON Et Al. The demurrer is not well taken. The motion as to Oma Clark is well taken for the reason she has no interest in the subject matter. The bill as to Oma Clark and W. H. Pedigo is dismissed. 23 Feb 1887. (Pp. 227-228)

JESSE T. HOLLIS versus JOHN B. ROBINSON. It appears that the present security is insolvent. It is ordered that the complainant answer the cross bill without process. 23 Feb 1887. (Pp. 228-229)

GILLY DURSE versus ISAAC DURSE. It was agreed that twenty dollars would be a reasonable fee for the Clerk for his services. 23 Feb 1887. (P. 230)

WILLIAM ROBINSON versus A. P. SMITH, Executor, Et Al. Vers S. Callicott is a minor without guardian. T. W. Wade is appointed guardian. 23 Feb 1887. (Pp. 231-232)

W. B. WOOD and wife versus G. W. WOOD. Defendant will have twenty days to pay one hundred dollars and costs. If necessary, writ of possession will be issued to the Sheriff. 23 Feb 1887. (Pp. 232-233)

J. VAUGHN Et Al versus B. M. CANTRELL Et Al. The Clerk will give an account as to how much land has been sold. 23 Feb 1887. (Pp. 233-234)

W. J. GIVAN versus G. WEST Et Al. Process has been served on Jessie Paty and W. E. Rich, Administrators of W. Grooms. 23 Feb 1887. (P. 235)

J. H. LOVE Et Al versus V. N. SMITH Et Al. There is no equity apparent upon the face of the bill as against the defendant. 23 Feb 1887. (Pp. 235-236)

E. A. COGGIN, Administrator, versus J. H. LOVE Et Al. The Clerk is ordered to pay over to H. M. Fite, Administrator of W. R. Coggin $150 of the funds in his hands. He is to determine if it is necessary to sell more land to pay the debts. 23 Feb 1887. (P. 237)

RACHEL ADAMS Et Al versus WILLIAM WATSON Et Al. The Clerk will take proof of the amount of available financial assets of the estate of Peter Adams. He is to determine if it will be necessary to sell the land. 23 Feb 1887. (Pp. 238-239)

JOHN JONES, Administrator, versus W. O. BURGER Et Al. The death of defendant S. O. Smithson was suggested. She died, intestate, since the commencement of this suit, leaving her only children, Lana E. Smithson, Jessie Smithson, John Smithson, and Bertha Smithson who are minors without guardian. A. J. Goodson is appointed as guardian. 24 Feb 1887. (Pp. 239-240)

T. C. ERVIN versus ELLA ERVIN. The bill is taken for confessed. Complainant and defendant were married to each other as charged. They had the children named in the bill. The defendant has been guilty of adultery as charged. Complainant as to chastity was good. The bonds of matrimony are dissolved. Complainant is given custody of the children. 24 Feb 1887. (Pp. 241-242)

E. B. ALLEN versus T. C. ALLEN Et Al. Motion to have a guardian for the minor defendants, to wit, Lee Allen, Luther Allen, and Cleborn Allen. J. W. Eaton is appointed as their guardian.

The bill is taken for confessed against the defendants, to wit, T. C. Allen, H. H. Allen, E. A. Allen, Anna Allen, Luther Love, Nancy Love, J. J. Mullican, R. F. Mullican, A. B. Atnip, H. G. Atnip, Enoch Atnip, and A. O. Allen. 24 Feb 1887. (Pp. 242-243)

R. L. PAGE versus B. R. PAGE Et Al. Complainant moved to make Margaret Trammel, wife of J. L. Trammel, a party defendant which is permitted. 24 Feb 1887. (P. 243)

A number of causes are continued. (Pp. 243-245)

CANTRELL & FORD versus E. A. COGGIN, Administrator. The court is pleased to order that the complainants receive from E. L. Bowers, Administrator of Jeremiah Coggin the sum of thirty-five dollars. 25 Feb 1887. (Pp. 245-247)

CALVIN JONES versus R. M. TITTSWORTH and J. E. CONGER. John E. Conger sold by deed the tract of land described in the bill to defendant R. M. Tittsworth who gave his promissory note. The said J. E. Conger endorsed the note. The Master will sell the land to satisfy the lien. 24 Feb 1887. (P. 249)

AARON CANTRELL, Administrator, Et Al versus SUSAN LOVE Et Al. The cause of Wilson versus Love is revived against Aaron Cantrell, Administrator, and the heirs of J. M. Love. Defendants H. K. Love, Wilson Taylor, John Taylor, Perry Taylor, and Cara Taylor are minors without guardian. B. G. Adcock is named their guardian. 24 Feb 1887. (Pp. 250-252)

A number of causes are continued. (Pp. 253-257)

S. W. McCLENNAN versus THOMAS J. SNEED. It is ordered that a deed be made to B. F. Bell for the land purchased. 24 Feb 1887. (P. 257)

G. W. PUCKETT versus G. W. MEDLEY. The death of J. J. Pedigo, one of the securities is suggested. 24 Feb 1887. (Pp. 258-259)

J. D. PHILLIPS Et Al versus PURE FOUNTAIN COLLEGE. 24 Feb 1887. (Pp. 259-260)

WILLIAM ROBINSON versus A. P. SMITH, Executor, Et Al. The bill is taken for confessed. The contract between complainant and Ann J. Callicott, dated 10 Dec 1884, is valid. 24 Feb 1887. (Pp. 261-263)

Report of the Clerk & Master to April Term 1886. (Pp. 264-267)

H. W. WILLIAMS versus W. B. PETTIE. William H. Magness, W. D. Carnes and wife Sarah E. have been made defendants in this cause. The said Magness is a citizen of Warren County and said Carnes is a citizen of Overton County. 24 Feb 1887. (P. 270)

J. M. FISHER and wife versus WILLIAM FARLER Et Al. The court decrees to Lucine Fisher is entitled to the lands mentioned in the pleadings as a homestead, it being the land owned by William A. Parker and complainant Lucine at the death of the said

William A. Parker. The court adjudged that the Will of said
Parker does not convey the land and homestead described in the
pleadings in these causes so as to defeat homestead rights of
complainant Lucine Fisher and that she is not by said will nor
the failure of complainant Lucine to dissent from said will.
The will of the said William A. Parker cannot be contested.
Complainants J. M. Fisher and wife, Lucine, recover of William
Farler. 26 Feb 1887. (Pp. 270-272)

A number of causes are continued. (P. 273)

J. A. JOHNSON Et Al versus MARTIN WAGGONER Et Al. 26 Feb
1887. (P. 274)

T. N. SMITH and wife versus H. C. TAYLOR Et Al. Final
Decree. 26 Feb 1887. (Pp. 275-276)

A number of causes are continued. (Pp. 276-280)

RACHEL ADAMS Et Al versus JACOB ADAMS Et Al. 26 Feb 1887.
(P. 280)

M. J. SMITH versus J. B. SMITH. Complainant moved to dismiss the bill. 26 Feb 1887. (P. 281)

AARON CANTRELL, Administrator, Et Al versus SUSAN LOVE Et
Al. Final Decree. 26 Feb 1887. (Pp. 281-286)

E. A. COGGIN, Administrator, versus J. H. LOVE Et Al. The
Clerk will pay over to the Administrator of W. R. Coggin $200.
26 Feb 1887. (Pp. 286-287)

G. W. ALLEN Et Al versus S. P. ELLIOTT Et Al. The title
to the land is divested out of W. A. Johnson and vested in J. P.
Johnson. 26 Feb 1887. (P. 287)

JANE SUMMERS versus GEORGE SUMMERS. Complainant dismisses
this suit. 26 Feb 1887. (P. 288)

JOSIE EMERY versus JOHN EMERY. Complainant dismisses this
suit. 26 Feb 1887. (P. 289)

M. C. Crawley is appointed as Clerk & Master. Clerk &
Master's official oath. 26 Feb 1887. (Pp. 289-300)

A number of causes are continued. (Pp. 300-301)

C. B. CANTRELL Et Al versus M. D. SMALLMAN. Judgment. 26
Feb 1887. (Pp. 302-303)

Chancery Court was held in the town of Smithville on the
third Monday in Aug, 1887, it being the fifteenth day of said
month. W. W. Wade, presiding. (P. 304)

J. R. NORTHCUTT next friend versus COLUMBUS C. PRICHARD.
Defendants Ethel Robinson and Cambell Robinson are minors without guardian. W. B. Corley is appointed guardian. 15 Aug
1887. (P. 304)

R. L. PAGE versus J. L. TRAMMELL Et Al. Defendant J. L.
Trammell, Administrator, agrees to pay complainant. This is
from the estate of Mary Walls. 15 Aug 1887. (P. 305)

H. L. PUCKETT, Administrator of Henry L. Puckett versus
W. J. HOLLIS Et Al. Defendant is allowed to take the oath of
pauperis. 15 Aug 1887. (P. 306)

B. M. WEBB versus M. BRAWER, Administrator. This bill is
filed to enjoin two small payments. 15 Aug 1887. (P. 306)

W. E. BARTLETT versus R. ALCORN Et Al. The papers in this
cause are lost. 15 Aug 1887. (P. 307)

JOE P. DAVIS versus T. J. DAVIS, Administrator Et Al. Defendant moved to dissolve the injunction. 15 Aug 1887. (Pp.
308-309)

J. A. JOHNSON versus MARTIN WAGGONER. Motion of complainant to amend the bill. 15 Aug 1887. (P. 310)

MATT BRISBO versus SYLVANUS PUCKETT. Defendant agrees to
surrender the mill. 15 Aug 1887. (P. 311)

JOHN ALCORN and wife versus H. ATNIP. Said Alcorn and wife
have already answered cross bill. 15 Aug 1887. (P. 312)

J. P. TITTSWORTH versus J. E. CONGER Et Al. Defendants
are to have time to file their answer. 15 Aug 1887. (P. 313)

M. T. VANATTA Et Al versus S. T. MOTTLEY Et Al. This cause
is continued. 15 Aug 1887. (Pp. 313-314)

W. J. GIVAN versus G. R. WEST Et Al. It is suggested that
Jesse Paty, Administrator of W. J. Givan has died. Charles Paty
is the Executor of Jesse Paty, a citizen of Cannon County. 15
Aug 1887. (Pp. 314-315)

J. T. HOLLIS versus JOHN B. ROBINSON. Complainant is permitted to retake his own deposition on the same facts. 15 Aug
1887. (Pp. 315-316)

JOE P. DAVIS versus T. J. DAVIS, Administrator of Solomon
Davis. The bill to make the heirs parties to this suit is not
presented at the present term of court. 15 Aug 1887. (P. 316)

W. B. STOKES versus F. M. SCHURER Et Al. The cross bill
does not present a proper case for the appointment of a receiver.
Defendants recover of complainant. 15 Aug 1887. (P. 317)

R. C. BONE versus J. T. ADAMSON Et Al. The depositions
taken in this suit are mislaid. Complainant is to have time to
file again. 15 Aug 1887. (P. 318)

T. A. TRACY Et Al versus JOHN CRIPS. The Clerk made a deed
to Thomas Young for the land mentioned in the pleadings. 15 Aug
1887. (P. 319)

T. J. FRAZIER next friend of Nancy Frazier versus T. B.
POTTER, Trustee. Relief is sought against defendants John Johnson and T. B. Potter, Trustee. 15 Aug 1887. (Pp. 320-321)

EMELINE FEREL versus RICHARD FEREL. Parties were married
and lived in DeKalb County. The defendant refused to provide for
the complainant. The bonds of matrimony are dissolved. Complainant's name is changed to Emeline Yates, her name before her

name before said marriage. 15 Aug 1887. (P. 322)

M. PACK versus A. BAIN. The Clerk is to give an account. 15 Aug 1887. (Pp. 322-323)

FRANCIS TURNER Et Al versus M. M. BRIEN. (The name is also written as Francis Turney.) The decree by the Chancellor is reversed by the Supreme Court. 15 Aug 1887. (Pp. 324-325)

M. A. STARK Et Al versus C. J. KING Et Al. The bill is taken for confessed as to all the other defendants, to wit, John H. Allen, W. G. Evins, Nancy Burkett, T. R. Huggins, Matilda Huggins, M. A. Evins, W. B. Preston, E. T. Lamberson, J. L. Hollinsworth, Mary Hollinsworth, and George Smith. 15 Aug 1887. (P. 326)

T. J. FRAZIER next friend of Nancy A. Frazier versus T. B. POTTER Et Al. 15 Aug 1887. (Pp. 327-328)

Report of Clerk & Master to August Term of court, 1887. (Pp. 328-329)

N. E. WARREN versus SQUIRE WARREN. 18 Aug 1887. (Pp. 330-331)

JOHN JONES, Administrator, versus W. O. BURGER Et Al. Defendants J. J. Jones and wife Josephine, Joseph W. P. Martin and Catherine D. Jones have yet to make defense. The bill is taken for confessed. 18 Aug 1887. (P. 331)

J. H. SAVAGE Et Al versus JAMES P. TUBB Et Al. Complainant pays the costs. 18 Aug 1887. (Pp. 332-334)

J. P. DAVIS versus T. J. DAVID, Administrator, Et Al. It appears to the court that this is a proper cause for an injunction. 18 Aug 1887. (Pp. 334-335)

J. W. GILBERT and wife versus T. B. POTTER, Trustee. Said Gilbert and wife, H. E., executed to T. B. Potter, Trustee, with power to sell a deed of trust to certain lands therein mentioned in the pleadings. The land is to be sold. 18 Aug 1887. (Pp. 336-338)

A number of causes are continued. (Pp. 339-340)

J. H. SAVAGE Et Al versus J. K. FISHER Et Al. Said J. K. Fisher is a non resident of the State of Tennessee. The bill is taken for confessed. 18 Aug 1887. (Pp. 340-341)

CAROLINE PETTY in her own right and as next friend versus JESSE PETTY Et Al. Caroline Petty paid all the purchase money, but Jesse Petty took title in himself when it should have jointly been in the name of Caroline and Jesse Petty. 18 Aug 1887. (Pp. 341-344)

R. E. SIMPSON Et Al versus M. M. BRIEN Et Al. The death of Helen Schurer was suggested. F. M. Schurer was admitted as her administrator. 19 Aug 1887. (Pp. 345-346)

WILLIAM ROBINSON versus A. P. SMITH, Executor of A. H. J. Callicott. Sale of a tract of land. 19 Aug 1887. (Pp. 346-348)

A number of causes are continued. (Pp. 348-349)

B. M. CANTRELL, Administrator, versus W. S. RENIC, Administrator, Et Al. There are assets belonging to the estate of G. W. Hathaway in the hands of the defendant. 18 Aug 1887. (Pp. 349-350)

L. B. RHODY next friend versus J. B. FRAZIER Et Al. 18 Aug 1887. (Pp. 350-351)

A. M. C. ROBINSON versus W. J. ROBINSON Et Al. The matters in this cause have been settled. 18 Aug 1887. (P. 351)

L. B. RHODY next friend versus J. B. FRAZIER Et Al. The statements and admissions in this cause have been lost or mislaid. 18 Aug 1887. (Pp. 352-353)

A. F. MAGNESS versus MATTIE E. MAGNESS. Final Decree. The bill is taken for confessed. The bonds of matrimony are dissolved. 18 Aug 1887. (P. 353)

B. M. WEBB versus M. BROWN, Administrator. It is ordered that complainant give other and better security. 18 Aug 1887. (P. 354)

A number of causes are continued. (Pp. 355-356)

JOHN D. BANE Et Al versus EDWIN PHILLIPS Et Al. Publication has been made in the LIBERTY HERALD. The bill is taken for confessed against Edwin Phillips and wife Sally, and John Gillwater and wife Callie. 18 Aug 1887. (Pp. 356-357)

CALVIN JONES versus R. M. TITTSWORTH Et Al. Report of sale. 19 Aug 1887. (Pp. 358-359)

W. L. HARDCASTLE, Administrator, versus JOHN WINDHAM Et Al. The entry should have appeared on the minutes of yesterday, but is entered now for then. 19 Aug 1887. Pp. 359-360)

ROBERT E. SIMPSON Et Al versus M. M. BRIEN Et Al. Upon the suggestion of M. M. Brien, Sr., W. A. Brien is the administrator of the said M. M. Brien. The Court decrees that defendant W. A. Brien as the Administrator of M. M. Brien, Sr. recover of the complainants. 19 Aug 1887. (Pp. 361-363)

A. V. MERRITT Et Al versus JOHN JOHNSON Et Al. On 30 Dec 1884, defendant John Johnson executed the deed to the land mentioned in the pleadings conditioned to repay to complainants as his securities. 19 Aug 1887. (Pp. 363-367)

POLLY CAPSHAW versus A. B. HATHAWAY. The complainant has not made out her case. The bill is dismissed. 19 Aug 1887. (P. 367)

H. S. GILL versus DEKALB COUNTY. The County is to pay the costs. 19 Aug 1887. (P. 368)

SARAH ADCOCK Et Al versus J. J. FORD. This cause is dismissed. 19 Aug 1887. (P. 368)

H. B. SMITH versus J. J. FORD. This cause is continued. 20 Aug 1887. (P. 369)

M. C. JACOBS versus L. D. JACOBS. Complainant has asked that the cause be dismissed. 20 Aug 1887. (Pp. 369-370)

M. J. SMITH versus J. B. SMITH. The law is with M. J. Smith. M. J. Smith will recover. 20 Aug 1887. (P. 370)

JOHN H. SAVAGE versus JAMES K. FISHER Et Al. Defendant did register and conveyed to W. H. Magness a trust deed on a tract of land. The land is ordered sold. 20 Aug 1887. (Pp. 371-374)

A. B. CHEATHAM versus G. W. CANTRELL. The County Surveyor is to survey the lands sold by the said G. W. Cantrell and wife to the said Cheatham. 20 Aug 1887. (Pp. 374-375)

E. B. ALLEN versus T. C. ALLEN, Executor, and others. The bill is taken for confessed. The complainants bill is so amended as to present the whole will and codicil of Alfred Allen deceased for construction. By consent, the rights of Anna Allen, widow of the deceased, to a homestead and year's support are submitted to the court for adjudication. 20 Aug 1887. (Pp. 375-378)

MARY A. RIGSBY versus J. D. RIGSBY. The Master will take possession of the property attached. 20 Aug 1887. (P. 378)

J. R. NORTHCUT and friend versus C. C. PRICHARD Et Al. The answer of W. B. Corley, Guardian for the minor children of John Robinson. The bill is taken for confessed. 20 Aug 1887. (P. 379)

MORGAN, THOMAS, & COMPANY versus OVERALL & HOLLANDSWORTH. 20 Aug 1887. (P. 380)

T. A. TRACY versus RUFUS BETHEL Et Al. In this cause, J. F. Smithson died and an amended bill has been filed to bring his children and widow before the court. Process was served. The bill is taken as confessed for C. B., J. D., and G. F. Smithson. All appeared except John Smithson, E. W. Smithson and wife Mary, John Pendleton and wife Clarindy, John Woodsides and wife Lou. The cause is set for hearing. 20 Aug 1887. (P. 381)

H. C. EASTHAM versus M. A. CROWLEY, Clerk. 20 Aug 1887. (Pp. 381-387)

T. A. TRACY versus RUFUS BETHEL Et Al. Final Decree. 20 Aug 1887. (Pp. 387-388)

W. L. HARDCASTLE, Administrator, versus JOHN WINDHAM Et Al. The Clerk will take proof and give an account. 20 Aug 1887. A guardian is appointed for the minor John Christian. 20 Aug 1887. (Pp. 389-390)

W. L. B. and J. M. LAWRENCE versus LEWIS B. and I. M. THOMPSON. This suit has been compromised. 20 Aug 1887. (Pp. 390-392)

WILLIAM VICK Et Al versus WILLIAM BYRD Et Al. No one has applied to become Administrator of Benjamin Thomas. The estate is insolvent. An amendment is added to the original bill. 20 Aug 1887. (P. 392)

T. C. HARPER Et Al versus S. H. SMITH Et Al. Motion by defendant to dismiss the suit. Overruled. 22 Aug 1887. (Pp. 392-393)

A number of causes are dismissed. (Pp. 393-394)

R. K. STEVENS versus JOHN MARTIN Et Al. Complainant recovers of John Martin, Jr.'s Administrator who is John H. Savage. 22 Aug 1887. (Pp. 394-398)

SARAH SHAW versus W. B. SHAW Et Al. In this cause, the pro confesso decree taken at a former term of this Court against Mrs. N. G. Tyree is set aside. 22 Aug 1887. (P. 398)

E. A. COGGIN, Administrator, versus J. H. LOVE, Administrator. 22 Aug 1887. (Pp. 398-399)

J. R. NORTHCUT Et Al versus COLUMBUS PRICHARD Et Al. Reasons are given why this cause should be dismissed. It appears on the face of the bill that Sanford Mann, father of complainants has a life estate in the land. The bill shows that Sanford Mann and Matilda Mann fraudulently sold the land mentioned. Matilda Mann in her lifetime for more than seven years ratified and confirmed said sale of land to defendants. 22 Aug 1887. (Pp. 400-401)

JOHN MARTIN, Executor of John Martin, Sr. versus W. C. MARTIN Et Al. This cause is ordered to be prosecuted in the name of John H. Savage, Administrator of John Martin. The Clerk will make a report. 22 Aug 1887. (Pp. 402-403)

JACOB ADAMS, Guardian, Et Al versus W. A. CATHCART, Administrator, Et Al. Defendant Cathcart moved the Court to be permitted to withdraw his answer concerning the estate of Leroy Braswell. 22 Aug 1887. (Pp. 403-405)

R. K. STEVENS versus JOHN H. SAVAGE, Administrator of John Martin. A compromise is reached. 23 Aug 1887. (Pp. 406-407)

J. J. FORD versus H. C. RUTLAND. The Clerk failed to affix his certificate to the depositions taken. The Court directs him to do so. 22 Aug 1887. (P. 408)

E. A. COGGIN versus J. H. LOVE, Administrator. 23 Aug 1887. (Pp. 408-410)

JANE VAUGHN Et Al versus B. M. CANTRELL Et Al. 23 Aug 1887. (Pp. 410-413)

G. W. PUCKETT versus G. W. MEDLEY. Decree. 23 Aug 1887. (Pp. 413-414)

R. T. FRISBY versus T. ADCOCK Et Al. A judgment was rendered against Thomas Frisby and his securities on his said first note in favor of the former Clerk & Master for $96.50. 23 Aug 1887. (Pp. 414-418)

W. L. B. and J. M. LAWRENCE versus LEWIS B. THOMPSON. 23 Aug 1887. (Pp. 418-420)

E. S. CLOSE versus T. N. CLOSE. 23 Aug 1887. (Pp. 420-424)

STATE OF TENNESSEE versus J. N. HAYS Et Al. This cause was again heard 22 Aug 1887 on motion of complainants to dismiss the bill. 23 Aug 1887. (P. 424)

J. L. COLVERT, Administrator, versus W. D. G. CARNES. The Clerk is to take an account and make a report. 23 Aug 1887. (Pp. 424-426)

STATE OF TENNESSEE versus J. N. HAYS Et Al. The bill is taken for confessed. 23 Aug 1887. (Pp. 426-427)

A number of causes are continued. (Pp. 427-429)

W. L. HARDCASTLE, Administrator, versus JOHN WINDHAM Et Al. 24 Aug 1887. (Pp. 429-430)

WILLIAM SELLARS Et Al versus L. P. WILLIAMS Et Al. Consolidated causes. Final Decree. The Clerk was to make a full settlement of the estate of Lee Smith which is in the hands of William Sellars the Administrator. 23 Aug 1887. (Pp. 430-441)

JAMES AYERS versus J. R. LAWRENCE. Complainant is trying to establish the line so as to allow defendants Lawrence and John Martin to erect a fence. 24 Aug 1887. (P. 442)

HENRY PUCKETT, Administrator, versus J. L. BROWN. The Clerk will advertise the land for sale. 24 Aug 1887. (Pp. 442-443)

B. M. WEBB versus M. BROWN, Administrator. The venue in this cause is transferred to the Chancery Court at Woodbury. 24 Aug 1887. (P. 444)

JAMES AYERS versus J. R. LAWRENCE. Petition of the said Ayers praying for an attachment for the body of defendant Lawrence for comtempt. The Court is of the opinion and so decrees that said defendant Lawrence has not violated the injunction granted in this cause. 24 Aug 1887. (P. 445)

G. W. MEDLEY versus G. W. PUCKETT. The cause was heard on motion of the defendant to dissolve the injunction. 24 Aug 1887. (Pp. 445-447)

JOHN JONES Et Al versus W. O. BURGER Et Al. The application of defendants for the appointment of a receiver was heard. The Court declined to appoint a receiver. 24 Aug 1887. (Pp. 447-448)

JAMES FORD versus JOHN and W. D. LOCKHART. Final Decree. It appears to the Court that the defendants are indebted to the complainant. 24 Aug 1887. (Pp. 448-449)

H. W. WILLIAMS versus W. B. PETTIE. It was agreed that the sale of the house and lot by D. G. Carnes and wife Sarah to W. B. Pettie on 1 Oct 1884 should be rescinded. 24 Aug 1887. (Pp. 449-451)

W. J. HOLLIS versus W. S. TYREE Et Al. The bill stands dismissed. 24 Aug 1887. (Pp. 451-452)

A number of causes are continued. (Pp. 452-453)

WILLIAM SELLARS, Executor of Matthew Sellars Et Al versus

L. P. WILLIAMS Et Al. On 20 Aug 1887, Charity Cathcart exercized fully her right to appear before the Supreme Court of Tennessee. 25 Aug 1887. (Pp. 453-460)

R. C. NESMITH versus J. J. FORD Et Al. The bill is taken for confessed for H. B. Smith and J. B. Robinson. 25 Aug 1887. (P. 460)

C. W. ANDERSON Et Al versus DAVID FISHER Et Al. Judgment. On 20 Mar 1886, C. W. Anderson executed a note for land in the cause. 25 Aug 1887. (Pp. 461-462)

M. A. CROWLEY. Financial Report. 25 Aug 1887. (Pp. 463-464)

A number of causes are continued. (Pp. 464-466)

J. S. GRIBBLE and others versus ELI ARNOLD Et Al. The bill is taken for confessed. 26 Aug 1887. (Pp. 466-467)

WILLIAM CLARK next friend versus E. L. MEGGERSON Et Al. The Clerk is to take proof and report back to court. 26 Aug 1887. (Pp. 468-472)

AARON CANTRELL, Administrator, Et Al versus SUSAN LOVE Et Al. At last term of court commissioners were appointed to lay off to Susan Love, widow of J. M. Love, one thousand dollars worth of land located in the 14th District. 26 Aug 1887. (Pp. 474-478)

W. L. HARDCASTLE, Administrator, versus JOHN WINDHAM Et Al. 26 Aug 1887. (Pp. 478-479)

J. L. COLVERT, Administrator of T. N. Christian versus G. P. M. WILLIAMS. Motion of complainant to have a receiver is disallowed. 26 Aug 1887. (P. 480)

L. B. RHODY next friend versus J. B. FRAZIER Et Al. Commissioners appointed to set apart a homestead and dower to complainant, Martha Rhody, in the lands of her former husband A. L. Frazier deceased. 26 Aug 1887. (Pp. 481-485)

T. H. ROBERTSON Et Al versus D. B. DAVIS Et Al. It appears to the Court that Max Baker, purchaser of Lot No. 5 has paid for said lot. The Clerk is ordered to make him a deed. 26 Aug 1887. (Pp. 485-486)

It is ordered by the Court that a special term of this court be held. Chancellor Wade is incompetent to preside. A Special Chancellor is called for. 26 Aug 1887. (P. 486)

(Page 487 is blank)

Chancery Court met in the town of Carthage on the third Monday in Dec 1887, it being the 19th day of said month. W. W. Wade, presiding. (P. 488)

JOHN D. BANE Et Al versus EDWIN PHILLIPS Et Al. The bill is taken for confessed against Edwin Phillips and his wife, Sally Phillips, and Joel Gittenwater and wife Callie, and W. T. Bone. 19 Dec 1887. (P. 489)

JAMES FORD versus JOHN and W. C. LOCKHART. Report of the sale of land by the Master to James Ford from the defendants. 19 Dec 1887. (Pp. 490-491)

JOHN D. BANE, Administrator, versus EDWIN PHILLIPS Et Al. The Clerk will make a report on how much is in the hands of the Administrator of A. Bane. 20 Dec 1887. (Pp. 492-495)

DAVID SMITH, Executor, Et Al versus JOHN T. STOKES Et Al. Judgment. 20 Dec 1887. (Pp. 496-497)

J. L. HOOD Et Al versus JAMES JONES Et Al. The bill is taken for confessed as to Hattie Hathaway; Mary, William R., Charley, George, and Sampson, minor heirs of George Hathaway; Sarah Hathaway, minor heir of James Hathaway all without guardian except the (Josie) Jones mentioned. Sorena Jones, formerly Serena Hathaway is their guardian who is also a defendant in this suit. 20 Dec 1887. (Pp. 497-498)

J. M. MALONE next friend versus JACOB ADAMSON Et Al. Final Decree. A number of consolidated causes. 20 Dec 1887. (Pp. 498-501)

JACOB ADAMS versus J. R. FUSON. 20 Dec 1887. (P. 502)

J. L. WOOD and wife versus JAMES JONES Et Al. The order, issued heretofore, appointing a guardian for the minor defendants is rescinded and for nothing held. 24 Dec 1887. (Pp. 503-504)

Chancery Court met in the town of Smithville at the Court-house on the third Monday in Feb 1888, it being the twentieth day of said month. W. W. Wade, presiding. (P. 1)

T. H. ROBERTSON and wife versus D. B. DAVIS Et Al. The decree of reference heretofore made in this cause is revived. 20 Feb 1888. (P. 1)

J. H. LOVE Et Al versus V. N. SMITH. This cause is dismissed without prejudice. 20 Feb 1888. (P. 1)

J. L. COLVERT, Administrator, versus W. D. G. CARNES Et Al. Sale of land is ordered. 20 Feb 1888. (P. 2)

J. L. WOOD and wife versus JOHN JONES Et Al. Sampson Hathaway is a minor without guardian. W. G. Crowley, a practicing attorney, is appointed guardian. 20 Feb 1888. (Pp. 2-3)

R. T. FRISBY versus TILLMAN ADCOCK, Guardian, Et Al. The title to the land is vested in William M. Turner instead of R. T. Frisby. 20 Feb 1888. (Pp. 4-5)

P. H. HANKINS versus W. R. PARISH Et Al. The death of W. R. Parish was suggested and admitted in court. 21 Feb 1888. (Pp. 5-6)

W. P. CONGER versus M. E. CONGER. Upon motion of the complainant, the bill is dismissed. 21 Feb 1888. (P. 6)

JAMES PRENTICE Et Al versus MARY A. FOSTER, Administratrix Et Al. Upon motion of defendant J. P. Stevens to change his attitude in this cause from that of a defendant to a complainant so as to charge and show that the estate of J. L. Foster is justly owning Stevens. 21 Feb 1888. (Pp. 6-7)

E. M. McDONALD for the use of R. E. Robinson versus T. J. CRIPS. Complainant asked leave of the court to execute an attachment. 21 Feb 1888. (P. 7)

MASON ATNIP, Guardian, versus JOHN HARRISON Et Al. The injunction heretofore granted in this cause to enjoin defendants from commiting waste on the lands is made perpetual. 21 Feb 1888. (Pp. 7-8)

WILLIAM and R. N. SELLARS versus G. W. BYFORD Et Al. R. N. Sellars agrees to pay all the cost incidental to making said Byford, George Hildreth, and Hiram Hildreth parties to this cause. 21 Feb 1888. (P. 9)

C. W. ANDERSON Et Al versus T. H. W. RICHARDSON Et Al. Complainant Anderson and wife had no authority to use the names of R. V. Gilbert and wife, Mary, as complinants in this bill. 21 Feb 1888. (P. 10)

W. B. STOKES versus F. M. SCHURER. Final Decree. The parties enter into a compromise. 21 Feb 1888. (Pp. 10-12)

JASPER RUYLE versus J. T. TURNEY Et Al. Charley Ward, Claudy Brown, and Lieh Ward are minors without guardian. W. G. Crowley, a practicing attorney is named guardian. 21 Feb 1888. (P. 12)

T. C. HARPER Et Al versus H. S. SMITH Et Al. The demurrer is overruled. 21 Feb 1888. (Pp. 12-13)

ELIZABETH WOODEN Et Al versus M. A. LYMAN Et Al. Motion by the complainant to have a receiver appointed to rent the lands in controversy. M. A. Lyman was appointed as receiver. 21 Feb 1888. (Pp. 13-14)

ELIZABETH JENKINS Et Al versus McADOO JENKINS Et Al. All the purchase money has been paid the Administrator of McAdoo Vanatta, the original purchaser. The Clerk is ordered to make the complainant Elizabeth Jenkins a deed to the tract of land described in the pleadings. 21 Feb 1888. (P. 14)

E. M. McDONALD for use of R. E. Robinson versus T. J. CRIPS. The injunction is dissolved. 22 Feb 1888. (Pp. 15-16)

DAVID SMITH'S Heirs versus JOHN T. STOKES. The Clerk is to pay to S. A. Smith, Executor of David Smith, the money that he has arising out of renting the lands. 22 Feb 1888. (Pp. 17-18)

JOHN GOODSON versus C. C. WRIGHT. P. T. Shores is appointed guardian to represent the minors in this suit. 22 Feb 1888. (P. 19)

MARY A. FOSTER, Administratrix, versus R. M. TITTSWORTH. Defendant to pay the costs. 22 Feb 1888. (Pp. 19-20)

S. S. KERR Et Al versus C. S. FRAZIER Et Al. The demurrer of the first three clauses is not well taken. As to the fourth clause, defendants so demurring are allowed to rely upon said clause in their answer. 22 Feb 1888. (Pp. 21-22)

R. B. WEST versus W. T. DOZIER. Final Decree. The parties have agreed to compromise and settle. 22 Feb 1888. (Pp. 22-24)

ANDREW CARR Et Al versus T. J. LEE Et Al. The death of T. J. Lee was suggested and admitted in open court. 22 Feb 1888. (Pp. 24-25)

ANDREW CARR Et Al versus T. J. LEE Et Al. The said T. J. Lee now has the following named parties living as his heirs, to wit, Mira Congo, formerly Lee, and her husband John Conger; Payton Terry and wife Sarah; J. P. Stevens and wife C. J.; Theodore Lee; Lawson Lee; and Pierce Lee, the above named are citizens of DeKalb County. Albert Lee is a citizen of Macon County. Thomas Lee is a citizen of Putnam County. Margaret Patterson is a citizen of Texas. Jeff Waller is a citizen of DeKalb County. Mat Waller, Darthula Waller, William Conger, Eden are citizens of Putnam County. Edna Exum, Isaac Exum, Mary M. Exum, John Exum, and Calvin Oakley are citizens of Smith County. 22 Feb 1888. (Pp. 25-26)

T. A. TRACY versus RUFUS BETHEL Et Al. Final Decree. The Clerk is to report the debts against the estate of Simpson Bethel. 22 Feb 1888. (Pp. 26-28)

J. H. OVERALL versus H. L. S. MAXWELL. This cause was filed to enjoin a cause in Circuit Court. It is dismissed. 22 Feb 1888. (Pp. 28-29)

CHANCERY MINUTES 1888-1889

A number of causes are continued. (Pp. 29-32)

G. R. WEST versus W. J. GIVAN. Consolidated causes. 23 Feb 1888. (Pp. 32-33)

J. M. EVANS versus N. E. EVANS. The charges in this bill are sustained by the proof. The bonds of matrimony are dissolved. 23 Feb 1888. (P. 34)

JOHN E. ROBINSON Et Al versus JAMES A. BARRETT Et Al. Consolidated causes. 23 Feb 1888. (Pp. 35-38)

JASPER RUYLE versus J. T. TURNEY Et Al. The Clerk is to determine whether the land can be partitioned. 23 Feb 1888. (P. 38)

ELENOR BENNETT versus JOHN C. BENNETT. The charges of adultery, cruel and inhuman treatment, and failing to provide for complainant and his family are true and fully sustained. The parties were married in DeKalb County in 1852. They have been citizens of the county and state ever since. Complainant is a woman of undoubted good character upon the subject of chastity as well as upon all other subjects. Defendant John C. Bennett is a man of the most violent temper and is not a suitable person to have the care and custody of the children, the last five set out in complainant's bill which are now single and living with complainant, to wit, Arminda C.; Thomas L. Phonzo and Alonzo who are twins; and Petaway Bennett. The bonds of matrimony are dissolved. 23 Feb 1888. (Pp. 38-41)

MARY ANN STARNES next friend versus J. M. STARNES Et Al. The fees have not been paid. Said Mary Ann has sixty days to pay or the land will be sold. 23 Feb 1888. (Pp. 41-42)

E. W. BASS and others versus T. J. SNEED and others. 24 Feb 1888. (Pp. 43-44)

OVERALL BROTHERS versus W. S. RENIC Et Al. Decree. 24 Feb 1888. (Pp. 44-45)

ISAAC WOOD versus CHARITY WOOD. The bill is taken for confessed. A hearing is set. 24 Feb 1888. (P. 46)

JOHN E. ROBINSON Et Al versus JAMES A. BARRETT Et Al. Consolidated causes. 24 Feb 1888. (Pp. 47-48)

W. A. BRIEN, Administrator, and in his own right versus G. R. WEST. Motion of the complainant to have some disposition of the property of G. R. West which has been attached. 24 Feb 1888. (Pp. 48-50)

MORGAN, THOMAS, & COMPANY versus OVERALL & HOLLINSWORTH. Decree. 24 Feb 1888. (P. 50)

MARTHA RHODY versus J. B. FRAZIER. 24 Feb 1888. (P. 51)

F. P. SANDERS versus J. A. SUMMERS Et Al. Complainant moved the court for an injunction to restrain the defendant from selling any goods within two miles of Hollinsworth, Tennessee. The court is of the opinion that this is a proper injunction. 24 Feb 1888. (Pp. 51-52)

J. M. VANTREASE versus A. J. VANTREASE. 24 Feb 1888. (Pp. 52-54)

RACHEL ADAMS Et Al versus WILLIAM WATSON Et Al. It is suggested that Jacob Adams is dead. W. N. Sellars is his administrator. 24 Feb 1888. (P. 55)

OVERALL BROTHERS versus W. S. RENICK. Motion. 24 Feb 1888. (P. 56)

JASPER RUYLE versus J. T. TURNEY Et Al. The Clerk reports that the lands cannot be partitioned between the parties to advantage. It is in the interest of the parties that the land be sold and the proceeds divided. 24 Feb 1888. It appears to the Court that Jasper Ruyle and Isaac Turney were joint owners of the land. Isaac Turney is now dead leaving the heirs as would be in complainant's bill. 24 Feb 1888. (Pp. 57-58)

JOHN D. BONE Et Al versus EDWIN PHILLIPS Et Al. The Clerk reports that it will be necessary to sell the lands to pay the debts against the estate of A. Bone. 24 Feb 1888. (Pp. 59-63)

W. E. BARTLETT Et Al versus R. S. ALCORN Et Al. Final Decree. The bill is taken for confessed. It appears from the levy and mortgages and other proofs that the mortgages named were made to secure the defendant for which Bartlett and Merritt were securities. Said levy was made upon the interest of defendant R. A. Smith in the Johnathan Smith lands alone and not upon the 28 acres named in said mortgage. 24 Feb 1888. (Pp. 63-66)

STATE OF TENNESSEE versus J. N. HAYS Et Al. The cause was dismissed. 24 Feb 1888. (P. 67)

MORGAN, THOMAS, & COMPANY versus OVERALL & HOLLINSWORTH. Decree. 25 Feb 1888. (Pp. 67-69)

JOE P. DAVIS versus T. J. DAVIS, Administrator. The parties have entered into a compromise. 25 Feb 1888. (Pp. 69-70)

W. L. HARDCASTLE, Administrator, versus JOHN WINDHAM Et Al. Decree. 25 Feb 1888. (Pp. 71-72)

JAMES L. WOOD Et Al versus JAMES JONES Et Al. Motion to have a guardian appointed for the minor defendants. 25 Feb 1888. (P. 72)

NANCY E. WARREN versus SQUIRE WARREN. It is ordered by the court that complainant make to B. M. Merritt a deed to the land. 25 Feb 1888. (P. 73)

J. M. MALONE next friend versus JACOB ADAMSON Et Al. Consolidated causes. 25 Feb 1888. (Pp. 73-74)

WILLIAM VICK Et Al versus W. and MARTHA BYRD Et Al. Defendant W. Byrd died, intestate, since the last term of court. No administrator has been appointed. It appears that he had no interest in the land named in the pleadings, but as husband of the widow entitled to homestead and dower. Said W. Byrd had no children by said widow. Defendants Andrew Thomas, James Vanatta, and William Thomas have been served. The bill is taken for confessed. 25 Feb 1888. (Pp. 75-76)

STATE OF TENNESSEE versus J. C. WATSON. Decree. 25 Feb 1888. (Pp. 77-78)

B. M. MERRITT Et Al versus (LUM) HUNT Et Al. The bill is taken for confessed. 25 Feb 1888. (Pp. 78-80)

JAMES L. WOOD Et Al versus JAMES JONES Et Al. Demurrer of John B. Robinson, Administrator of W. L. Hathaway and A. H. Robinson. The cause is dismissed. 25 Feb 1888. (P. 81)

C. W. ANDERSON Et Al versus T. H. RICHARDSON Et Al. A sale was entered of record supported by affidavit that complainant C. W. Anderson show his authority for making R. V. Gilbert and Mary Gilbert complainants in his bill. The bill is dismissed as to R. V. Gilbert and Mary Gilbert. 25 Feb 1888. (Pp. 81-82)

STATE OF TENNESSEE versus W. G. CROWLEY. 25 Feb 1888. (Pp. 83-84)

MOSES PACK versus A. D. BAIN. Final Decree. Defendant is indebted to complainant. A sale of land is ordered. 25 Feb 1888. (Pp. 85-86)

S. F. WATSON versus J. C. WATSON. Defendant is to pay over to complainant. 25 Feb 1888. (Pp. 86-87)

T. J. FRAZIER next friend versus T. B. POTTER, Trustee, Et Al. Report of sale. 25 Feb 1888. (Pp. 87-88)

J. J. FORD versus SARAH ADCOCK Et Al. Final Decree. Defendants Jeff Vaughn and Martha Vaughn recover of the complainants. 25 Feb 1888. (Pp. 88-89)

T. A. TRACY versus RUFUS BETHEL Et Al. Report on payments to Bethel heirs. 25 Feb 1888. (Pp. 89-90)

J. L. COLVERT, Administrator versus W. D. CARNES Et Al. Decree. Report by the Clerk. 25 Feb 1888. (Pp. 90-92)

Financial report of the Clerk & Master. 25 Feb 1888. (Pp. 92-93)

T. A. TRACY versus RUFUS BETHEL. Report of sales. 25 Feb 1888. (Pp. 93-97)

J. L. COLVERT, Administrator, versus W. D. G. CARNES Et Al. Report of sale. 25 Feb 1888. (Pp. 97-103)

H. FRAZIER versus W. A. DUNLAP. 25 Feb 1888. (Pp. 104-105)

C. W. L. HALE Et Al versus W. H. JONES Et Al. 25 Feb 1888. (Pp. 105-106)

J. L. WOOD and wife versus JAMES JONES Et Al. 25 Feb 1888. (Pp. 107-108)

F. P. SANDERS versus J. A. SUMMERS Et Al. The injunction is dissolved. 25 Feb 1888. (P. 108)

W. C. ODOM versus J. W. HENDERSON. All the equity in complainant's bill has been met. 25 Feb 1888. (P. 109)

T. A. TRACY versus RUFUS BETHEL. The order as to taxes is revived and the Master will report to whom taxes are due. 25 Feb 1888. (P. 110)

JOHN JONES, Administrator, versus W. O. BURGER Et Al. Final Decree. The lands claimed under the contract belong to the heirs of Nancy R. Jones subject alone to the payment of such debts and liabilities as may be against her estate. The Court declines to allow complainant John Jones anything for improvements. 25 Feb 1888. (Pp. 111-113)

Chancery Court met in the town of Smithville on the second Monday in Aug 1888, it being the 13th day of said month. W. W. Wade, presiding. 13 Aug 1888. (P. 114)

S. R. LOWERY versus R. B. WEST Et Al. All the equities set up in the original bill have been met. The Court is of the opinion that the law is with the cross bill. 13 Aug 1888. (Pp. 114-116)

A number of causes are continued. (Pp. 117-119)

JAMES PRENTICE Et Al versus MARY A. FOSTER Et Al. Decree. Complainant recovers of the defendant who is the administratrix of J. L. Foster. 13 Aug 1888. (Pp. 120-121)

WILLIAM VICK versus MARTHA BYRD Et Al. 13 Aug 1888. (P. 122)

The Honorable W. W. Wade is incompetent to hear and determine certain causes. T. J. Fisher is appointed Special Chancellor. 13 Aug 1888. (Pp. 123-125)

GUS PARKER versus JOSEPH HILL. The bill is taken for confessed. Complainant recovers of defendant. 13 Aug 1888. (Pp. 126-127)

Chancery Court met in the town of Smithville on the third Monday in Aug 1888, it being the 20th day of said month. T. J. Fisher, presiding. (P. 128)

N. E. MAYNARD versus E. MAYNARD Et Al. Final Decree. The Clerk is to determine what property E. Maynard owned at the commencement of this suit who was not covered by the deed of trust to Matilda Maynard and her children. 20 Aug 1888. (Pp. (Pp. 128-131)

J. L. COLVERT, Administrator, Et Al versus JAMES STALEY Et Al. 20 Aug 1888. (Pp. 131-132)

A. L. SHERRILL and wife versus W. G. CROWLEY Et Al. The bill is taken for confessed. 20 Aug 1888. (Pp. 133-134)

B. M. MERRITT Et Al versus (LEM) HUNT Et Al. The Master will sell the property as directed. 20 Aug 1888. (P. 134)

T. H. WEST versus T. E. WEST. J. L. Dinwiddie is the administrator of the Estate of T. W. West. The cause was made by agreement of the parties. 20 Aug 1888. (Pp. 134-135)

J. L. COLVERT, Administrator of T. N. Christian versus G. P. M. WILLIAMS. 20 Aug 1888. (Pp. 135-137)

JOHN D. BONE, Administrator of A. Bone, versus EDWIN
PHILLIPS Et Al. John D. Bone became the purchaser of the A.
Bone tract of land. 21 Aug 1888. (Pp. 138-141)

JAMES GEORGE versus SAM SNOW Et Al. Defendant Sam Snow
has reconveyed to complainant James George by deed executed by
said Snow and wife the land mentioned in the bill. 21 Aug 1888.
(Pp. 141-142)

A number of causes are continued. (Pp. 142-143)

JASPER RUYLE versus J. T. TURNEY Et Al. The Master will
take proof and report back what would be a fair price for the
said land. 21 Aug 1888. (Pp. 144-145)

H. A. HILL versus PAT GARRETY. H. A. Hill has filed a bill
alleging fraud in the title of a piece of land he bought of
Pat Garrety. 21 Aug 1888. (Pp. 145-147)

W. W. SELLARS Et Al versus A. L. OVERALL Et Al. Defendants
H. L. Overall, Charles Overall, P. C. Overall, Callie Overall,
and Nola Overall are minors without guardian. A. J. Goodson is
appointed their guardian. 21 Aug 1888. (Pp. 147-148)

D. B. HAGER, Guardian, versus A. AVANT Et Al. 21 Aug 1888.
(Pp. 148-149)

J. J. FORD versus N. BAXTER Et Al. The injunction in this
cause is dissolved. 21 Aug 1888. (Pp. 149-150)

DOBSON JOHNSON versus MONROE NEAL Et Al. Defendant moved
to dismiss the bill in this cause so far as it involves Charles
Cooper's estate because it is not filed for the purpose of
having an administrator appointed. 22 Aug 1888. (P. 151)

R. C. NESMITH Et Al versus J. J. FORD Et Al. 22 Aug 1888.
(Pp. 151-152)

H. DENTON Et Al versus MONROE INGE Et Al. Because of the
matter of incompetence of the Chancellor, the venue is changed
to McMinnville. 22 Aug 1888. (Pp. 153-154)

JAMES H. HICKMAN versus H. P. KEMP Et Al. Defendants recover of the complainant. 22 Aug 1888. (Pp. 154-155)

T. J. WHITE versus NANCY WHITE. The bill is taken for
confessed. A hearing is set. 22 Aug 1888. (P. 156)

T. J. WHITE versus NANCY WHITE. Final Decree. Report of
the Clerk. 22 Aug 1888. (Pp. 157-159)

SARAH SHAW Et Al versus W. B. SHAW Et Al. Final Decree.
Report of the Clerk. It is in the manifest interest of all
the heirs of John W. Shaw deceased that the land be sold and
the funds divided among the heirs. 22 Aug 1888. (Pp. 159-
165)

J. A. FUSON Et Al versus STATE OF TENNESSEE for use of
DeKalb County. 22 Aug 1888. (Pp. 165-168)

J. D. PHILLIPS Et Al versus PURE FOUNTAIN COLLEGE Et Al.
23 Aug 1888. (P. 168)

J. D. PHILLIPS Et Al versus PURE FOUNTAIN COLLEGE Et Al.
The injunction in this cause has been dissolved. The order
directing a sale of the college has been revived. The Clerk
will sell said property. 23 Aug 1888. (Pp. 168-169)

The following proceedings were had before the Honorable
W. W. Wade, regular Chancellor. (P. 169)

G. W. PUCKETT versus G. W. MEDLEY. This cause is continued.
23 Aug 1888. (P. 169)

W. A. BRIEN, Administrator of M. M. Brien, Sr. versus G. R.
WEST Et Al. The injunction is dissolved and the attachments
are charged. 23 Aug 1888. (Pp. 169-170)

MARION TRAPP Et Al versus J. T. TRAPP Et Al. Final Decree.
All the equities set up in the original bill have been met.
John Trapp at the time of making the deed of gift, to wit, 14
Oct 1882 was incompetent to transact his ordinary services on
account of being an imbecile. Said deed should be set aside
on account of fraud, undue influence, etc. It is decreed by
the Court that J. T. Trapp and Isaac Denton be subrogated to
the rights and equities of the said John Trapp under said deed.
J. T. Trapp and Isaac Denton recover of M. V. Trapp. 23 Aug
1888. (Pp. 170-173)

W. H. CHEEK & COMPANY versus J. S. DUNLAP Et Al. 24 Aug
1888. (Pp. 174-175)

W. J. HOLLIS versus R. C. HAYS, Executor of W. J. and S. M.
Isbell. The Master is to take an account of the said estates
and report at next term. 24 Aug 1888. (Pp. 175-176)

ROBERT SMITH Et Al versus T. J. M. LEE Et Al. The Court
orders that the complainants execute land with good securities.
24 Aug 1888. (P. 177)

M. J. MALONE Et Al versus DAVID MALONE Et Al. It appears
to the court that James N. Fisher who was a minor has arrived
at his majority. He is allowed to act in the future as his
own man. 24 Aug 1888. (Pp. 177-178)

A number of causes are continued. (Pp. 178-179)

WASHINGTON J. HOLLIS versus R. C. HAYS. Decree. The
Clerk is to report what property of W. J. Isbell came to the
hands of either defendant or Sarah M. Isbell as Executor and
Executrix of W. J. Isbell or should have come to them. 24 Aug
1888. (Pp. 180-189)

W. J. HOLLIS versus W. S. TYREE Et Al. 24 Aug 1888. (Pp.
189-192)

SARAH SHAW Et Al versus W. B. SHAW Et Al. B. G. Adcock
represented C. L. Shaw, Minnie Shaw and   Shaw who are minors.
He is allowed a fee of ten dollars for his services. 24 Aug
1888. (P. 193)

MARION TRAPP Et Al versus J. T. TRAPP Et Al. 24 Aug 1888.
(Pp. 193-194)

J. M. FITE Et Al versus J. T. HOLLIS Et Al. The Court is of the opinion that Margret E. Witt, now Bennett, has the right to have her special legacy with interest from the date the will was probated paid to her before the other heirs take anything that the personal assets in the hands of Hollis amounting to $291.53 was decreed to J. M. Fite, T. D. Fite, Margret Witt by this court on 29 Jul 1873 which was affirmed by the Supreme Court. 24 Aug 1888. (Pp. 194-195)

JOHN H. SAVAGE versus T. C. ALLEN. Final Decree. The Court is of the opinion and so decrees that the true N. E. corner of Grant No. 5678 to Catherine Long for 2000 acres is at the place on the Eagle Bottom Road about three miles from Smithville. 24 Aug 1888. (Pp. 196-197)

W. J. HOLLIS versus R. C. HAYS, Executor. 24 Aug 1888. (Pp. 197-198)

HANNAH TAYLOR versus C. H. GRIFFITH Et Al. The minor defendants C. H. Griffith, Mary Griffith, Helen Griffith are minors without guardian. R. C. Nesmith is appointed as guardian. 24 Aug 1888. (P. 199)

A. D. PACK versus MARY E. JOHNSON. It is ordered that process be served on defendant. 24 Aug 1888. (P. 199)

W. W. SELLARS, Administrator, Et Al versus H. L. OVERALL Et Al. The bill is taken for confessed. Jacob Adams was dead before the filing of the bill in this cause. W. W. Sellars was and is his administrator. Complainants and defendants were and are his only heirs and distributees. Jacob Adams in his lifetime was the owner of 140 acres of land. He conveyed the same to P. C. and J. B. Adams who at the instance of the heirs and administrators expressed a willingness to cancel said conveyance and allow the title thereto to be divested out of them and vested in the said heirs or the purchaser at the sale in this cause. Jacob Adams died intestate in DeKalb County. He was the owner of but little personal estate. He was considerably in debt. 24 Aug 1888. (Pp. 200-202)

WADE HUDDLESTON versus ADALINE HUDDLESTON. The defendant declined to answer the cross bill. The same is taken for confessed. The Court decrees that complainant Adaline be divorced from defendant Wade Huddleston. She is to have custody of the child mentioned in the cross bill. 24 Aug 1888. (P. 203)

PAT GARRETY versus JENNIE BYFORD Et Al. Defendants Laura Byford, Macon Byford, Kate Byford, (Matt) Byford are minors without guardian. B. M. Webb is appointed as guardian. 24 Aug 1888. (P. 204)

A number of causes are continued. (Pp. 204-205)

W. VICK Et Al versus W. BYRD Et Al. Benjamin Thomas has died intestate in DeKalb County. No one has applied to administer his estate. J. A. Nesmith is appointed as administrator. 24 Aug 1888. (Pp. 205-206)

JOHN B. ROBINSON versus W. B. STOKES. 24 Aug 1888. (P. 206)

W. E. BENNETT versus J. C. BENNETT Et Al. The law is with the defendants. The injunction is dissolved. 24 Aug 1888. (Pp. 207-208)

RACHEL ADAMS versus WILLIAM WATSON Et Al. The bill is taken for confessed. 25 Aug 1888. (Pp. 209-210)

L. Y. DAVIS Et Al versus LAWRENCE DRIVER Et Al. The Chancellor is incompetent to try this cause. 25 Aug 1888. (P. 210)

W. VICK Et Al versus W. BYRD Et Al. Benjamin Davis has died intestate. His estate was insolvent. This is declared to be a creditor's bill. 25 Aug 1888. (Pp. 211-212)

W. E. BENNETT versus JOHN C. BENNETT. The divorce was granted in the original bill. The question of alimony for the causes therein set forth in said bill of duress of complainant and for fraud which motion by the Court overruled. Complainant may have the preference of renting the land in controversy for the year 1889. 25 Aug 1888. (Pp. 212-213)

DELIA VANTREASE versus SAM VANTREASE. Defendant is to pay complainant eight dollars per month as alimony. 25 Aug 1888. (Pp. 213-214)

A number of causes are continued. (Pp. 214-216)

WILLIAM VICK Et Al versus CAROLINE BARGER Et Al. John Barger died intestate. His estate is insolvent. This cause is declared to be a creditor's bill. 25 Aug 1888. (Pp. 216-217)

W. W. SELLARS, Administrator, versus H. L. OVERALL Et Al. 25 Aug 1888. (Pp. 217-221)

WILLIAM VICK Et Al versus CAROLINE BARGER Et Al. J. A. Nesmith has been appointed administrator of the Estate of John Barger. 25 Aug 1888. (P. 221)

JORDAN LEAGUE versus JANE LEAGUE. Final Decree. The defendant has failed to make defense. The bill is taken for confessed. It appears to the Court that defendant Jane has been guilty of adultery with divers persons. Complainant is a man of good character upon the subject of virtue as well as other subjects. The bonds of matrimony are dissolved. 25 Aug 1888. (Pp. 221-222)

JAMES AYERS versus JOHN LAWRENCE. Complainant has a right of way through the premises set out in the bill and which has been obstructed by defendant by putting a fence across the same at one place and a gate at another. The Court rules that complainant has the right of way in the lane. This is located at Temperance Hall and Liberty Road. 25 Aug 1888. (Pp. 222-223)

ISABELLA YOUNG versus ANDERSON YOUNG. It was ordered that alimony be allowed. 25 Aug 1888. (P. 224)

Financial report of the Clerk & Master. 25 Aug 1888. (Pp. 224-225)

W. W. SELLARS, Administrator, Et Al versus H. L. OVERALL Et Al. 25 Aug 1888. (Pp. 225-226)

(Page 227 is blank)

Chancery Court met in the town of Smithville on the third Monday, it being the eighteenth day of Feb 1889. Special Chancellor R. A. Cox presiding. (P. 228)

R. A. Cox takes his oath of office from H. W. Williams, Clerk & Master of Jackson County. 18 Feb 1889. (P. 229)

S. S. KERR Et Al versus C. S. FRAZIER Et Al. T. J. Frazier is administrator of the Estate of A. E. Frazier. 18 Feb 1889. (P. 229)

H. C. EASTHAM versus R. B. WEST. Final Decree. The cause is dismissed. 18 Feb 1889. (Pp. 230-231)

JASPER ALEXANDER, Guardian versus C. L. RHODA Et Al. The bill shows that the legal title to the land mentioned has been in Isaac Alexander and wife and the parties to whom they conveyed the same for more than seven years before this suit was filed. Complainant's bill is dismissed. 18 Feb 1889. (Pp. 231-232)

A number of causes are continued. (Pp. 232-234)

J. B. FRAZIER versus H. FRAZIER. Defendants Henry Frazier, (Andrew) Frazier, Charlie Frazier are minors without guardian. W. G. Crowley is appointed as guardian. 19 Feb 1889. (P. 234)

A number of causes are continued. (Pp. 234-238)

A. B. FLIPPEN, Administrator, Et Al, versus T. F. BOWMAN, Administrator, Et Al. Most of the defendants are non residents of DeKalb County. 19 Feb 1889. (P. 239)

GRACY C. ROBINSON versus JAMES H. ROBINSON. The bill is taken for confessed. 19 Feb 1889. (P. 239)

P. CLEMMONS versus ALCORN, MADDUX, JAMES & COMPANY. 19 Feb 1889. (Pp. 240-241)

DELIA BARRETT versus WILLIAM BARRETT. Final Decree. The bill is taken for confessed. Parties were married as charged. Defendant has been guilty of cruel and inhuman treatment and has failed to provide for the complainant. Complainant is divorced from the defendant. The said Delia Barrett is restored to her maiden name of Delia Spurlock. 19 Feb 1889. (Pp. 241-242)

AARON CANTRELL, Administrator versus SUSAN LOVE Et Al. 19 Feb 1889. (P. 243)

H. L. HANEY Et Al versus JOHN BRAGG Et Al. Defendants Vietta Haney, Pink Murphy, Paralee Haney, and Martha Haney are all minors without guardian. 19 Feb 1889. (Pp. 243-244)

J. L. COLVERT, Administrator versus G. P. M. WILLIAMS. Report of sale. 19 Feb 1889. (Pp. 244-246)

J. D. PHILLIPS Et Al versus PURE FOUNTAIN COLLEGE Et Al. 19 Feb 1889. (Pp. 246-248)

B. M. MERRITT versus (LUM) HUNT Et Al. 19 Feb 1889. (P. 248)

A. B. FLIPPEN, Administrator Et Al versus T. F. BOWMAN, Administrator, Et Al. The note is justly due and owing to the estate of H. G. Flippen. The Court orders that Complainant A. B. Flippen, Administrator of the estate of Henry Flippen recover of the Defendant T. F. Bowman, Administrator of the estate of Henry Rutland. 19 Feb 1889. (Pp. 248-250)

A number of causes are continued. (Pp. 248-253)

JAMES PRENTICE Et Al versus MARY A. FOSTER Et Al. Report of sale. (Pp. 253-254)

DELIA VANTREASE versus SAMUEL VANTREASE. The bill is taken for confessed. A hearing is set. 19 Feb 1889. (P. 255)

HIRAM HILDRETH, Guardian. Ex Parte. Hiram Hildreth was on 8 Apr 1886 appointed as the guardian of Dora Ann Hildreth, minor child of ( ) Hildreth deceased. This is a minor cause for a report. 19 Feb 1889. (Pp. 255-256)

R. H. COOK versus W. B. CORLEY Et Al. Final Decree. The bill is taken for confessed. Defendants are indebted to the complainant. 19 Feb 1889. (Pp. 256-258)

J. B. FRAZIER Et Al versus H. FRAZIER Et Al. There is a necessity for the sale of the land mentioned in the pleadings. 20 Feb 1889. (Pp. 258-259)

ANDREW CARR Et Al versus T. J. LEE Et Al. The defendants give bond. 20 Feb 1889. (P. 260)

A number of causes are continued. (Pp. 260-262)

S. M. CROWDER versus ELIZA EATON. The demurrer is not well taken. Defendant is allowed time to answer. 21 Feb 1889. (P. 262)

ALLEN WRIGHT versus JAMES BLANKENSHIP, Administrator. The death of James Blankenship, the administrator of S. Griffin, was suggested. J. J. Ford has been appointed as the administrator of S. Griffin. 21 Feb 1889. (Pp. 263-264)

C. B. CANTRELL Et Al versus M. D. SMALLMAN Et Al. 21 Feb 1889. (Pp. 265-266)

A. D. PACK versus M. E. JOHNSON Et Al. The Clerk is to give a report. 21 Feb 1889. (P. 267)

HANNAH TAYLOR versus C. H. GRIFFITH Et Al. Complainant has married J. M. Evans since this suit was filed. The suit is revised in the name of J. M. Evans. The bill is taken as confessed as to Elias Taylor, M. T. Walker, (Bedy) Taylor, Jno Taylor, Charles Taylor, Lucinda Taylor, adult defendants. 21 Feb 1889. (Pp. 267-268)

SAMUEL BRASWELL, Guardian, versus JACOB ADAMS Et Al. Charlie Overall, Callie Overall, Bob Overall, and Nolie Overall have been served with process. They are minors without guardian. Alvis Avant has been appointed as guardian. 21 Feb 1889. (P. 268)

WILLIAM PACK versus WILLIAM SELLARS Et Al. Compromise. 21 Feb 1889. (Pp. 268-270)

WILLIAM BENNETT versus RACHEL BENNETT. This cause is taken for confessed. Rachel Bennett has been guilty of divers acts of adultery and abandonment as charged. The bonds of matrimony are dissolved. 21 Feb 1889. (Pp. 270-271)

THOMAS PARSLEY and wife versus WILLIAM FOSTER. Process has been served. The bill is taken for confessed. 21 Feb 1889. (P. 271)

JACOB ADAMS, Guardian.Et Al versus W. A. CATHCART, Administrator, Et Al. The Court is of the opinion that all the minor heirs of Leroy Braswell should be made defendants and be represented by regular guardian. Several causes should be consolidated with this cause. 21 Feb 1889. (Pp. 271-274)

SARAH SHAW versus W. B. SHAW Et Al. The Clerk is to report as to whether the lands of John W. Shaw can be divided among his heirs. He is to report whether it is in the interest of the minor heirs to confirm the sale of 100 acres belonging to Sarah Shaw. 21 Feb 1889. (Pp. 274-278)

T. J. WADE versus T. J. FRAZIER Et Al. Motion is made for the appointment of a guardian for the minor defendants, to wit, Ada Frazier, Willie Frazier, Ed Frazier, and Bettie Hall. There is a committee man for Defendant Nancy A. Frazier. J. W. Eaton is appointed as guardian. 22 Feb 1889. (Pp. 278-279)

T. M. SCHURER, Administrator, versus J. W. FOUTCH Et Al. It is suggested that the land in this pleading has been materially damaged by trespassers. The parties guilty of trespassing are ordered to pay the Receiver. 22 Feb 1889. (Pp. 279-280)

W. C. ODOM versus M. J. REDMAN Et Al. The defendant Eva Redman is a minor without guardian and has been served with process. T. J. Fisher is appointed as guardian. 22 Feb 1889. (P. 280)

HANNAH TAYLOR versus C. H. GRIFFITH Et Al. Final Decree. The land mentioned in the pleadings belongs to the complainant. Defendants have no interest in the land whatever. 22 Feb 1889. (Pp. 282-283)

T. A. TRACY versus RUFUS BETHEL Et Al. J. P. Tittsworth has bought the interest of John Smithson in the funds in this cause. 22 Feb 1889. (P. 284)

J. S. GRIBBLE Et Al versus ELI ARNOLD Et Al. Final Decree. Court is of the opinion that complainants were entitled to recover of defendants Nancy Adcock and Harriet Webb. 22 Feb 1889. (Pp. 285-286)

A number of causes are continued. (Pp. 286-287)

JOHN SCURLOCK Et Al versus MARTHA JOHNSON Et Al. Defendants W. J. Johnson, J. R. Johnson, D. Johnson, Mary Johnson, H. Johnson, and Alman Johnson are minors without guardian. 22 Feb 1889. (P. 288)

JOHN GLEASON, Guardian. Ex Parte. The Clerk will report the condition of the property so as to determine if it is in the interest of the minors to have their money invested in said property as a home. He is to determine if it is in a good neighborhood, convenient to good schools, etc. 22 Feb 1889. (P. 289)

JOHN SCURLOCK Et Al versus MARTHA JOHNSON Et Al. The Clerk is to report whether the land can be partitioned or not. 22 Feb 1889. (P. 289)

THOMAS PARSLEY versus W. W. FOSTER Et Al. Complainant re-covers of defendant the tract of land mentioned in the bill. 22 Feb 1889. (Pp. 289-290)

A number of causes are continued. (Pp. 290-291)

R. CANTRELL versus R. C. NESMITH Et Al. All the defendants have been served with process. The bill is taken for confessed. Defendants Minerva James, E. P. James, David James, and John James, Jr. are minors without guardian. A. J. Goodson is ap-pointed as guardian. 22 Feb 1889. (Pp. 291-292)

A. D. PACK versus W. E. JOHNSON Et Al. Report of sale. 22 Feb 1889. (Pp. 292-295)

D. B. HAGER versus A. AVANT Et Al. Final Decree. Report of sale. 22 Feb 1889. (Pp. 295-297)

ROBERT CANTRELL versus R. C. NESMITH Et Al. Clerk is to report what personal estate, if any, is in the hands of the Administrator of David James deceased. 22 Feb 1889. (Pp. 297-300)

SALLIE BANKS versus JOHN BANKS. Defendant has been absent more than two years without just cause. He has failed to pro-vide for complainant. The bonds of matrimony are dissolved. 23 Feb 1889. (P. 300)

JOHN SCURLOCK Et Al versus MARTHA JOHNSON Et Al. Report of the Master. 23 Feb 1889. Isaac Johnson is dead and has no no administrator and has no estate to administer. All the complainants and defendants except John Scurlock, Webb, and Avant are the only heirs of the said Isaac Johnson deceased. (Pp. 301-303)

MARY H. POTTER versus E. POTTER. The bill is taken for confessed. A hearing is set. 23 Feb 1889. (Pp. 303-304)

ISABELL FITTS versus T. W. FITTS. 23 Feb 1889. (P. 304)

ROBERT JOHNSON versus SARAH JOHNSON. This cause is dis-missed. 23 Feb 1889. (P. 304)

ISBELL FITTS versus T. W. FITTS. The bill is taken for confessed. This cause is set for hearing. 23 Feb 1889. Many years ago, complainant and defendant were married to each other. They lived together as man and wife in DeKalb County. Defen-dant has abandoned complainant and neglects and refuses to live with or provide for her. The bonds of matrimony are dissolved. 23 Feb 1889. (Pp. 306-307)

RACHEL ADAMS Et Al versus WILLIAM WATSON Et Al. Final Decree. 23 Feb 1889. (Pp. 308-310)

W. H. HAYS and wife verus H. G. RAY, Administrator Et Al. A compromise has been reached. Complainants agree to dismiss this bill and disclaim any title as purchaser to J. H. Ray's two fields. Mentions Julia Rays upper field. 23 Feb 1889. (Pp. 311-313)

W. J. HOLLIS versus R. C. HAYS. Report of the Clerk & Master. 23 Feb 1889. (Pp. 313-320)

W. T. MAXWELL Et Al versus J. D. ROBINSON Et Al. The guardian is to be allowed to make a defense. 23 Feb 1889. (P. 320)

DELIA C. VANTREASE versus SAM VANTREASE. Final Decree. The bonds of matrimony have been dissolved. Complainant is to have custody of the two children free from the control of the defendant. Complainant is to have leave to take his children home with him three days at any one time as often as once a motion if he desires to do so. He is to call at the complainant's gate in a quiet and peaceable manner and call for the children if they are willing to go with him without being forced to go. The complainant is required to send them to him or take them to him. 23 Feb 1889. (Pp. 320-322)

ALLEN WRIGHT versus JOHN R. TURNER Et Al. 23 Feb 1889. (P. 322)

HANNAH TAYLOR versus C. H. GRIFFITH Et Al. Defendants recover of complainant. 23 Feb 1889. (Pp. 323-324)

G. W. PUCKETT versus G. W. MEDLEY Et Al. Defendant's exceptions are not well taken. 23 Feb 1889. (Pp. 324-326)

M. E. BENNETT versus J. C. BENNETT Et Al. 23 Feb 1889. (Pp. 326-327)

RACHEL ADAMS, Administrator, versus WILLIAM WATSON and wife. 23 Feb 1889. (P. 328)

SAMUEL BRASWELL, Guardian, versus JACOB ADAMS and PETER Adams Et Al. All of the defendants have been served. The bill is taken for confessed. 23 Feb 1889. (Pp. 329-334)

B. C. VAUGHN versus JAMES VAUGHN Et Al. Motion of defendants to discharge the injunction on account of the oath prescribed for paupers. 23 Feb 1889. (P. 334)

MOSES PACK versus A. D. BAINE. Report of sale. 23 Feb 1889. (Pp. 335-336)

JOHN GLEASON, Guardian. Ex Parte. The title to the house and lot is good. The buildings are good. The property is located in the central portion of the town of Liberty near churches and schools and will likely increase, rather than deminish, in value. It is manifestly in the interest of the parties to purchase said property for a house. 23 Feb 1889. (Pp. 337-338)

JASPER RUYLE versus J. T. TURNEY Et Al. Sale of land. 23 Feb 1889. (Pp. 338-340)

(Page 341 is blank)

Chancery Court met in the town of Smithville at the Courthouse on the third day of Jun 1889, it being the first Monday in said month as prescribed by law. W. W. Wade, presiding. (P. 342)

ELIZABETH STOGLIN versus PERRY STOGLIN. Process has been served. The bill is taken for confessed. 3 Jun 1889. (P. 342)

WADE HUDDLESTON versus ADALINE HUDDLESTON. The answer of G. R. Smith who was garnished in this cause. The said Huddleston is the owner of a two horse wagon. The wagon is to satisfy the judgment. 3 Jun 1889. (P. 343)

F. M. SCHURER, Administrator, versus J. W. FOUTCH Et Al. Ella Eaton, Jane Eaton, Jessie Eaton, and Willie Eaton are minors without guardian. J. W. Eaton, a practicing attorney, is appointed as guardian. 4 Jun 1889. (P. 344)

RACHEL ADAMS versus WILLIAM WATSON Et Al. Report of the Clerk. 5 Jun 1889. (P. 345)

On 17 Jun 1889, it being the day to which the special term of court had adjourned, W. W. Wade failed to attend on account of physical disability. T. W. Wade was elected Special Chancellor. (P. 446)

SARAH SHAW Et Al versus W. B. SHAW Et Al. Report of sale. 17 Jun 1889. (Pp. 347-352)

ROBERT CANTRELL versus A. P. JAMES Et Al. Decree confirming report of sale. 17 Jun 1889. (Pp. 353-355)

RACHEL ADAMS versus WILLIAM WATSON Et Al. 17 Jun 1889. (Pp. 355-356)

The Clerk is ordered to record all decrees, etc. 17 Jun 1889. (P. 357)

(Page 358 is blank)

Chancery Court met in the town of Smithville at the Courthouse on the second Monday, the same being the twelfth day of Aug 1889. W. W. Wade, presiding. W. W. Wade announced his disability to hold this term of court by reason of physical disability. J. S. Gribble was appointed as Special Chancellor. (P. 359)

JANE FOUTCH versus G. R. WEST Et Al. Judgment. 12 Aug 1889. (P. 360)

A number of causes are continued. (Pp. 361-363)

ISAAC W. SANDLIN versus F. M. FOUTCH. The death of F. M. Foutch is suggested. Prudie Foutch, John Foutch, Bella Foutch, and Reason Foutch are his only heirs and are minors. 12 1889. (Pp. 362-363)

CHANCERY MINUTES 1888-1889

M. LANCASTER versus C. S. FRAZIER. The death of M. Lancaster was suggested. No steps have been taken to revive the suit. 12 Aug 1889. (P. 363)

A. J. VANTREASE Et Al versus MATTIE N. WOOD Et Al. The death of A. J. Vantrease was suggested. Thomas Vantrease has qualified as administrator. This cause is revived in the name of the administrator. 12 Aug 1889. (Pp. 363-364)

PEOPLE'S NATIONAL BANK versus W. G. CROWLEY Et Al. 13 Aug 1889. (P. 365)

T. W. SHIELDS versus W. W. WADE. The bill is taken for confessed. Complainant recovers from the defendant. 13 Aug 1889. (Pp. 366-367)

JOHN D. BONE versus EDWIN PHILLIPS. Judgment. 13 Aug 1889. (Pp. 367-369)

T. H. ROBERTSON versus D. B. DAVIS Et Al. 13 Aug 1889. (Pp. 368-369)

T. DRIVER Et Al versus H. P. KEMP Et Al. 13 Aug 1889. (P. 371)

W. W. SELLARS, Administrator, versus H. L. OVERALL Et Al. 13 Aug 1889. (Pp. 372-374)

J. H. TITTSWORTH versus JOHN HALLUM. Complainant has failed to prepare this cause for trial. Defendant recovers from the complainant. 13 Aug 1889. (P. 375)

M. E. BENNETT versus J. C. BENNETT. Judgment. 14 Aug 1889. (Pp. 376-377)

L. E. JONES versus A. D. FOUST. There is no grounds for an attachment. 14 Aug 1889. (P. 377)

T. W. WEST versus T. E. WEST. Final Decree. The death of T. W. West was suggested. J. L. Dinwiddie is the administrator. These causes are settled by compromise. 14 Aug 1889. (Pp. 377-380)

JOHN H. SAVAGE versus T. C. ALLEN Et Al. It was agreed by the solicitors that the cause be settled finally. 14 Aug 1889. (P. 380)

JOHN D. BONE, Administrator, versus EDWIN PHILLIPS. Judgment. 14 Aug 1889. (Pp. 381-382)

RACHEL ADAMS Et Al versus WILLIAM WATSON Et Al. 14 Aug 1889. (Pp. 383-384)

E. WOODEN Et Al versus W. LYMAN Et Al. Motion to revive this cause in the name of J. J. Ford, Administrator of E. Wooden. It, appearing to the court that E. Wooden is dead, it is so ordered. 14 Aug 1889. (P. 385)

M. E. BENNETT versus J. C. BENNETT. Report of sale. 14 Aug 1889. (Pp. 386-388)

W. F. MAXWELL and wife versus JAMES D. ROBINSON Et Al.

It appears that John B. Robinson is a suitable person to act as guardian for the minor defendants to the cross bill, Allie Robinson, Charlie Robinson, Bettie Robinson, and Daniel Robinson. 14 Aug 1889. (Pp. 388-389)

S. M. CROWDER versus ELIZA EATON Et Al. The complainant suggested the death of the defendant which was admitted. Defendant died intestate. D. A. Eaton has been appointed as administrator of her estate. 15 Aug 1889. (Pp. 389-390)

SARAH SHAW versus W. B. SHAW Et Al. 15 Aug 1889. (Pp. 390-392)

M. V. TRAPP versus J. T. TRAPP. Final Decree. The Court decrees that the parcel of land set apart to the estate of Jobe Trapp is to be sold by the Clerk. The Clerk will pay over to M. V. Trapp to satisfy in full all demands that she has against the estate. 15 Aug 1889. (Pp. 392-400)

T. W. WEST versus T. E. WEST. John B. Robinson is receiver in this cause. It was suggested that said Robinson has been put to trouble and expense. He is entitled to compensation. 15 Aug 1889. (Pp. 400-401)

JOHN JOHNSON Et Al versus T. J. FRAZIER Et Al. Nancy A. Frazier is a woman of insane mind so much so as to render her incompetent for want of mental capacity to take care of herself or property. Defendants Willie, Ed, and Ada Frazier are minors without guardian. W. G. Crowley is appointed as guardian. 15 Aug 1889. (P. 401)

JOHN B. HOLCOMB versus B. S. ST. JOHN Et Al. Judgment. 15 Aug 1889. (P. 402)

W. H. HAYS and wife versus T. W. WADE Et Al. The defendants are allowed time for their answer. 15 Aug 1889. (P. 403)

HERMAN BROTHERS & COMPANY versus HUNT & McCLENNAND. 15 Aug 1889. (P. 404)

JOHN ALCORN and wife versus H. G. ATNIP. Final Decree. 15 Aug 1889. (Pp. 404-406)

F. M. SCHURER, Administrator, versus J. W. FOUTCH Et Al. J. W. Eaton is appointed as guardian for the minor defendants. 16 Aug 1889. (P. 407)

E. GARRISON versus A. TUGGLE Et Al. Defendants Tuggle and wife agree to surrender possession of the land to the complainants on 1 Dec 1889 in as good order as it now is except natural decay. 16 Aug 1889. (Pp. 408-410)

STATE OF TENNESSEE versus SAM VANTREASE. Contempt. The costs of this cause have not been adjudicated. 16 Aug 1889. (P. 410)

J. B. FRAZIER versus H. FRAZIER Et Al. Report of sale. 16 Aug 1889. (Pp. 411-413)

J. R. NORTHCUT Et Al versus C. C. PRICHARD. This cause is continued. 16 Aug 1889. (P. 414)

E. WOODEN versus M. A. LYMAN Et Al. The bill is taken for confessed. The land cannot be partitioned without injury to the several heirs. 16 Aug 1889. (Pp. 415-416)

MARY E. STOGLIN versus J. P. STOGLIN. The bill is taken for confessed. The charges are fully sustained. The bonds of matrimony are dissolved. 16 Aug 1889. (P. 417)

MERCER & COFFEE versus GEORGE ALLEY Et Al. The interest of defendant Bybee in the land has been ordered to be sold. 16 Aug 1889. (Pp. 418-419)

JOHN H. SAVAGE versus JAMES K. FISHER Et Al. The death of A. T. Fisher is suggested. Mary A. Fisher is his widow. Palestine Fisher, B. H. Fisher, S. C. Fisher, R. L. Fisher, J. K. Fisher, W. H. Fisher, and M. F. Fisher are his heirs. 18 Aug 1889. (P. 420)

MARY H. POTTER versus EVIN POTTER. Process has been served. The bill is taken for confessed. Defendant abandoned complainant and failed to provide for her. He has been guilty of cruel and inhuman treatment toward her. The bonds of matrimony are dissolved. Complainant is restored to her maiden name of Mary H. Cantrell. 18 Aug 1889. (P. 421)

J. L. WOOD and wife versus JAMES JONES Et Al. 18 Aug 1889. (Pp. 421-424)

W. L. HARDCASTLE, Administrator, versus JOHN WINDHAM Et Al. Final Decree. 18 Aug 1889. (Pp. 424-435)

J. H. CAMERON Et Al versus E. V. STALEY Et Al. Decree. 17 Aug 1889. (Pp. 435-436)

MERCER & COFFEE versus GEORGE ALLEY Et Al. 17 Aug 1889. (Pp. 437-439)

Court met pursuant to adjournment. George H. Morgan was appointed as Special Chancellor. 19 Aug 1889. (Pp. 440-442)

F. D. WARREN Et Al versus A. T. PHILLIPS Et Al. Decree. (P. 442)

M. A. CRAWLEY versus J. T. EXUM Et Al. This cause involves directly the questions concerning a public office and as to the eligibility and qualifications of Defendant Exum as Clerk & Master. It is a proper cause to be advanced on the docket. 19 Aug 1889. (P. 443)

M. A. CRAWLEY versus J. T. EXUM Et Al. It is ordered that a jury be empaneled to consider the issues. 21 Aug 1889. (Pp. 444-447)

JOHN W. HICKS Et Al versus SPIRAL HALE. Complainant is enjoined from taking possession of the land. 21 Aug 1889. (P. 447)

S. M. CROWDER versus ELIZA EATON. W. A. Williams is made a defendant. 21 Aug 1889. (P. 448)

Court adjourned until tomorrow morning. 21 Aug 1889. (P. 448)

JOHN MARTIN, Executor, versus W. C. MARTIN Et Al. Final settlement of the estate of John Martin, Sr. John H. Savage as administrator on the estate of William Martin will show what is due B. M. Cantrell as administrator of John Martin, Sr. 22 Aug 1889. (Pp. 449-450)

WILLIAM SELLARS Et Al versus L. P. WILLIAMS Et Al. Consolidated causes. 22 Aug 1889. (Pp. 450-454)

JACOB ADAMS versus J. R. FUSON. This cause was heard before the Supreme Court. 22 Aug 1889. (Pp. 455-458)

M. E. BENNETT versus JOHN C. BENNETT Et Al. The Clerk & Master has taken a judgment against complainant for the rent of the land in controversy. 22 Aug 1889. (P. 459)

SAMUEL BRASWELL versus JACOB and PETER ADAMS Et Al. Report of the Clerk & Master. 22 Aug 1889. (Pp. 460-466)

H. B. SMITH versus J. J. FORD. Final Decree. Complainant is indebted to defendant in a larger sum than he claimed against the defendant. The defendant in open court agrees to relinquish his claim against complainant. Complainant's bill is dismissed and defendant recovers of complainant. 21 Aug 1889. (P. 466)

T. J. POTTER, Administrator, Et Al versus NANCY DAVIS. Parties agree on a compromise. 21 Aug 1889. (P. 467)

THOMAS ESTES versus WILLIAM BLAIR and wife. Final Decree. Parties agree on a compromise. 22 Aug 1889. (Pp. 468-470)

GRACY ROBINSON versus JES ROBINSON. The bill is taken for confessed. 22 Aug 1889. (Pp. 470-471)

E. GRACY versus J. W. GRACY. This cause is compromised. 22 Aug 1889. (P. 471)

H. DENTON Et Al versus MALONE Heirs Et Al. Mary Fisher since the bill was filed has intermarried with John Ward. They reside in Smith County. The complainants are permitted to amend so as to make said John Ward a defendant. It appears that David Hardcastle, John Medley and wife, John Reed and wife, Andrew Savage and wife Mary, J. N. Fisher, and James Fisher have been served. The bill is taken for confessed and set for hearing. 22 Aug 1889. (P. 472)

JOHN GOODSON versus C. C. WRIGHT. This cause is continued. 22 Aug 1889. (Pp. 472-473)

JOHN H. SAVAGE Et Al versus J. K. FISHER Et Al. R. Cantrell is made a party to complainants. 22 Aug 1889. (P. 473)

S. A. SMITH, Executor, versus JOHN T. STOKES. 22 Aug 1889. (Pp. 474-475)

L. P. WILLIAMS Et Al versus WILLIAM SELLARS Et Al. Consolidated causes. 22 Aug 1889. (Pp. 475-478)

M. C. FERRELL versus JAMES FERRELL. The bill is taken for confessed. The bonds of matrimony are dissolved. Complainant is restored to her maiden name of M. C. Priestly. 22 Aug 1889. (Pp. 478-479)

ALICE VANATTA versus JAMES VANATTA. Final Decree. The bill is taken for confessed. Complainant and defendant were married together in DeKalb County. Defendant has failed and refused to provide for complainant. He has abandoned her and neglected to provide for her as charged. Complainant is restored to all the rights and privileges of a single woman. 22 Aug 1889. (Pp. 480-481)

J. M. FISHER and wife versus W. B. FARLER Et Al. 22 Aug 1889. (P. 482)

A. B. CHEATHAM versus G. W. CANTRELL. The proof fails to show how much of the eight acre tract is within the fence of G. W. Cantrell and how long the same has been enclosed. 22 Aug 1889. (P. 483)

CHESLEY TURNER Et Al versus T. P. WEST Et Al. Complainants are without equity in this bill. 22 Aug 1889. (Pp. 484-485)

A number of causes are continued. (Pp. 485-486)

P. T. SHORES versus MAGGIE SHORES. The complainant wishes to amend his bill so as to charge that defendant attempted to maliciously take the life of complainant on the night of 12 Apr 1889 and at other times in DeKalb County. The Court was pleased to sustain said motion. 22 Aug 1889. (P. 486)

G. W. MEDLEY versus G. W. PUCKETT. 22 Aug 1889. (Pp. 486-489)

PATRICK CAMERON versus W. H. MAGNESS Et Al. Complainant failed to bring his suit against said defendant within three years after the complainant arrived at his majority. Complainant's bill is dismissed. 22 Aug 1889. (P. 489)

BETTIE MORGAN versus LEE MORGAN. The bill is taken for confessed. A hearing is set. 22 Aug 1889. (P. 490)

A number of causes are continued. (Pp. 490-492)

W. T. MAXWELL Et Al versus J. D. ROBINSON Et Al. The Court decrees that the deed executed 23 Mar 1880 by J. D. Robinson to his wife, N. P. Robinson, and their children is invalid and not binding upon the parties. 22 Aug 1889. The Court rules that said J. D. Robinson has his tenancy by courtesy in said land. The Court further decrees that complainant Eliza Maxwell and defendants Ollie Robinson, Charlie Robinson, Bettie Robinson, and Daniel Robinson are owners and tenants in common of said land subject to the interest of said J. D. Robinson. The Court decrees that complainant Eliza Maxwell and the other defendants, except defendants J. D. Robinson and W. H. Hays are entitled to have the land in controversy partitioned if it can be done. If not, to be sold. 23 Aug 1889. (Pp. 492-494)

A number of causes are continued. (Pp. 494-495)

W. T. MAXWELL and wife versus J. D. ROBINSON Et Al. 23 Aug 1889. (Pp. 495-496)

J. J. FORD versus PALLAS SMITH Et Al. 23 Aug 1889. (P. 497)

AARON CANTRELL, Administrator, Et Al versus SUSAN LOVE. 23 Aug 1889. (Pp. 497-498)

W. D. PRICHARD Et Al versus J. M. LOVE Et Al. 23 Aug 1889. (Pp. 498-500)

T. W. WADE versus NANCY FRAZIER Et Al. 23 Aug 1889. (Pp. 501-502)

W. L. HARDCASTLE, Administrator, versus JOHN WINDHAM Et Al. 23 Aug 1889. (P. 503)

PEOPLE'S BANK versus W. G. CRAWLEY Et Al. 23 Aug 1889. (P. 504)

J. M. FISHER and wife versus M. A. CRAWLEY. 23 Aug 1889. (P. 505)

A number of causes are continued. (P. 506)

B. C. VAUGHN versus JAMES VAUGHN Et Al. The parties have agreed to a compromise. 24 Aug 1889. (Pp. 507-515)

JACOB ADAMS Et Al versus M. A. CATHCART Et Al. Consolidated causes. 24 Aug 1889. (Pp. 515-526)

PARALEE PACK versus V. W. ANDERSON. Paralee Pack and William Pack agree to let L. G. Love have three-fifth's of the corn raised on about twenty acres of their land where they now live on the Caney Fork River. 24 Aug 1889. (Pp. 526-528)

JACOB ADAMS versus M. A. CATHCART Et Al. 24 Aug 1889. (P. 529)

STATE versus M. A. CRAWLEY, Clerk & Master. 24 Aug 1889. (Pp. 529-531)

W. F. VANATTA versus S. T. MOTTLEY Et Al. The Court is of the opinion that complainants are not entitled to recover the land described in the pleadings. 24 Aug 1889. (Pp. 531-533)

J. L. COLVERT, Administrator, versus REBECCA CHRISTIAN. 24 Aug 1889. (Pp. 533-534)

T. E. BRATTEN versus R. A. SMITH. There is a lien on the land described in complainant's bill and defendant is allowed sixty days to pay said amount and if not, the land will be sold. 24 Aug 1889. (Pp. 534-535)

J. J. FORD versus PALLAS SMITH Et Al. 24 Aug 1889. (Pp. 535-537)

A. L. SHERRILL and wife versus W. G. CRAWLEY Et Al. 24 Aug 1889. (Pp. 537-539)

E. S. CLOSE Et Al versus T. N. CLOSE, Administrator, Et Al. 24 Aug 1889. (Pp. 539-540)

ANN BLACKBURN versus JOE H. BLACKBURN Et Al. Complainant is allowed to amend her bill to charge that William Blackburn, the husband of complainant died seized and possessed of the land out of which complainant is asking dower. 24 Aug 1889. (P. 540)

CHANCERY MINUTES 1888-1889

A number of causes are continued. (Pp. 541-545)

E. W. TAYLOR versus L. R. TAYLOR. Complainant's bill is dismissed. 24 Aug 1889. (P. 545)

M. F. VANATTA Et Al versus S. T. MOTTLEY Et Al. Petition of complainant for a rehearing. 24 Aug 1889. (P. 546)

There being no further time allowed by law to hold the present term of this court, the court is adjourned until the first Monday in Nov 1889. 24 Aug 1889. (P. 547)

Chancery Court met in the town of Smithville at the Court-house on the first Monday in Nov 1889, it being the fourth day of said month. W. W. Wade, presiding. (P. 1)

A. A. TURRANTINE and wife versus P. L. POWELL Et Al. In this cause, it is agreed that defendants Starnes and Powell have till Dec Rules 1889 to answer the bill filed in this matter. 4 Nov 1889. (P. 1)

MARTHA JOHNSON versus W. S. JOHNSON Et Al. The bill is taken for confessed. J. H. Johnson, Patrick Johnson, C. M. Johnson, W. C. Johnson, Nancy E. Johnson, S. E. Johnson, and T. F. Johnson are minors without guardian. 4 Nov 1889. (P. 2)

E. GARRISON versus H. TUGGLE. Sale of a tract of land. 4 Nov 1889. (Pp. 3-4)

J. D. BONE versus EDWIN PHILLIPS. J. D. Bone is the pur-chaser of the land. 4 Nov 1889. (Pp. 5-6)

James Staley and Etta Staley of Scottsborough County, Alabama appoint J. H. Windham of Smithville their power of at-torney. 4 Nov 1889. (P. 7)

DOBSON JOHNSON versus MANERVA NEAL Et Al. The bill is dismissed. 4 Nov 1889. (Pp. 8-9)

J. L. WOOD and wife versus JAMES JONES Et Al. Report of sale. 5 Nov 1889. (Pp. 10-12)

MERCER & COFFEE versus BYBEE & ALLEY. 5 Nov 1889. (Pp. 12-13)

JOHN H. SAVAGE versus W. G. CRAWLEY Et Al. Change of venue is asked on account of the fact that Chancellor W. W. Wade was counsel to W. G. Crawley and brother in law to J. B. Crawley, defendants. This cause is transferred to Warren County. 6 Nov 1889. (Pp. 14-15)

L. WOODEN and wife DELIA versus T. E. BRATTEN Et Al. A compromise was reached. 6 Nov 1889. (Pp. 15-17)

PEOPLE'S BANK versus W. G. CRAWLEY Et Al. It appears to the Court that Chancellor Wade married a daughter of Defendant W. G. Crawley who is sister of the defendant John B. Crawley. Chancellor Wade is therefore incompetent to hear this cause. 6 Nov 1889. (Pp. 17-18)

I. M. SANDLIN versus F. M. FOUTCH. Prudie Foutch, John Foutch, Belle Foutch, and Reason Foutch are minor defendants before the Court by service of process. It appears that W. G. Crawley, an attorney at this bar, represented the ancestor, F. M. Foutch, in his life time in this cause. He is a suitable person to serve as guardian. 6 Nov 1889. (Pp. 18-20)

P. T. SHORES versus MAGGIE SHORES. The charges in the original bill are not sustained by the proof. The charges in the cross bill of Maggie Shores charging him with cruel and in-human treatment towards his said wife and that conduct was so cruel that rendered it unsafe and improper for her to cohabit with him and be under his dominion and control. He has rendered such indignities to her that render her condition intolerable. He has abandoned and neglected her as is sustained by the proof. The bonds of matrimony are dissolved. The defendant will be allowed at all reasonable times to see his children and will be permitted to render such aid to their support and education as he may desire. 6 Nov 1889. (Pp. 21-22)

R. K. (   ) versus JOHN MAXWELL Et Al. Chancellor Wade, being incompetent to hear this cause, P. T. Shores is appointed as Special Chancellor. 6 Nov 1889. (Pp. 23-24)

E. W. TAYLOR versus L. R. TAYLOR. Sale of a tract of land. 6 Nov 1889. (Pp. 24-25)

C. A. BAILIFF Et Al versus THOMAS DRIVER. Nancy Bailiff, during her life, sold to Defendant Driver a tract of land in the 16th District. C. A. Bailiff, Administrator of Nancy Bailiff, recovers of the said Driver $92 and all costs in this cause. 6 Nov 1889. (Pp. 25-26)

Court adjourned until tomorrow morning at ten o'clock. 6 Nov 1889. (P. 27)

JOSEPH MOSS versus JOHN EXUM. Petition for the issuance of a habeas corpus for the release of Isaac Exum illegally restrained by the defendant. 7 Nov 1889. (P. 28)

W. D. PRICHARD Et Al versus J. M. LOVE Et Al. A report settling the matter fully as between the security of E. A. Coggin, Administrator of Jenny Coggin was had before the Clerk 6 Jul 1885. It appears from the decree confirming said report that C. Starnes and W. D. Prichard were indebted the amount of $20 and W. D. Prichard indebted to the amount of $43.95. 7 Nov 1889. (Pp. 29-30)

JOSEPH MOSS versus JOHN EXUM. The cause stands dismissed. Petition and his security will pay the costs. 7 Nov 1889. (P. 31)

STATE OF TENNESSEE versus M. T. MARTIN Et Al. It appears to the court that the action of defendant Martin in refusing to report to defendant Evans, Trustee of the 25th School District, was sustained by the law from the fact that the County Court has no jurisdiction to legally establish a school district. A. J. Goodson, former Superintendent of the common schools, on 10 Aug 1888 appointed T. J. Hass and others as free school directors for the 25th District. Said directors on 24 Jan 1889 contracted with J. H. (   ) to teach school in District No. 1. The establishment by the County Court of the school district is null and void and held for nothing. 7 Nov 1889. (Pp. 32-34)

S. M. CROWDER versus ELIZA EATON. 7 Nov 1889. (P. 35)

J. L. WOOD and wife versus JAMES JONES Et Al. William M. Wilcox and wife Maude are residents of Knox County, Indiana. The said Maude Wilcox is the daughter of W. L. Hathaway. Said Wilcox and wife appoint R. C. Nesmith their power of attorney. 12 Nov 1889. (Pp. 36-37)

J. W. GILBERT versus G. B. CANTRELL. Final Decree. This cause is settled by compromise. 12 Nov 1889. (P. 38)

STATE OF TENNESSEE versus M. A. CROWLEY. Final Decree. James T. Exum's appointment as Clerk & Master on 20 May 1889 is valid and binding. Said Exum is the lawful Clerk & Master. 12 Nov 1889. (Pp. 38-40)

(Pages 41 and 42 are blank)

Chancery Court was held in the town of Smithville on the third Monday in Feb 1890, it being the seventeenth day of said month. W. W. Wade, presiding. (P. 43)

JOHN SCURLOCK versus MARTHA JANE JOHNSON. Order for deed. 17 Feb 1890. (Pp. 43-44)

JOHN C. HOLCOMB Et Al versus B. S. ST. JOHN Et Al. The interest of the parties to a tract of land is divested out of them and vested in John H. Savage. 17 Feb 1890. (Pp. 44-45)

JOHN E. ROBINSON and wife versus JAMES BARRETT, Executor, Et Al. This cause was heard by the Supreme Court. 17 Feb 1890. (Pp. 46-50)

MERCER & COFFEE versus GEORGE ALLEY Et Al. Commissioners are to report whether the interest of Defendant Bybee in the lands mentioned in the pleadings were sold, and if so, to whom and at what price. 17 Feb 1890. (Pp. 50-52)

T. DRIVER Et Al versus H. P. KEMP Et Al. The Clerk is to pay to S. W. McClennand his account against Cintha Kemp the deceased for her burial expenses, the amount of his account out of the funds now in his hands that was from the proceeds of the sale of her land, there being no personal assets to pay the same. 17 Feb 1890. (P. 52)

Court met next on Wednesday morning. 19 Feb 1890. (P. 53)

Court met next on Friday morning. 21 Feb 1890. (P. 54)

Court met next on Saturday morning. 22 Feb 1890. (P. 55)

E. WOODEN versus WOODEN. It is decreed by the Court that all the interest the heirs of Mary Wooden deceased have in the lands mentioned in the pleadings is divested out of them and vested in M. A. Lyman. 22 Feb 1890. (Pp. 56-57)

I. M. SANDLIN versus F. M. FOUTCH Et Al. All the interest of the heirs of Francis Foutch in a tract of land is divested out of them and vested in I. M. Sandlin. 22 Feb 1890. (P. 57)

JOHN H. SAVAGE versus W. G. CRAWLEY Et Al. Consolidated causes. 22 Feb 1890. (Pp. 58-59)

JOHN J. SHIELDS versus HANNAH SHIELDS. The bill is taken for confessed. The allegations are fully sustained. The bonds of matrimony are dissolved. 22 Feb 1890. (P. 60)

SARAH SHAW versus W. B. SHAW. Judgment against the defendant. 22 Feb 1890. (P. 60)

A. A. TURRENTINE and wife versus E. L. POWELL Et Al. The complainant agreed to abandon all claims to the land deeded to Mary Ann Starnes, Martha Jane Powell, and Sylvanus Stokes. The said Powell and wife, Starnes and wife, and Stokes agree to surrender all claims to any part of the land embraced in the deed of gift made by John T. Stokes to his wife and the children named in said deed, dated 22 Jun 1880. It appears to the court that said compromise is manifestly to the advantage of the minors. 22 Feb 1890. (Pp. 61-63)

EVA CUNNINGHAM versus GRANT CUNNINGHAM. Final Decree. The bill is taken for confessed. The complainant's charge of failure to provide by the defendant is sustained. The bonds of matrimony are dissolved. Complainant is restored to her maiden name of Eva Woodridge. 22 Feb 1890. (P. 64)

(Page 65 is blank)

Chancery Court met in the town of Smithville on the second Monday in Aug 1890, it being the eleventh day of said month. B. M. Webb, presiding. (P. 66)

A number of causes are continued. 11 Aug 1890. (Pp. 66-67)

JOHN JONES, Administrator, versus W. O. BURGER Et Al. This cause is heard by the Supreme Court. 11 Aug 1890. Complainant and defendant, Catherine Jones, were entitled to an account for services rendered to their mother under their contract. Neither John Jones nor Catherine Jones take any interest in the personal estate of their mother except their interest as distributees nor any interest in the John L. Patterson land except as heirs of Nancy R. Jones deceased. 11 Aug 1890. (Pp. 68-70)

BETTIE MORGAN versus LEE MORGAN. The charges in the complainant's bill are fully made out by the proof. The bonds of matrimony between complainant and defendant are dissolved. Complainant is restored to her maiden name of Bettie Merritt. 11 Aug 1890. (P. 71)

A number of causes are continued. (Pp. 71-73)

S. T. MOTTLEY versus M. A. CRAWLEY Et Al. The death of complainant was suggested and admitted. E. S. Vance is the administrator. The suit is revived in the name of the said Vance. 11 Aug 1890. (P. 73)

L. VANATTA Et Al versus S. T. MOTTLEY. The death of S. T. Mottley is suggested. Foster Mottley and Ellen Vance are the only heirs of the said S. T. Mottley. E. L. Vance is the husband of the said Ellen Vance and administrator of the estate. The Sheriff of Wilson County is directed to summon said Foster Mottley, Ellen Vance, and E. L. Vance to appear at the next term of this court. 11 Aug 1890. (Pp. 73-74)

ELEANOR F. RICH versus WILLIAM RICH. A cross bill will be filed. 11 Aug 1890. (Pp. 74-75)

MARY LOCKHART versus A. J. LOCKHART. Defendant is allowed time. 11 Aug 1890. (P. 75)

ANDREW CARR Et Al versus T. J. LEE Et Al. Process has been served for Albert Lee, Thomas Lee, Matt Waller, Darthula Waller, William Conger, Kittie Conger, Edna Exum, Isaac Exum, Mary Exum, John Exum, and C. O. Exum and returned not found. The bill is taken for confessed. 11 Aug 1890. (P. 75)

A number of causes are continued. (P. 76)

A. B. FLIPPEN, Administrator, Et Al versus T. F. BOWMAN, Administrator, Et Al. This cause was appealed to the Supreme Court. There is error in refusal of the Chancellor to grant a new trial to the end that the heirs of M. P. Rutland be brought before the court. 11 Aug 1890. (Pp. 77-79)

P. H. HANKINS versus W. R. PARISH. The heirs of W. R. Parish are Lucine Parish, E. G. Parish, D. A. Parish, S. S. Parish, T. V. Parish, E. M. Parish, J. W. Parish, T. L. Parish, M. D. Parish, Mizzie Parish, and Dovie Parish. The heirs have not shown any reason why the cause should not be revived against them. The cause is ordered revived. 11 Aug 1890. (Pp. 79-80)

A. B. FLIPPEN, Administrator, Et Al versus T. F. BOWMAN, Administrator, Et Al. It is ordered that the attitude of complainants A. W. Clifford and wife Mary, formerly Flippen; H. L. Flippen; George Thomas and wife Pauline be changed from that of complainants to defendants. 12 Aug 1890. (P. 81)

JOHN GOODSON Et Al versus G. C. WRIGHT. The Clerk is to report whether or not the family settlement and compromise set out in the bill as to advancements of real estate among the heirs of J. R. P. Goodson is manifestly to the interest of the minor G. C. Wright. 12 Aug 1890. (P. 82)

T. J. POTTER, Executor, Et Al versus NANCY A. DAVIS. The Court decreed that all the lands mentioned in the pleadings be sold to pay debts and all costs and the remainder, if any, be equally divided between defendant and devisees, to wit, Hannah L. Mullican and Nancy Davis. 12 Aug 1890. (P. 83)

DAVE ADCOCK versus ELIZABETH ADCOCK. The bill is taken for confessed. Defendant has failed to make defense. The Court was of opinion that the proof fully sustains the charge that defendant has been guilty of adultery. The bonds of matrimony are dissolved. 12 Aug 1890. (P. 84)

A number of causes are continued. (Pp. 84-87)

JOHN H. SAVAGE Et Al versus JAMES K. FISHER Et Al. The parties have entered into a compromise. 12 Aug 1890. (Pp. 87-92)

ISAAC ALEXANDER Et Al versus AARON Frazier, Executor, Et Al. It appeared to the court that Ammon Frazier and J. B. Frazier should be charged with the amount of funds paid to them. 12 Aug 1890. (Pp. 92-93)

A number of causes are continued. (Pp. 93-94)

A. A. TURRANTINE, Administrator, versus L. P. POWELL. 12 Aug 1890. (Pp. 94-97)

JACOB ADAMS Et Al versus M. A. CATHCART, Administrator, Et Al. G. W. Cathcart agrees to dismiss his appeal in the Supreme Court and agrees to accept in full satisfaction of all his claims against the estate of Lee Braswell deceased. 12 Aug 1890. (Pp. 97-100)

A. E. LOCKHART versus A. J. LOCKHART. Complainant states, "I regret very much my divorce suit against my husband A. J. Lockhart. I wish to have it dismissed." 12 Aug 1890. (P. 100)

BETTIE MOORE versus WILLIAM MOORE. It appears to the court that complainant has sustained the charges in her bill. The bonds of matrimony between Bettie Moore and William Moore are dissolved. The eighteen acres are decreed to the said Bettie Moore. All the children are decreed to the complainant. 12 Aug 1890. (Pp. 100-101)

JOHN H. SAVAGE versus J. K. FISHER Et Al. 12 Aug 1890. (P. 101)

A. B. CHEATHAM versus G. W. CANTRELL Et Al. The court decrees that the eight acres are not included in the transaction. 12 Aug 1890. (Pp. 302-303)

JOHN GOODSON Et Al versus GROVER C. WRIGHT. The heirs of J. R. P. Goodson agree to a compromise. 12 Aug 1890. (Pp. 103-106)

P. H. HANKINS Et Al versus W. R. PARISH Et Al. The bill is taken for confessed. 12 Aug 1890. (Pp. 108-109)

A number of causes are continued. (P. 107)

WILEY SANDERS versus MALETTA McDOWELL. This cause is dismissed. 12 Aug 1890. (P. 110)

WILLIAM SELLARS versus SECOND NATIONAL BANK, Lebanon. The death of complainant is suggested. The suit is revived in the name of R. M. Sellars, Executor of the said William Sellars. 12 Aug 1890. (P. 111)

JENNIE CATHCART versus F. M. CATHCART. The bill is taken for confessed. A hearing is set. 12 Aug 1890. (P. 112)

JENNIE CATHCART versus F. M. CATHCART. The complainant fully sustained all the charges made in her bill. The bonds of matrimony are dissolved. The said Jennie's name is changed to Jennie Byford. 12 Aug 1890. (Pp. 112-113)

JOHN GOODSON versus C. C. WRIGHT Et Al. Consolidated causes. 12 Aug 1890. (Pp. 113-114)

M. TRAPP Et Al versus J. T. TRAPP Et Al. Report of the sale. 12 Aug 1890. (Pp. 114-117)

S. T. MOTTLEY versus JOSEPH CLARKE Et Al. The death of S. T. Mottley was suggested. A motion was made to revive the suit in the name of the heirs. E. L. Vance is the administrator of the said S. T. Mottley. Foster Mottley and Ella Vance are his only heirs. The said Foster is a minor. E. L. Vance is his guardian. 12 Aug 1890. (P. 117)

DeKalb County Bar passes a resolution in praise of James A. Jones for his services as Special Chancellor. 15 Aug 1890. (P. 118)

NANCY ADCOCK versus MACK ADCOCK. Final Decree. The bill is taken for confessed. It appears to the court that the charge of cruel and inhuman treatment on the part of defendant to complainant was fully sustained by the proof. The bonds of matrimony are dissolved. Complainant is restored to her maiden name of Nancy Turner. 15 Aug 1890. (Pp. 119-120)

MARTHA LOUIS versus THOMAS LOUIS. The bill is taken for confessed. Defendant has failed and refused to provide for the complainant. The bonds of matrimony are dissolved. 15 Aug 1890. (P. 121)

JAMES ROGERS versus SALLIE ROGERS. Process has not been executed yet. 15 Aug 1890. (P. 121)

J. B. FRAZIER versus PEOPLE'S NATIONAL BANK, McMinnville. Request to change the venue of this cause to Warren County. 15 Aug 1890. (Pp. 121-123)

W. W. SELLARS, Administrator, versus H. L. OVERALL Et Al. By consent, the claim of $25 due J. L. Hollandsworth for coffin will be paid him by the Clerk. 15 Aug 1890. (P. 122)

S. T. MOTTLEY versus JOSEPH CLARKE Et Al. The Court is of the opinion that Mary A. Hollandsworth's title to the 50 acre tract mentioned in the pleadings is superior to the title of complainant. There is no fraud in the claim. E. L. Vance, Administrator of S. T. Mottley, recovers of defendant Joseph Clarke. 15 Aug 1890. (Pp. 123-124)

BERRY DEMOVILLE & COMPANY versus IRA W. KING, JR. and IRA W. KING, SR. 15 Aug 1890. (Pp. 125-127)

W. T. MAXWELL and wife versus JAMES D. ROBINSON Et Al. 16 Aug 1890. (Pp. 128-129)

PLEAS WATTS versus WILLIAM PACK. The bill is taken for confessed. 16 Aug 1890. (Pp. 129-130)

J. N. ALEXANDER, Guardian, versus C. L. RHODA Et Al. 16 Aug 1890. (Pp. 130-131)

JOHN W. HICKS Et Al versus SPIRAL HALE. The demurrer was not well taken. 16 Aug 1890. (P. 131)

SARAH HILL versus MELSELO HILL. The bill is taken for confessed. The Court is of the opinion that the proof sustains the charge. Defendant wilfully and maliciously deserted complainant. He has absented himself from her without reasonable cause for more than two years. He refused and neglected to provide for her. The bonds of matrimony are dissolved. It is ordered that Rhoda Ann Hill, the child mentioned in the bill as the issue of said complainant and defendant be decreed to the complainant. 16 Aug 1890. (Pp. 131-132)

Whereas a vacancy exists in the office of Chancellor of the

Fifth Chancery Division occasioned by the death of Honorable
W. W. Wade, Chancellor, Robert L. Taylor, Governor of the State
of Tennessee, commissions Honorable B. M. Webb to fill the office of Chancellor. 31 Jul 1890. (Pp. 132-133)

PLEAS WATTS versus WILLIAM M. PACK. The bill is taken for
confessed. Complainant recovers of the defendant. A sale is
ordered for the land attached. 18 Aug 1890. (Pp. 134-135)

JENNIE CATHCART versus T. M. CATHCART. Chancellor Webb is
incompetent to hear this cause. J. W. Eaton is appointed as
Special Chancellor. The note shall be paid out of the property
attached. 18 Aug 1890. (Pp. 135-136)

STANTON HANEY Et Al versus W. G. ESTES Et Al. Process has
been served on John Colvert and wife Nannie and P. T. Shores.
The bill is taken for confessed. 18 Aug 1890. (Pp. 137-140)

M. C. VANATTA Et Al versus N. S. VANATTA Et Al. It is
ordered that the injunction be quashed. Complainant's bill is
dismissed as to complainants Mary and Dora. 18 Aug 1890. (P.
140)

S. M. CROWDER versus D. A. EATON, Administrator. Motion
of defendant to have a receiver appointed to take charge of all
the lands mentioned in the cause. It appears to the court that
this is a proper cause for a receiver. 18 Aug 1890. (Pp. 141-
142)

A. J. VANTREASE, Administrator, Et Al versus MATTIE N. DOSS
Et Al. 18 Aug 1890. (P. 143)

ED CURTIS Et Al versus WILLIAM CURTIS. The Clerk is to take
proof and report back. 18 Aug 1890. (Pp. 143-144)

ELEANOR F. RICH versus WILLIAM RICH. It has been previously
decreed that the bonds of matrimony were dissolved. It is also
decreed that the household property and real estate be sold. 18
Aug 1890. (Pp. 144-145)

JACOB ADAMS Et Al versus M. A. CATHCART Et Al. Survey of
the lands of Leroy Braswell deceased which are to be sold. 18
Aug 1890. (Pp. 145-150)

SARAH ADCOCK versus DAVID ADCOCK. There is a compromise as
to alimony. 18 Aug 1890. (Pp. 150-152)

GRACY C. ROBINSON versus J. H. ROBINSON. Complainant and
defendant were married together as husband and wife. The defendant has abandoned complainant as charged. He wilfully and
maliciously turned her out of doors. He has been guilty of cruel
and inhuman treatment toward her. The bonds of matrimony are
dissolved. Defendant is not a proper person to have the care
and custody of the child. Its welfare is best secured with the
mother. Complainant's name is changed from Gracy C. Robinson
to Gracy New. Defendant is enjoined from molesting her or the
child. 18 Aug 1890. (Pp. 152-153)

(P. 154 is blank)

Chancery Court began and held at the office of the Clerk & Master of said court by reason of the unsafe condition of the Courthouse. Court was held on the third Monday in Feb 1891, it being the sixteenth day of said month. B. M. Webb, presiding. (P. 155)

W. E. BARTLETT versus E. A. COGGIN Et Al. It appears to the court that T. S. Christian and John Christian were before the court by service of spa. 16 Feb 1891. (P. 155)

C. C. JOHNSON versus AMERICA BENNETT Et Al. Motion of the complainant for the appointment of a guardian for the minor defendant Bettie Bennett. J. W. Eaton is appointed as guardian for the said Bettie Bennett. 16 Feb 1891. (P. 156)

W. H. MERRITT Et Al versus JAMES MANNERS Et Al. Order publication. 16 Feb 1891. (Pp. 156-157)

MARTHA RHODY VERSUS C. L. RHODY. Final Decree. The complainant's bill is dismissed. Certain property of the defendant has been attached in this cause. If the defendant fails to pay the costs, then the Sheriff will seize the property attached. 16 Feb 1891. (P. 157)

A number of causes are continued. (P. 158)

J. M. BOZARTH versus M. B. BOZARTH. M. B. Bozarth is a minor without guardian. B. G. Adcock is appointed as guardian. 16 Feb 1891. (P. 158)

JOHN B. ROBINSON versus M. E. WADE Et Al. (Mont) Wade and Ida Belle Wade are minors without guardian. T. W. Wade is appointed as guardian. 16 Feb 1891. (Pp. 158-159)

ANN BLACKBURN versus J. H. BLACKBURN Et Al. Mattie Pledger is a minor without guardian. J. W. Eaton is appointed as guardian. 16 Feb 1891. (P. 159)

JAMES THOMAS versus EFFIE THOMAS. Given time to answer. 16 Feb 1891. (Pp. 159-160)

ANN BLACKBURN VERSUS J. H. BLACKBURN. Defendants J. H. Blackburn, G. S. Blackburn, Henry Blackburn, W. B. Blackburn, John Martin and wife Jane, W. T. Blackburn, and J. F. Blackburn have agreed in writing to enter their appearances. All have failed to make a defense. The bill is taken for confessed. 16 Feb 1891. (P. 160)

ED CURTIS Et Al versus WILLIAM F. FOUTCH Et Al. Comfirmation of sale. 16 Feb 1891. (Pp. 160-163)

F. H. ROBERTSON and wife versus D. B. DAVIS Et Al. Report of Clerk & Master. 16 Feb 1891. (Pp. 163-167)

IRA W. KING Et Al versus E. S. BOWERS Et Al. Final Decree. Process has been served. The bill is taken for confessed. 16 Feb 1891. (Pp. 167-168)

KIRCH BROTHERS versus N. M. FOUTCH Et Al. The death of Thomas Foutch was suggested. Levi Foutch, Jr. is the administrator. 16 Feb 1891. (Pp. 168-169)

A number of causes are continued. (Pp. 169-170)

W. C. GREEN versus MARTHA SMITH Et Al. Russell Smith and wife are non residents of the State of Tennessee. Process to be served. 16 Feb 1891. (P. 170)

SUSAN ATNIP Et Al versus BENJAMIN ATNIP Et Al. This cause is referred to the Clerk for a report. 16 Feb 1891. (P. 170)

A number of causes are continued. (Pp. 171-173)

ANN BLACKBURN versus J. H. BLACKBURN. This cause is rescinded. 16 Feb 1891. (P. 174)

ANN BLACKBURN versus J. H. BLACKBURN Et Al. Mattie Pledger is a minor without guardian. J. W. Eaton is appointed as her guardian. 17 Feb 1891. (Pp. 175-176)

J. H. GARRISON Et Al versus W. H. MERRITT, Executor, Et Al. Final Decree. This cause is dismissed at costs of complainants. 17 Feb 1891. (Pp. 176-177)

JOHN JONES Et Al versus W. O. BARGER Et Al. Decree reference. 17 Feb 1891. (Pp. 177-179)

JACOB ADAMS versus M. A. CATHCART Et Al. Decree on report of no sale. 17 Feb 1891. (P. 179)

A. B. FLIPPEN, Administrator, Et Al versus T. F. BOWMAN, Administrator, Et Al. Defendant W. P. Rutland died some time since, leaving Ida Rutland, his widow; and Ford Rutland and W. A. Rutland as his only children. This cause is revived against said Ida Rutland, Ford Rutland, and W. A. Rutland. Complainants also suggested the death of Defendant T. C. Rutland whose death was admitted in open court. 17 Feb 1891. (Pp. 179-181)

J. B. WEST versus W. W. WADE Et Al. The death of W. W. Wade was suggested. T. W. Wade is his executor. 17 Feb 1891. (P. 182)

A number of causes are continued. (Pp. 182-183)

J. L. COLVERT, Administrator, Et Al versus JOHN B. ROBINSON Et Al. Decree suppressing depositions. 17 Feb 1891. (Pp. 183-184)

J. A. JOHNSON versus MARTIN WAGGONER Et Al. Decree to supply papers. 17 Feb 1891. (Pp. 185-186)

A. J. VANTREASE, Administrator, Et Al versus JOHN D. BONE, Administrator, Et Al. Decree reference. 17 Feb 1891. (P. 186)

W. S. VANATTA versus M. C. VANATTA Et Al. The demurrer is not well taken. 17 Feb 1891. (Pp. 186-187)

JOHN C. BENNETT Et Al versus WILLIAM SELLARS Et Al. The death of W. H. Sellars was suggested and proven. He left minor children and heirs whose names are unknown. They are non residents. Process is to be served through the LIBERTY HERALD. 17 Feb 1891. (P. 188)

A number of causes are continued. (Pp. 188-189)

A. S. McCLENNAND Et Al versus W. A. McCLENNAND Et Al.   The
death of C. Trammel is suggested.   J. L. Trammel and W. A. Trammel are his administrators.   This cause is revived in the name
of the administrators.   17 Feb 1891.   (P. 189)

E. S. CLOSE Et Al versus T. N. CLOSE Et Al.   Report on the
rented land.   17 Feb 1891.   (Pp. 190-191)

J. M. GILBERT versus B. H. COOKE & COMPANY.   Decree dismissing bill.   18 Feb 1891.   (Pp. 192-193)

JOHN H. SAVAGE versus JAMES K. FISHER Et Al.   Report on
land sale.   18 Feb 1891.   (Pp. 193-196)

FANNIE SEAWELL Et Al versus REBECCA CHRISTIAN Et Al.   James
Christian is a minor without guardian.   L. C. Young is appointed
as his guardian.   The cause was then heard on the demurrer of
T. N. Christian's Administrator.   18 Feb 1891.   (Pp. 196-197)

F. D. WARREN Et Al versus A. T. PHILLIPS Et Al.   Report of
Clerk.   18 Feb 1891.   (Pp. 197-203)

FANNIE SEAWELL Et Al versus REBECCA CHRISTIAN Et Al.   Upon
motion of complainant, Laura Seawell, to amend her affidavit in
a reasonable time so as to show that owing to her poverty, she
is unable to give the bond required for the injunction.   18 Feb
1891.   (P. 204)

JAMES HERALD versus G. W. MEDLEY and wife Et Al.   Final
Decree.   The parties have compromised and settled this suit.
18 Feb 1891.   (Pp. 205-207)

A number of causes are continued.   (Pp. 208-210)

P. C. ADAMS Et Al versus F. M. JOHNSON Et Al.   On motion of
Defendant Johnson, the court discharges the injunction absolute-
ly in so far as it seeks to enjoin defendant from going into
possession of the land.   18 Feb 1891.   (Pp. 210-211)

AARON CANTRELL Et Al versus SUSAN LANE Et Al.   W. N. Wilson
and R. M. Cantrell became the purchasers of the home tract of
land of John M. Love deceased.   19 Feb 1891.   (P. 212)

A number of causes are continued.   (Pp. 212-214)

PAT GARRETY versus JENNIE BYFORD Et Al.   The Clerk will report to the next term of court.   19 Feb 1891.   (Pp. 214-215)

W. C. ODOM versus M. J. REDMAN Et Al.   The Clerk will report on the personal assets of the estate of A. S. Redman.   19
Feb 1891.   (P. 215)

JACOB ADAMS versus J. R. FUSON.   Decree on the report of
the Clerk & Master.   19 Feb 1891.   (Pp. 216-218)

W. W. WADE Et Al versus T. B. POTTER, Trustee, Et Al.
Final Decree.   W. W. Wade was entitled to have a credit on the
judgment.   19 Feb 1891.   (Pp. 218-219)

SUSAN ATNIP Et Al versus BENJAMIN ATNIP Et Al.   This cause
is dismissed as to M. B. Atnip, B. F. Wilkerson and wife, and
T. B. Potter.   19 Feb 1891.   (Pp. 219-223)

C. C. ROBINSON versus MARY P. ROBINSON. The bill is taken for confessed. A hearing is set. 19 Feb 1891. (P. 223)

JAMES RODGERS versus SALLIE RODGERS. Final Decree. The bill is taken for confessed. The charge of wilful and malicious abandonment is sustained. The bonds of matrimony are dissolved. 19 Feb 1891. (Pp. 223-224)

E. WOODEN versus W. A. LYMAN. Judgment on a note. 19 Feb 1891. (Pp. 224-225)

E. F. RICH versus WILLIAM RICH. Report of sale. 19 Feb 1891. (Pp. 226-227)

R. (FERN) versus E. (FERN). The bonds of matrimony are dissolved. 19 Feb 1891. (P. 228)

C. S. FRAZIER Et Al versus A. J. EDWARDS Et Al. Final Decree. Complainants are entitled to the relief sought. 19 Feb 1891. (Pp. 229-230)

T. J. SIMPSON versus THOMAS MARKS. Decree dissolving injunction. 19 Feb 1891. (Pp. 230-231)

J. R. WEST versus W. W. WADE Et Al. Final Decree. The injunction is dissolved. 19 Feb 1891. (Pp. 231-232)

J. L. COLVERT, Administrator, versus JOHN B. ROBINSON. Petition of complainant for a new trial. 19 Feb 1891. (Pp. 233-235)

JOHN MARTIN versus W. C. MARTIN. Decree reviving order reference. 19 Feb 1891. (Pp. 236-237)

G. W. MEDLEY versus G. W. PUCKETT. Final Decree. Complainant is the legal owner of and entitled to the possession of the lands mentioned in the pleadings. 19 Feb 1891. (Pp. 237-238)

PLEAS WATTS versus WILLIAM PACK. Report of sale. 19 Feb 1891. (Pp. 239-240)

A. L. SHERRILL and wife versus W. G. CRAWLEY Et Al. Report of sale. 19 Feb 1891. (Pp. 240-241)

STANTON HANEY versus W. G. ESTES. Decree on report of sale. 19 Feb 1891. (Pp. 242-243)

BETTIE MOORE versus WILLIAM MOORE. Decree on report of sale. 19 Feb 1891. (Pp. 243-244)

W. H. HAYS versus T. W. WADE Et Al. Final Decree. Complainant is entitled to the relief sought. 19 Feb 1891. (Pp. 244-246)

JOHN B. ROBINSON versus J. B. FRAZIER, Guardian. Final Decree. Defendant Frazier as guardian took charge and control of the ward's property. He received the rents and profits of their land. Said guardian has failed to properly account for the money. 19 Feb 1891. (Pp. 246-247)

JOHN HALLUM versus S. W. A. HOOPER. The law is with the defendant. 19 Feb 1891. (Pp. 247-248)

GRIBBLE, WEBB, & AVANT versus G. R. WEST Et Al. Final Decree. The bill is taken for confessed. 20 Feb 1891. (Pp. 248-249)

W. W. WADE Et Al versus T. B. POTTER, Trustee. Decree rescinding. 20 Feb 1891. (P. 251)

C. C. ROBINSON versus MARY P. ROBINSON. Complainant is entitled to the relief sought. The bonds of matrimony are dissolved. 21 Feb 1891. (Pp. 251-252)

JOHN EMORY versus JOSIE EMORY. Final Decree. The bill is taken for confessed. It appears that the defendant has been guilty of adultery with various persons at divers times and places in DeKalb County since her marriage with the complainant. There are two children born to complainant and defendant. Defendant is not a suitable person to have the care and control of said children. The bonds of matrimony are dissolved. 21 Feb 1891. (Pp. 252-253)

C. C. JOHNSON versus AMERICA BENNETT Et Al. Decree on report. The sale of the land by Thomas and J. R. Bennett to complainant Johnson was a verbal and void sale and the same is for nothing. 21 Feb 1891. (Pp. 254-256)

E. NORTHCUT versus M. NORTHCUT. Decree to dissolve the injunction. 21 Feb 1891. (P. 257)

STATE versus W. G. EVANS. Final Decree. The court is of the opinion that the reasons for defendant's failure to file the paymentf of the school warrants are not good and sufficient causes. 21 Feb 1891. (Pp. 258-259)

R. MARLER Et Al versus J. A. EATON. Final Decree. Motion of complainant to appoint a receiver. 21 Feb 1891. (Pp. 259-261)

JOHN B. ROBINSON versus J. N. FITTS. Final Decree. The parties have agreed to a compromise. 21 Feb 1891. (P. 261)

T. J. MITCHELL versus G. W. PRESLEY. Decree on petition to appoint a receiver. 21 Feb 1891. (Pp. 262-263)

J. J. FORD versus WILLIAM BASS. Decree dismissing bill. 21 Feb 1891. (Pp. 264-265)

Financial Report of the Clerk & Master. 21 Feb 1891. (Pp. 266-267)

(Page 268 is blank)

Chancery Court was held at the office of the Clerk & Master by reasons of the unsafe conditions of the Courthouse. The Court was held on the first Monday in Mar 1891, it being the second day of said month. B. M. Webb, presiding. (P. 269)

JOHN E. ROBINSON Et Al versus J. A. BARRETT, Executor, Et Al. Order for deed. 2 Mar 1891. (Pp. 269-271)

BERRY DEMANIUS & COMPANY versus IRA W. KING, JR. and IRA W. KING, SR. Report of receiver. 2 Mar 1891. (Pp. 271-273)

M. E. BENNETT versus J. C. BENNETT. Decree on report of rents. 2 Mar 1891. (P. 274)

R. A. SMITH Et Al versus E. M. CUBBINS. Final Decree. The defendant has paid to the complainant the claim sued for. 2 Mar 1891. (Pp. 275-276)

PATRICK GARRETY versus J. M. BAILIFF Et Al. Motion of defendants to withdraw their answer. 3 Mar 1891. (Pp. 276-277)

John F. Frazier appeared in open court and asked to be sworn and admitted as an attorney and solicitor of said court. 3 Mar 1891. (P. 277)

HELEN SCHURER, Administratrix of Charles Schurer, versus MARTIN FOUTCH and W. G. CRAWLEY, Administrators of J. N. Eaton. Final Decree. A decree has been entered settling the amount of the debt from Martin Foutch to the estate of Charles Schurer. 3 Mar 1891. (Pp. 278-280)

S. M. CROWDER versus D. A. EATON, Administrator, Et Al. Decree as to renting. 4 Mar 1891. (Pp. 281-282)

W. E. BARTLETT versus E. A. COGGIN Et Al. Final Decree. 4 Mar 1891. (Pp. 282-284)

PARALEE PACK versus V. W. ANDERSON Et Al. Motion of complainant to have a lien declared in his favor on the land and property mentioned and attached. 4 Mar 1891. (Pp. 284-285)

T. J. MITCHELL versus P. W. PRESLEY Et Al. The complainant filed his amended bill and defendant his demurrer. 4 Mar 1891. (Pp. 285-287)

William T. Smith will serve as Special Chancellor to hear those causes in which Chancellor Webb is incompetent. 4 Mar 1891. (Pp. 287-289)

G. W. MARTIN versus S. W. McCLENNAND Et Al. It appears to the court that the judgment or decree that is enjoined by this bill was obtained by fraud and therefore is null and void. 4 Mar 1891. (P. 289)

B. H. COOKE & COMPANY versus HUNT & McCLENNAND. 4 Mar 1891. (Pp. 289-290)

G. W. MEDLEY versus G. W. PUCKETT. Order for writ of restitution. 5 Mar 1891. (P. 291)

J. B. ROBINSON versus THOMAS DRIVER Et Al. Reference. 5 Mar 1891. (Pp. 291-292)

STATE versus FREE SCHOOL DIRECTORS. Final Decree. Application of complainant to revive this cause in the name of R. G. Nelson, husband of Relator Amanda Nelson, formerly Amanda Bozarth. Said Relator had intermarried with said R. G. Nelson since this suit was brought and is a necessary party. So ordered. Said Relator Amanda Bozarth was entitled to have the warrant of $50 drawn on the Trustee of DeKalb County by defendants, the Directors of the Eight School District. 5 Mar 1891. (Pp. 293-294)

M. A. STARK Et Al versus C. J. KING Et Al. Under the will of James Allen, at the time of his death, the widow, now C. J. King, took only a life estate in all the property, both real and personal. She has the right of possession during her natural life. The investing of the personal estate into lands by the defendant C. J. King was an improper use of the money. The title to said lands is divested out of said C. J. King and husband and vested in the heirs of James Allen. 5 Mar 1891. (Pp. 295-297)

PATRICK GARRETY versus J. M. BAILIFF Et Al. C. A. Bailiff and J. S. Braswell are added as defendants. 5 Mar 1891. (Pp. 297-298)

JOHN JOHNSON Et Al versus T. J. FRAZIER Et Al. Reference. 6 Mar 1891. (P. 299)

HERMAN BROTHERS & COMPANY versus HUNT & McCLENNAND. 6 Mar 1891. (P. 300)

JAMES P. TUBB versus A. AVANT Et Al. Decree to supply papers. 6 Mar 1891. (Pp. 301-302)

MARY LOCKHART versus A. J. LOCKHART. Final Decree. Defendant recovers all the costs in this cause. 6 Mar 1891. (P. 302)

J. M. PAGE versus TENNESSEE PAGE. Rollin Page and Ham McGinnis are introduced to prove the mental condition of Defendant Tennessee Page. 6 Mar 1891. (Pp. 303-304)

J. M. PAGE next friend versus TENNESSEE PAGE. Final Decree. The verdict of the jury was warranted from the facts. Complainant and his security pay all the costs of this cause. The Court sustains the verdict of the jury as to the mental capacity of the defendant. County Court sets apart a year's support for defendant Tennessee Page after the death of Thomas Page. 6 Mar 1891. (Pp. 304-305)

E. W. TAYLOR versus L. R. TAYLOR. Reviewing order. 6 Mar 1891. (Pp. 305-306)

PARALEE PACK versus V. W. ANDERSON. Final Decree. 6 Mar 1891. (Pp. 306-308)

G. W. MEDLEY versus G. W. PUCKETT. Decree as to writ of restitution. 7 Mar 1891. (Pp. 310-311)

A number of causes are continued. (Pp. 311-312)

E. S. CLOSE versus T. N. CLOSE, Administrator. Final Decree. 7 Mar 1891. (Pp. 313-314)

W. J. JONES versus E. S. BOWERS. Final Decree. The bill is taken for confessed. 7 Mar 1891. (Pp. 314-315)

ED CURTIS Et Al versus WILLIAM F. FOUTCH Et Al. Decree on report. 7 Mar 1891. (Pp. 316-317)

J. L. D. LEE versus J. M. LEE. Final Decree. The case has been compromised. 7 Mar 1891. (P. 316)

A. A. TURRANTINE versus P. L. POWELL Et Al. 7 Mar 1891.

(Pp. 318-319)

J. M. PAGE versus TENNESSEE PAGE. The petitioner ask the Court to have Tennessee Page brought before him for inspection and examination. 7 Mar 1891. (Pp. 319-320)

JOHN D. BONE Et Al versus W. B. BRIDGES Et Al. Final Decree. The Court is of the opinion that the law is with the defendants. 7 Mar 1891. (Pp. 320-321)

G. W. MEDLEY versus G. W. PUCKETT. Decree declining to grant appeal. 7 Mar 1891. (Pp. 321-322)

H. DENTON Et Al versus MALONE Heirs. Final Decree. 7 Mar 1891. (P. 323)

W. W. SELLARS Et Al versus H. L. OVERALL Et Al. 7 Mar 1891. (Pp. 324-325)

SAMUEL WALKER versus JOHN B. TAYLOR. Final Decree. 7 Mar 1891. (Pp. 325-326)

M. A. STARK Et Al versus C. J. KING Et Al. 7 Mar 1891. (Pp. 326-327)

The Court orders the Clerk to enroll all the papers in causes pending in this court. 7 Mar 1891. (Pp. 327-328)

J. P. TITTSWORTH versus J. E. CONGO Et Al. Final Decree. 7 Mar 1891. (Pp. 329-330)

JAMES WINDHAM versus R. J. CHRISTIAN Et Al. The charges made in complainant's bill are fully sustained by the proof. All the rights and title to a house and lot is divested out of the defendants, the widow and children of T. N. Christian is divested out of them and vested in the complainant. 7 Mar 1891. (P. 331)

W. B. CORLEY versus T. W. SHIELDS. Final Decree. Defendant recovers of complainant. 7 Mar 1891. (P. 332)

A number of causes are continued. (P. 333)

E. F. RICH versus WILLIAM RICH. Decree as to special commissioner. 7 Mar 1891. (P. 334)

C. L. RHODY Et Al versus J. B. FRAZIER Et Al. Final Decree. 7 Mar 1891. (P. 335)

SAMUEL BRASWELL, Guardian versus JACOB and PETER ADAMS. Decree of reference. 7 Mar 1891. (Pp. 335-336)

T. C. HARPER Et Al versus S. H. SMITH Et Al. Final Decree. The equities of the bill are sustained. 7 Mar 1891. (Pp. 336-337)

J. L. COLVERT, Administrator, Et Al versus JAMES STALEY Et Al. 7 Mar 1891. (Pp. 337-343)

FANNIE SEAWELL Et Al versus REBECCA CHRISTIAN Et Al. Decree modifying the injunction. J. L. Colvert does not consent to this decree. 7 Mar 1891. (Pp. 344-345)

M. F. VANATTA Et Al versus S. T. MOTTLEY Et Al. Decree praying appeal. 7 Mar 1891. (Pp. 345-346)

At the closing of the special term of the Chancery Court at this place, presided over by the Honorable William T. Smith of Sparta, there was a meeting of the bar to adopt suitable resolutions of respect to Judge Smith. 7 Mar 1891. (P. 346)

Order as to special term. 7 Mar 1891. (P. 347)

(Page 348 is blank)

Chancery Court met at the Courthouse in the town of Smithville on the second Monday in Aug 1891, it being the tenth day of said month and the time fixed by law. B. M. Webb, presiding. (P. 349)

YERG SCOTT Et Al versus M. T. HALL Et Al. Defendant E. M. Hall is a minor without guardian. H. A. Bratten is appointed as guardian. 10 Aug 1891. (Pp. 349-350)

H. S. TAYLOR and wife versus ELIZABETH TAYLOR Et Al. At the July Rules 1891, W. G. Crawley was appointed as guardian for Bettie Ann Taylor, Horace L. Taylor, and Edgar Lewis Taylor. Mary Isbell Taylor and Defendant Hezekiah Taylor are the adopted daughter and son of John C. Taylor by order of the DeKalb County Court. 10 Aug 1891. (Pp. 350-351)

A number of causes are continued. (Pp. 352-353)

Financial report of the Clerk & Master. 10 Aug 1891. (P. 353)

A. J. VANTREASE versus WILLIAM ROBINSON. 10 Aug 1891. (Pp. 354-355)

GILBERT CLARKE versus W. B. PRESTON. Judgment over costs. 10 Aug 1891. (P. 355)

AARON CANTRELL Et Al versus JAMES PIRTLE Et Al. Decree appointing J. B. Moore as guardian for James Pirtle who is a minor. (P. 10 Aug 1891. (P. 356)

IRA W. KING, SR. Et Al versus IRA W. KING, JR. Et Al. An account is taken with Dr. T. P. Davis. 10 Aug 1891. (Pp. 356-358)

W. H. and B. M. MERRITT, Executors, Et Al versus JAMES ( ) Et Al. It was the mainfest interest of testator John Merritt by his last will and testament to make his daughter equal to the advancements made by him to his other heirs. Each of the heirs of John Merritt have been advanced the sum of $500 by the said John Merritt during his life. The daughters of John Merritt were advanced, to wit, Elizabeth J. Johnson, Sarah Garner, Mary Hall, and Elizabeth Conger. There is not sufficient proof to show an advancement to his daughter Josephine Wester. 10 Aug 1891. (Pp. 359-361)

A number of causes are continued. (P. 362)

A. A. TURRANTINE versus P. L. POWELL Et Al. It appears

to the court that John T. Stokes in his life time made a deed
of gift to his wife, E. P., and his children, viz. J. M.,
Jeff D., R. L., Thomas, Benton, and   Stokes. Since his
death, the said E. P. intermarried with A. A. Turrantine who
administered all of said estate. Since the death of John T.
Stokes and before the filing of the bill, two of the children,
that is to say Benton and   Stokes died unmarried and intestate and without issue. John T. Stokes left surviving him
and who are now living children by his first wife, that is to
say, Sylvanus Stokes, Elizabeth Heflin. There are also the
heirs of Tennessee Driver who was a daughter of said deceased.
E. P. Turrantine is entitled to one sixth. Robert Lee Stokes
is entitled to one sixth. Two sixth's is due to Thomas B.
Stokes and   Stokes. 11 Aug 1891. (Pp. 362-364)

CATHERINE SMITH versus RAS SMITH Et Al. Complainant has
asked that her cause be dismissed. 11 Aug 1891. (P. 365)

A number of causes are continued. (Pp. 365-368)

WILLIAM LINDER Et Al versus JOHN LINDER Et Al. John
Linder and Isaac Linder are heirs of Low Linder. There are
other children whose names and residences are unknown. The
heirs of Aaron Linder and wife, their names and residences
are unknown. J. B. Moore is appointed as guardian to represent them. 11 Aug 1891. (P. 369)

J. M. BOZARTH Et Al versus M. B. BOZARTH. Complainants
James M. Bozarth, Isaac Bozarth, L. F. Bozarth, Samuel Bozarth,
Elijah Bozarth, Mary Goff, John M. Bozarth, and defendant
M. B. Bozarth are entitled by descent to a tract of land in
the 14th District. 12 Aug 1891. (Pp. 369-370)

W. C. GILBERT and wife versus PHILA A. SEAWELL. Defendant Phila A. Seawell in her own right and as trustee sold
complainants the land mentioned in the deed from T. L. Seawell
to Phila A. Seawell, but by fraud, accident, or mistake the
deed failed to convey in her own right and as trustee, but
they show us facts in the bill to constitute fraud, accident,
or mistake nor does the bill allege which it was. 11 Aug 1891.
(Pp. 371-372)

J. I. BURTON Et Al versus LAWSON MAYNARD. Complainants
and defendant are tenants in common. The Clerk is to report
whether it is best for the land to be sold or partitioned. 12
Aug 1891. (Pp. 372-373)

J. B. MORGAN versus DAVID TAYLOR Et Al. Complainant and
defendants are tenants in common. The Clerk is to report as
to whether the land should be partitioned or sold. 11 Aug
1891. (P. 379)

H. S. TAYLOR and wife versus ELIZABETH TAYLOR Et Al.
Complainants and defendants moved the Court to strike from the
file the plea heretofore filed. 12 Aug 1891. (P. 375)

WILLIAM LINDER versus JOHN LINDER Et Al. The bill is
taken for confessed. 11 Aug 1891. (P. 376)

ERASTUS SMITH versus CATHERINE SMITH. Final Decree. The bill is taken for confessed. It appears to the Court that defendant Catherine Smith has failed to make defense of the charges. The bonds of matrimony are dissolved. Complainant is decreed the two children mentioned in complainant's bill. Said Catherine will be permitted to see said children whenver she desires to do so. 13 Aug 1891. (Pp. 377-378)

W. H. and B. H. MERRITT, Executors, Et Al versus JAMES MANES Et Al. 13 Aug 1891. (Pp. 378-383)

JOHN A. EVANS versus JOSIE R. HALL Et Al. Defendants Josie R. Hall and Helen Brien will have time to answer the bill. Service will be ordered against Eleanor Bennett, Thomas Bennett, and Amanda Bennett. 13 Aug 1891. (Pp. 383-384)

R. L. STOKES versus J. M. STARNES. R. L. Stokes is in feeble health and is married and has a wife, one child, and will be twenty-one years old next June. He has no means of support except what funds are in the hands of the Clerk. The wife of the said R. L. Stokes is also in feeble health. They are in destitute circumstances. It is decreed by the Court that the Clerk pay over to the said Robert L. the amount of $12 due him. 13 Aug 1891. (Pp. 384-385)

AMERICA BENNETT Et Al versus C. C. JOHNSON Et Al. 13 Aug 1891. (Pp. 386-389)

AMANDA BANDY versus THOMAS BANDY. The bill is taken for confessed. Defendant has failed and refuses to provide for complainant. The bonds of matrimony are dissolved. 13 Aug 1891. (Pp. 389-390)

MARY LAWRENCE VERSUS CHARLIE LAWRENCE. The bonds of matrimony are dissolved. Complainant's name is changed to Mary Ponder. 13 Aug 1891. (P. 390)

AMERICA BENNETT Et Al versus C. C. JOHNSON Et Al. Final Decree. 13 Aug 1891. (Pp. 390-393)

IRA W. KING, SR. Et Al versus IRA W. KING, JR. Et Al. 13 Aug 1891. (Pp. 394-395)

T. J. MITCHELL versus P. W. and J. J. PRESLEY. Complainant's bill is dismissed. 13 Aug 1891. (Pp. 395-397)

JANE RANKHORN versus C. M. RANKHORN. Defendant will be allowed time to make defense. 13 Aug 1891. (P. 397)

J. B. MORGAN Et Al versus MARY TAYLOR Et Al. The Court is of the opinion that partition of the land is not possible. 15 Aug 1891. (Pp. 398-399)

ELIZABETH PASS versus M. PASS. Final Decree. The bill is taken for confessed. Defendant has been convicted of a crime which by the laws of the State render him infamous. Complainant is therefore entitled to a divorce. The bonds of matrimony are dissolved. Complainant is restored to her maiden name of Elizabeth Paris. The children are committed to the complainant. 15 Aug 1891. (Pp. 399-401)

JAMES THOMAS versus EFFIE THOMAS. It appears to the Court that the complainant fully sustained the charge in his bill. The bonds of matrimony are dissolved. 15 Aug 1891. (P. 402)

YERG SCOTT Et Al versus M. T. HALL Et Al. This is a proper cause for partition between complainant and his wife, Martha D., and defendant E. M. Hall representing the other share. 15 Aug 1891. (Pp. 403-404)

WILLIAM LINDER Et Al versus JAMES LINDER Et Al. The lands mentioned in the pleadings cannot be partitioned. The same should be sold. 15 Aug 1891. (Pp. 404-406)

A number of causes are continued. (Pp. 406-408)

W. M. ROGERS versus J. H. BLACKBURN Et Al. The bill is taken for confessed. 16 Aug 1891. (Pp. 409-410)

W. B. BRIDGES Et Al versus G. R. WEST Et Al. The proof is that the trustee has held possession of the lot for more than twenty years. Defendants have no prescriptive right of way over said lot. 16 Aug 1891. (Pp. 410-411)

J. M. BOZARTH Et Al versus M. B. BOZARTH Et Al. 16 Aug 1891. (Pp. 411-414)

J. J. BURTON Et Al versus LAWSON MAYNARD. The parties mentioned in the pleading, namely J. I. Burton, J. E. Burton, Henry Burton, Sarah F. Watson, Sophronia Fox, Lawson Maynard, and Ruth Maynard are holding the land as tenants in common. The land cannot be partitioned. 17 Aug 1891. (Pp. 414-415)

LODASKIE JONES versus DICK JONES. The Court is of the opinion that complainant has failed to sustain the charges in her bill. The Complainant has sustained the charge of adultery. The bonds of matrimony are dissolved. 17 Aug 1891. (P. 416)

MILLIE MAYNARD versus WILLIAM H. MAYNARD. The bill is taken for confessed. It appears to the Court that the charges of adultery made in complainant's bill are fully sustained. The bonds of matrimony are dissolved. Complainant is restored to her maiden name of Millie Dyer. A girl child has been born to complainant. Complainant is to have custody of the child. 17 Aug 1891. (P. 417)

JOHN B. ROBINSON and wife versus M. E. WADE Et Al. This is the cross bill of Mont Wade and Ida Bell Wade by their guardian. 17 Aug 1891. (Pp. 417-418)

WILLIAM LINDER Et Al versus JAMES LINDER Et Al. 17 Aug 1891. (Pp. 418-419)

E. CURTIS versus WILLIAM FOUTCH Et Al. Complainant Curtis is not liable for rents of the land mentioned in the cause. 17 Aug 1891. (Pp. 420-421)

J. L. COLVERT, Administrator of T. N. Christian, versus JOHN B. ROBINSON Et Al. 18 Aug 1891. (P. 422)

A number of causes are continued. (Pp. 423-424)

PAT GARRETY versus JENNIE BYFORD. Jennie Byford is a minor without guardian. B. M. Webb is appointed as her guardian. 19 Aug 1891. (P. 424)

F. H. ROBINSON Et Al versus D. B. DAVIS Et Al. The Court directed that the Master make to George C. Puckett a deed to 145 acres. 19 Aug 1891. (Pp. 424-425)

JACOB ADAMS versus J. R. FUSON. Report by the Clerk. 19 Aug 1891. (Pp. 426-428)

W. W. SELLARS, Administrator, versus H. L. OVERALL Et Al. 19 Aug 1891. (Pp. 429-431)

A number of causes are continued. (Pp. 431-432)

JOHN JONES, Administrator, versus W. O. BURGER Et Al. Report of the Clerk. Catherine Jones is entitled to pay for her services under contract until the date of Nancy R. Jones' death. 20 Aug 1891. (Pp. 433-442)

J. L. COLVERT, Administrator, versus JAMES STALEY Et Al. Consolidated causes. 20 Aug 1891. (Pp. 442-444)

A number of causes are continued. (Pp. 444-446)

T. W. WEST versus T. E. WEST. The $407 note executed by T. W. West has been delivered up. 20 Aug 1891. (Pp. 446-449)

AARON CANTRELL, Administrator, versus SUSAN LOVE Et Al. 20 Aug 1891. (P. 450)

JOHN MARTIN Et Al versus W. C. MARTIN Et Al. 20 Aug 1891. (Pp. 451-454)

T. C. HARPER versus G. A. HARPER Et Al. Complainant is entitled to a sale of the land. 21 Aug 1891. (Pp. 455-456)

H. L. HANEY versus JOHN BRAGG Et Al. 21 Aug 1891. (Pp. 457-458)

T. W. WEST versus T. E. WEST. 21 Aug 1891. (Pp. 458-462)

T. W. WADE versus J. B. FRAZIER. The parties agree to submit the matter for arbitration. 21 Aug 1891. (Pp. 462-464)

W. S. TYREE Et Al versus C. S. FRAZIER Et Al. The bill is taken for confessed. 21 Aug 1891. (Pp. 464-465)

W. W. WADE Et Al versus T. B. POTTER, Trustee. 21 Aug 1891. (Pp. 465-468)

J. M. MALONE Et Al versus JACOB ADAMS Et Al. 21 Aug 1891. (P. 469)

J. L. COLVERT, Administrator, versus JAMES STALEY Et Al. 21 Aug 1891. (Pp. 470-472)

LAURA SEAWELL Et Al versus R. CHRISTIAN Et Al. T. W. Wade is relieved of any liability to complainants. 21 Aug 1891. (P. 472)

J. L. COLVERT versus JAMES STALEY Et Al. 21 Aug 1891.

Sale of land. 21 Aug 1891. (Pp. 473-475)

W. C. ODUM versus M. J. REDMAN Et Al. The Court is of the opinion that the allegations in complainant's bill are not sustained. 21 Aug 1891. (Pp. 475-476)

ANN BLACKBURN versus J. H. BLACKBURN. It appears that William Blackburn died about 13 Mar 1889, the equitable owner of 90 acres of land in the 2nd District. Complainant was his lawful wife. She is entitled to dower. 21 Aug 1891. (Pp. 477-479)

G. W. MEDLEY versus G. W. PUCKETT. The injunction is modified. 21 Aug 1891. (Pp. 479-480)

J. B. ROBINSON next friend versus J. B. FRAZIER Et Al. 21 Aug 1891. (Pp. 480-482)

Court adjourned until tomorrow morning. 21 Aug 1891. (P. 483)

PAT GARRETY versus JENNIE BYFORD. It is agreed that W. B. Corley is to have a fee. 21 Aug 1891. (P. 485)

E. WOODEN versus M. A. LYMAN Et Al. The lands mentioned in the proceedings was the property of Mary Wooden and descended to her heirs subject to the debts. M. A. Lyman is the administrator of said Mary Wooden. J. W. Eaton is the guardian of the minors. 22 Aug 1891. (Pp. 486-487)

NANCY MARSHALL versus ANDREW MARSHALL. The bill is taken for confessed. The Court is of the opinion that the charges made in complainant's bill of abandonment by the defendant are sustained by the proof. The bonds of matrimony are dissolved. Complainant is given custody of the two children. 22 Aug 1891. (Pp. 487-488)

JOHN W. HICKS Et Al versus L. HALL. 22 Aug 1891. (P. 490)

METE ANN GRAHAM versus JAMES GRAHAM. The bill is taken for confessed. The charges in complainant's bill are sustained. The bonds of matrimony are dissolved. Complainant is given custody of the child. 22 Aug 1891. (Pp. 490-491)

JOHN B. ROBINSON and wife versus M. E. WADE Et Al. 22 Aug 1891. (Pp. 492-493)

M. C. VANATTA versus W. S. VANATTA. The Clerk is to take an account. 22 Aug 1891. (Pp. 493-494)

ELMAR F. RICH versus WILLIAM RICH. The proceeds from the sale of the land belongs equally to complainant and defendant. 22 Aug 1891. (P. 495)

A number of causes are continued. (Pp. 495-497)

A. A. TURRANTINE Et Al versus P. L. POWELL Et Al. 22 Aug 1891. (P. 491)

Court adjourned until next term of court. B. M. Webb, Chancellor. 22 Aug 1891. (P. 498)

Bratten, H. A. 126
Bratten, Isaac 12,13
Bratten, Matilda 47
Bratten, T. E. 108,110
Brawer, M. 79
Brent, Samuel 29
Breshears, E. A. 53,68
Bridges, M. B. 52
Bridges, W. B. 41,125,
129
Brien, G. R. 89
Brien, Helen 128
Brien, M. M. 1,12,27,
32,37,39,40,57,69,70,
73,80,81
Brien, M. M., Sr. 37,
81,94
Brien, Manson M. 2,3,
7,8,20,33
Brien, Paschal W. 2
Brien, W. A. 81,89,94
Brien, W. W. 3
Brisbo, Matt 79
Britten, Isaac 15
Britton, Jane 56
Brown, Claudy 87
Brown, J. L. 84
Brown, M. 81,84
Brown, N. S. 8
Brown, W. H. 67
Browning, Benjamin F. 17
Browning, Benjamin T. 14
Browning, Lucinda 8,14
Bryant, Lewis 23,26
Bryant, Washington 23,26
Burgen, Abraham 1
Burger, W. O. 76,84,92,
113
Burkett, Nancy 80
Burks, Richard P. 26
Burtin, Charles 22,23
Burtin, John 22,23
Burton, C. F. 75
Burton, C. T. 52,54,60,66
Burton, Celia C. 28
Burton, Charles 27
Burton, Henry 27,129
Burton, J. E. 129
Burton, J. I. 127,129
Burton, J. J. 129
Burton, John 27
Burton, Mary 27
Burton, William 34
Butcher, Martha 20,32
Butcher, Richard 3,4,6,7

Butler, Lent 4
Bybee, George D. 50
Bybee, Joseph L. 31
Byers, Elizabeth 3
Byford, G. W. 87
Byford, Jennie 115,120,130,131
Byford, Kate 95
Byford, Laura 95
Byford, Macon 95
Byford, Matt 95
Byrd, Martha 90,92
Byrd, W. 90,96
Byrd, William 82
Calicott, John J. 43
Callicot, Anne 35
Callicot, J. J. 35,45,51
Callicot, Vera 43
Callicot, W. F. 35,42,45,50
Callicott, A. H. 70,80
Callicott, Ann H. 64,77
Callicott, Ann J. 51,52,55
Callicott, J. J. 64
Callicott, Vera S. 76
Callicott, W. F. 55,61
Cameron, J. H. 49,52,54,58,60,67,
71,75,100
Cameron, James H. 35,37,38,39,72
Cameron, Lula V. 49
Cameron, Mary E., Jr. 49
Cameron, Mary E., Sr. 49
Cameron, Patrick 107
Campbell, J. N. 39
Campbell, William 21,25,32
Candler, Martha J. 13,16,17,19
Cannady, John C. 7
Cantrell, Aaron 13,24,77,78,85,
97,108,120,126,130
Cantrell, Abram 1
Cantrell, B. M. 39,40,41,43,51,
54,56,59,60,64,65,75,76,81,83,
106
Cantrell, Bela D. 64
Cantrell, C. A. 43,51,53
Cantrell, C. B. 44,56,65,68,72,
78,98
Cantrell, Calvin B., Jr. 44,68
Cantrell, Canny 10
Cantrell, Charles A. 44,68
Cantrell, Cleopatra 64
Cantrell, E. T. 73
Cantrell, Edna F. 44
Cantrell, Edner F. 68
Cantrell, Eliza J. 64
Cantrell, Elizabeth 24
Cantrell, Emma F. 44,68

135

Cantrell, Ephraim 24
Cantrell, G. B. 112
Cantrell, G. W. 107,115
Cantrell, Hannah 3
Cantrell, Hiram 41,74
Cantrell, I. 42
Cantrell, Isaac 44,68,
  69,74
Cantrell, J. H. 38,51
Cantrell, James 24
Cantrell, Jennie 72
Cantrell, John 1,24,54
Cantrell, Martha 10,13,
  24,68
Cantrell, Mary A. 68
Cantrell, Mary H. 105
Cantrell, Mary L. 44
Cantrell, Moses 24,64
Cantrell, Nancy A. 44
Cantrell, Nancy O. 73
Cantrell, Patsy A. 24
Cantrell, R. 100,106
Cantrell, R. M. 120
Cantrell, Rachel 24
Cantrell, Robert 10,29,
  34,58,68,100,102
Cantrell, Samantha 64
Cantrell, Smith 13,24
Cantrell, T. L. 73
Cantrell, T. P. 64
Cantrell, Virginia 44,68
Cantrell, Walter J. 44,
  68
Cantrell, William 13,24
Cantrell, William B. 3
Cantrell, William H. 44,
  68
Cantrell, William R. 10
Cantrell, Zollie H. 73
Caplinger, Samuel 1,3
Capshaw, Polly 69,81
Carnes, D. G. 84
Carnes, Mary 39
Carnes, Sarah 84
Carnes, Sarah E. 77
Carnes, W. D. 77,84,91
Carr, Andrew 88,98,114
Carter, John R. 71
Carter, Martha 71
Cartwright, J. H. 75
Cartwright, J. N. 48
Casey, Clary 20
Casey, Samuel 20
Cathcart, Charity 37,46,
  85

Cathcart, F. M. 115
Cathcart, G. W. 115
Cathcart, George 62
Cathcart, Jennie 115,116
Cathcart, M. A. 36,51,57,108,
  115,117,119
Cathcart, Mathew 62
Cathcart, R. H. 37
Cathcart, T. M. 117
Cathcart, W. A. 83,99
Cheatham, A. B. 82,107,115
Cheatham, Archable B. 20
Cheatham, G. W. 82
Cheatham, Joel E. 4,6,7
Cheatham, Martha 20
Cheek, W. H. 94
Chrisman, Isaac 32
Christian, James 37,47,60,120
Christian, John 37,47,60,82,118
Christian, R. 130
Christian, R. J. 64,125
Christian, Rebecca 37,47,60,70,
  108,120,125
Christian, T. N. 35,37,40,47,49,
  53,55,60,64,67,85,92,120,125,
  129
Christian, T. S. 47,118
Christian, Thomas 37,60
Christian, Thomas S. 47,74
Christian, William 37,47
Christian, William F. 74
Christie, Thornton 31
Chysm, L. 69
Claiborn, John B. 19,20
Clark, Gilbert 73,126
Clark, J. 7
Clark, J. E. 39
Clark, John E. 40
Clark, Joseph 2,4,5,6,7,8,9,11,
  14,15,17,18,19,39,45,51,54,115,
  116
Clark, Oma 75
Clark, William 75,85
Clayborn, J. F. 45
Clayborn, J. T. 36,53,57,62
Clayborn, Mary 58
Clemmons, P. 97
Clifford, A. W. 114
Clifford, Mary 114
Close, E. 50
Close, E. S. 54,67,72,83,108,120,
  124
Close, E. W. 64
Close, J. S. 64,67
Close, John 72

Floyd, R. B. 36,41
Floyd, William 2,4,21,
  26,27
Ford, Daniel 1
Ford, J. J. 39,40,53,
  54,55,59,60,62,63,
  66,67,68,70,75,81,
  83,85,91,93,98,103,
  106,107,108,122
Ford, James 84,86
Foster, Annie 45
Foster, B. T. 40,63
Foster, Charles 45
Foster, E. T. 63
Foster, Edmund 6
Foster, Edward 8
Foster, Edward T. 6
Foster, Fannie 45
Foster, Flora 45
Foster, Frierson 45
Foster, J. L. 87,92
Foster, James F. 34
Foster, Jesse 45
Foster, Joel 13
Foster, Lina 6,8
Foster, M. L. 63
Foster, Mary A. 87,88,
  92,98
Foster, Mary L. 40,45
Foster, Mathew 30
Foster, Mattie 45
Foster, Sauky 45
Foster, Sidney 45
Foster, W. W. 100
Foster, William 99
Foust, A. D. 103
Foutch, Amos 22,24
Foutch, Bella 102
Foutch, Belle 110
Foutch, Elijah 72
Foutch, F. L. 63
Foutch, F. M. 50,55,
  69,102,110,112
Foutch, Francis 69,112
Foutch, J. W. 72,99,
  102,104
Foutch, Jane 48,49,58,
  102
Foutch, John 102,110
Foutch, Levi, Jr. 118
Foutch, Martha 72
Foutch, Martin 43,123
Foutch, N. M. 118
Foutch, Nancy 22,24
Foutch, Prudie 102,110

Foutch, Reason 102,110
Foutch, Thomas 118
Foutch, William 129
Foutch, William F. 118,124
Fox, Sophronia 129
Francis, Mary A. 54
Francis, William 54,57,64,71
Frazer, Henry 4,5
Frazer, John 5
Frazer, A. 39
Frazier, A. E. 97
Frazier, A. L. 43,55,85
Frazier, Aaron 45,114
Frazier, Ada 99,104
Frazier, Ammon 114
Frazier, Andrew 97
Frazier, C. S. 58,67,88,97,103,
  121,130
Frazier, Charlie 97
Frazier, Ed 99,104
Frazier, H. 91,97,98,104
Frazier, Henry 55,97
Frazier, J. B. 43,54,55,67,81,85,
  89,97,98,104,114,116,121,125,
  130,131
Frazier, J. R. 55
Frazier, John F. 123
Frazier, Mary 43
Frazier, Nancy 79,108
Frazier, Nancy A. 80,99,104
Frazier, T. J. 79,80,91,97,99,104
Frazier, Willie 99,104
Frisby, R. T. 41,64,83,87
Frisby, T. 74
Frisby, Thomas 75,83
Fuson, J. A. 93
Fuson, J. R. 62,63,64,72,75,86,
  106,120,130
Fuston, David 69
Garner, Sarah 126
Garrety, Pat 93,95,120,130,131
Garrety, Patrick 123,124
Garrison, Angelena 33
Garrison, Charlot 1
Garrison, E. 104,110
Garrison, Eliza 33
Garrison, Elizabeth C. 11
Garrison, Elizabeth J. 11
Garrison, Franklin 1
Garrison, G. M. 26
Garrison, J. H. 119
Garrison, James L. 33
Garrison, Joel M. 26
Garrison, L. 54
Garrison, L. F. 70

140

Magness, Leroy 3,10
Magness, Martha 3
Magness, Mattie 60
Magness, Mattie E. 81
Magness, Olah D. 60
Magness, P. G. 10
Magness, Peggy G. 3
Magness, R. M. 59
Magness, Richard 3,10
Magness, Robert 60
Magness, Sallie A. 59
Magness, W. H. 63,82,
 107
Magness, William H. 3,
 4,10,41,42,45,51,52,
 58,70,77
Malone, David 44,46,49,
 50,94
Malone, J. M. 68,71,74,
 86,90,130
Malone, Jesse 32
Malone, M. J. 39,49,94
Malone, Monroe 39
Malone, Nancy 57
Malone, Rebecca 33
Malone, S. 57
Malone, Sam H. 44
Malone, Thomas 26,31,
 34
Manes, James 128
Mangrum, Joseph 64
Mangrum, Minerva 64
Mann, Matilda 83
Mann, S. 74
Mann, Sanford 68,83
Manners, James 118
Manners, William 40
Manson, Elisha 5
Manson, Kitty 5
Marchbanks, Calvin 24
Marchbanks, Josephine 24
Marcum, M. C. 67
Marks, Thomas 121
Marler, R. 122
Marshall, Andrew 131
Marshall, Nancy 131
Martin, A. 51
Martin, Elizabeth J. 17
Martin, G. W. 123
Martin, James 22
Martin, Jane 118
Martin, John 3,4,5,6,8,
 20,21,25,32,65,69,83,
 84,106,118,121,130
Martin, John, Jr. 4,7,83

Martin, John, Sr. 83,106
Martin, Joseph W. 80
Martin, M. B. 65
Martin, M. T. 111
Martin, Mary 30
Martin, Mary E. 17
Martin, Mathew 30
Martin, P. M. 42
Martin, Patsy 20
Martin, W. C. 65,83,106,121,130
Martin, William 3,106
Martin, William C. 3,4
Mason, John 31
Mason, R. W. 68
Mathews, Moses 13,16,19
Mathis, Moses 17
Maxwell, Eliza 107
Maxwell, H. L. 55,62,65,75,88
Maxwell, John 111
Maxwell, W. F. 103
Maxwell, W. T. 101,107,106
Maynard, A. E. 56
Maynard, Andrew 10
Maynard, E. 56,59,64,66,92
Maynard, Ezekiel 65
Maynard, F. 54
Maynard, Lawson 127,129
Maynard, M. A. 66
Maynard, Millie 129
Maynard, Matilda 92
Maynard, N. E. 59,92
Maynard, Nancy E. 56,64,65
Maynard, Ruth 129
Maynard, T. 60,75
Maynard, Thomas 52,66
Maynard, William 62
Maynard, William H. 129
Meacham, Bettie 45
Medley, G. W. 42,43,62,65,77,83,
 84,94,101,107,120,121,123,124,
 125,131
Medley, George W. 37,38
Medley, John 106
Medlin, Riley 32
Meggerson, E. L. 75,85
Melchore, Joseph 30
Merritt, A. V. 81
Merritt, B. H. 128
Merritt, B. M. 90,91,92,97,126
Merritt, Bettie 113
Merritt, John 126
Merritt, W. H. 118,119,126,128
Milsted, Jane 68
Milsted, John 68
Mitchell, Joseph 51

Stark, M. A. 80,124,125
Stark, T. H. 51
Starnes, J. M. 89,128
Starnes, Mary A. 89,113
Stevens, C. J. 88
Stevens, J. P. 88
Stevens, R. K. 83
Stoglin, Elizabeth 102
Stoglin, J. P. 105
Stoglin, Mary E. 105
Stoglin, Perry 102
Stokes, Benton 127
Stokes, E. P. 68,127
Stokes, J. M. 127
Stokes, Jeff D. 127
Stokes, John T. 42,50,
    68,86,88,106,113,127
Stokes, Jordan 2,4,5
Stokes, Paralee 2
Stokes, R. L. 127,128
Stokes, Robert L. 128
Stokes, Sylvanus 113,
    127
Stokes, Thomas 127
Stokes, Thomas B. 127
Stokes, W. B. 35,36,45,
    47,49,79,87,95
Stokes, William B. 13
Stone, Dillard G. 24
Stone, Samuel 16
Stone, W. B. 53,61
Stroud, David 10
Sullivan, Anne 13
Sullivan, Dewane 24
Sullivan, Herbert H. 5,
    24
Sullivan, Lucian B. 24
Sullivan, Mary A. 4,5,
    6,8
Sullivan, Susan 24
Sullivan, William 13
Summers, George 78
Summers, J. A. 89,91
Summers, Jane 78
Talifaro, John B. 9
Talifaro, Mary 9
Tallafara, John B. 25
Tallafaro, JOhn B. 10
Tallafaro, Mary 10
Talley, C. H. 6
Talley, William R. 63
Tapp, Benjamin 1
Tate, James 4
Taylor, A. 59
Taylor, Andrew 56

Taylor, B. B. 45,53
Taylor, Bedy 98
Taylor, Bettie A. 126
Taylor, Cara 77
Taylor, Charles 98
Taylor, David 65,127
Taylor, E. W. 32,109,111,124
Taylor, Edgar L. 126
Taylor, Elias 98
Taylor, Elizabeth 65,126,127
Taylor, Ezekiel W. 18,20
Taylor, H. C. 65,78
Taylor, H. S. 126,127
Taylor, Hannah 95,98,99,101
Taylor, Hezekiah 126
Taylor, Horace L. 126
Taylor, James A. 12
Taylor, John 77,98
Taylor, John B. 32,125
Taylor, John C. 126
Taylor, L. R. 109,111,124
Taylor, Lucinda 98
Taylor, M. T. 98
Taylor, Malinda 71,74
Taylor, Mary 65,128
Taylor, Mary I. 126
Taylor, Perry 77
Taylor, Robert L. 117
Taylor, Wilson 77
Terry, Payton 88
Terry, Sarah 88
Thomas, Andrew 90
Thomas, Benjamin 82,95
Thomas, Effie 118,129
Thomas, George 114
Thomas, James 118,129
Thomas, Leroy P. 21
Thomas, Martha 50,63
Thomas, Pauline 114
Thomas, William 90
Thomason, Araminta 24
Thomason, Pleasant A. 3,8,17,20,24
Thompson, A. H. 51
Thompson, Etta 51
Thompson, I. M. 82
Thompson, James P. 11
Thompson, Lewis B. 82,83
Thompson, Louis B. 70
Thompson, R. A. 1
Thompson, William B. 18
Thompson, William C. 25
Tittsworth, J. H. 103
Tittsworth, J. P. 79,99,125
Tittsworth, R. M. 77,81,88
Tracy, T. A. 47,53,79,82,88,91,

Young, Isaac 24
Young, Isabella 96
Young, J. 5
Young, Jane 24
Young, John 6,7,13,24
Young, Patty 24
Young, Pleasant 24
Young, Polly 24
Young, Rachel 24
Young, Thomas 79
Young, William 24
Young, William H. 30
Youngblood, Mary 3
Youngblood, Ransom A. 3

www.ingramcontent.com/pod-product-compliance
Lightning Source LLC
Chambersburg PA
CBHW031856200326
41597CB00012B/429